Understanding Concepts of Business Strategy

Understanding Concepts of Business Strategy

R. Duane Ireland
Texas A&M University

Robert E. Hoskisson
Arizona State University

Michael A. Hitt
Texas A&M University

Australia · Brazil · Canada · Mexico · Singapore · Spain · United Kingdom · United States

Understanding Concepts of Business Strategy, 1st Edition
R. Duane Ireland, Robert E. Hoskisson, and Michael A. Hitt

VP/Editorial Director:
Jack W. Calhoun

VP/Editor-in-Chief:
Dave Shaut

Sr. Publisher:
Melissa S. Acuña

Executive Editor:
John Szilagyi

Sr. Developmental Editor:
Mardell Toomey

Marketing Manager:
Rob Bloom

Marketing Communications Manager:
Jim Overly

Sr. Production Project Manager:
Emily Gross

Manager of Technology, Editorial:
Vicky True

Technology Project Editor:
Kristen Meere

Web Coordinator:
Karen Schaffer

Manufacturing Coordinator:
Doug Wilke

Production House:
Lachina Publishing Services

Printer: C&C

Sr. Art Director:
Tippy McIntosh

Internal Designer:
Christy Carr

Cover Designer:
Craig Ramsdell,
Ramsdell Design

Cover Images:
Terry Vine and Manfred Rutz,
Getty Images

Photography Manager:
John Hill

Photo Researcher:
Seidel Associates

Printed in China
1 2 3 4 5 09 08 07 06 05

ISBN 0-324-30604-0
(International Student Edition)

Library of Congress Control Number: 2005922997

For more information about our products, contact us at:

Thomson Learning Academic Resource Center

1-800-423-0563

Thomson Higher Education
5191 Natorp Boulevard
Mason, OH 45040
USA

To our son, Scott: Your courage and perseverance continue to inspire me. Following in your footsteps, I'll always try to be on that hill with everything I've got. I love you, Scott. Dad

R. Duane Ireland

To my wife, Kathy: Your lifetime of sacrifice for our family has made a major difference in my life and the lives our children. I love you so very much.

Robert E. Hoskisson

To my little granddaughter, Michelle (Michellebell): Your smiles light up my day. I love you. PaPa

Michael A. Hitt

Brief Contents

Contents

chapter_4
The Firm 68

Part 3 strategic thinking 91

chapter_5
Business-Level Thinking 92

chapter_6
Product Strategies 116

chapter_7
Mergers and Acquisitions 140

chapter_8 Global Competition 160

chapter_9

Strategic Alliances 184

Preface

Firms are important to all of us. As customers, we buy products (goods and services) from them; as employees, we work for them; as suppliers, we sell raw materials to them; and, as perhaps many of us would agree, firms often are a vital part of the communities in which we live. Thus, for many reasons, all of us benefit when firms perform well. Think about it this way. When firms are successful, they are (1) producing, selling, and servicing products that customers want to buy, (2) providing employees with good-paying jobs, and (3) contributing in various ways to the communities in which they are located. But what influences a firm's performance? Why do some perform exceptionally well while others fail to perform adequately and end up in bankruptcy?

The strategic management process, the focus of this book, strongly influences firm performance. Stated simply, firms with executives who understand how to effectively use the strategic management process tend to succeed, while those with executives who do not, depend more on luck and often experience deteriorating performance that leads to failure. As you'll understand from reading this book, firms use the strategic management process to examine various alternatives in order to decide *what* objectives they should try to accomplish as well as *how* to pursue those objectives.

Our purpose in writing this text is to present to you, our readers, a succinct and action-oriented explanation of how to manage a firm strategically. As such, we cover a broad array of concepts in nine concisely written chapters. As you examine the following list of features, we think you will agree that this book is reader-friendly.

Let's examine some examples of how this book is accessible to you, our readers.

- The writing style is lively, engaging, and application-oriented. You'll find examples in each chapter of how firms that you likely know actually use strategic management concepts and tools. These examples bring the strategic management process to life and highlight its relevance to real firms around the globe.
- Each chapter is organized around **"Knowledge Objectives"** at the beginning of each chapter that clarify what you can expect to learn.
- We open each chapter with a feature called **"Focusing on Strategy."** Each "Focusing on Strategy" illustrates how a particular company uses the part of the strategic management process explained in the chapter. This feature quotes a strategic manager or observer of the strategic management process and brings strategic management issues to life by showing their application in actual firms.

- In each chapter, we also include a feature (**"Understanding Strategy—Learning from Success"**) to explain how one or more actual firms have benefited by successfully using a particular part of the strategic management process. We include a related feature in each chapter (**"Understanding Strategy—Learning from Failure"**) to explain how one or more firms suffered poor performance because of their failure to effectively use one or more parts of the strategic management process.
- To increase the book's visual appeal, full color is used to enhance the presentation of the concepts presented in the book's nine chapters. The full-color format enables us to include interesting color photographs to further illustrate each chapter's content. Captions describing the strategic actions illustrated by each photograph provide an additional way to actively engage you with aspects of the strategic management process that are explained in the chapter.

Acknowledgments

The feedback and guidance provided by our reviewers for this text were especially helpful. We are grateful for their insights about how to present you with an interesting, accessible, and complete explanation of strategic management.

Todd Alessandri
Syracuse University

Kunal Banerji
Florida Atlantic University

Rocki-Lee DeWitt
University of Vermont

Bahman Paul Ebrahimi
University of Denver

Cameron M. Ford
University of Central Florida

Tamela D. Ferguson
University of Louisiana at Lafayette

Steven Hamilton
University of Alaska, S.E.

Reza Karim
California State University, Fullerton

Franz W. Kellermanns
Mississippi State University

Joseph T. Mahoney
University of Illinois at Urbana-Champaign

Brett P. Matherne
University of Dayton

Paul Mallette
Colorado State University

Donald Neubaum
University of Central Florida

Daewoo Park
Xavier University

Laura H. Poppo
Virginia Tech

Jude Rathburn
University of Wisconsin, River Falls

Mitrabarun Sarkar
University of Central Florida

Katsuhiko Shimizu
University of Texas, San Antonio

Thomas D. Sigerstad
Frostburg State University

f. l. Smith
Emporia State University

Laszlo Tihanyi
Texas A&M University

Klaus Uhlenbruck
University of Montana

Our focus group participants helped us a great deal in understanding instructors' and students' needs in teaching and learning about strategic management in an action-oriented manner. We are grateful for the excellent observations the following scholar-teachers provided.

Donald Baack
Pittsburg State University

Rick Crandall
University of North Carolina, Pembroke

Fred Doran
University of Mississippi

Chuck Englehart
Salem International University

Steven Hamilton
University of Alaska, S.E.

Ed Murphy
Embry Riddle University

Tyge Payne
University of Texas at Arlington

Bill Ritchie
Florida Gulf Coast University

Michelle Slagle
University of South Alabama

Eva Smith
Spartanburg Technical College

Supplements

We also want to express our sincere appreciation for the excellent support we've received from our editorial and production team at South-Western. In particular, we want to thank John Szilagyi, our editor; Mardell Toomey, our senior developmental editor; Emily Gross, our senior production project manager; and Rob Bloom, our marketing manager. We are truly grateful for their dedication, professionalism, and commitment to work closely with us to prepare a high-quality book and an excellent and comprehensive package of support materials. It has been a great team effort.

Test Bank (available at http://aise.swlearning.com)

Prepared by Jude Rathburn, University of Wisconsin, River Falls. More than 1,000 test bank questions are linked to each chapter's knowledge objectives and are ranked by difficulty (easy, medium, difficult) and question type (definitional, conceptual, application). We have included many application questions throughout, as well as scenario-based questions that focus on helping students learn to think and act strategically. The test bank material is also available in computerized ExamView® format for creating custom tests in both Windows and Macintosh formats.

ExamView® (available at http://aise.swlearning.com)

The ExamView test creation software, which is an easy-to-use Windows-based program, contains all of the questions in the printed test bank. Instructors can add or edit questions, instructions, and answers, and select questions by previewing them on the screen, selecting them randomly, or selecting them by number. Instructors can also create and administer quizzes online, whether over the Internet, a local area network (LAN), or a wide area network (WAN).

Instructor's Manual and Transparency Masters (available at http://aise.swlearning.com)

Prepared by Janelle Dozier. The Instructor's Manual, organized around each chapter's knowledge objectives, includes ideas about how to approach each chapter and how to reinforce essential principles with extra examples. Included are lecture outlines, and detailed answers to end-of-chapter discussion questions.

About the Authors

R. Duane Ireland

R. Duane Ireland holds the Foreman R. and Ruby S. Bennett Chair in Business in the Mays Business School, Texas A&M University. He teaches courses at all levels (undergraduate, master's, doctoral, and executive). He has won multiple awards for his teaching during his career. His research, which focuses on diversification, innovation, corporate entrepreneurship, and strategic entrepreneurship, has been published in a number of journals including *Academy of Management Journal, Academy of Management Review, Academy of Management Executive, Administrative Science Quarterly, Strategic Management Journal, Journal of Management, Human Relations,* and *Journal of Management Studies.* His published books include *Competing for Advantage* (2004), *Strategic Management: Competitiveness and Globalization,* sixth edition (2005), and *Mergers and Acquisitions: A Guide to Creating Value for Stakeholders* (2001). He is coeditor of *The Blackwell Entrepreneurship Encyclopedia* (2005) and *Strategic Entrepreneurship: Creating a New Mindset* (2001). He is serving or has served as a member of the editorial review boards for a number of journals such as *Academy of Management Journal, Academy of Management Review, Academy of Management Executive, Journal of Management, Journal of Business Venturing, Entrepreneurship Theory and Practice, Journal of Business Strategy,* and *European Management Journal.* He has coedited special issues of *Academy of Management Review, Academy of Management Executive, Journal of Business Venturing, Strategic Management Journal,* and *Journal of High Technology and Engineering Management.* He received awards for the best article published in *Academy of Management Executive* (1999) and *Academy of Management Journal* (2000). In 2001, his article published in *Academy of Management Executive* won the Best Journal Article in Corporate Entrepreneurship Award from the U.S. Association for Small Business & Entrepreneurship (USASBE). He is a Research Fellow in the National Entrepreneurship Consortium. He received the 1999 Award for Outstanding Intellectual Contributions to Competitiveness Research from the American Society for Competitiveness and the USASBE Scholar in Corporate Entrepreneurship Award (2004) from USASBE. Currently, he is an Associate Editor for *Academy Management Journal.* Previously, he served as a representative-at-large on the Board of Governors of the Academy of Management.

Robert E. Hoskisson

Robert E. Hoskisson is a Professor of Strategic Management and he holds the W. P. Carey Chair in the Department of Management at the W. P. Carey School of Business at Arizona State University. He was formerly on the faculty at the University of Oklahoma as well as Texas A&M University. He also has a special appointment at the University of Nottingham in the United Kingdom. He received his Ph.D. from the University of California–Irvine. His interest in strategic management topics has allowed him to teach overview as well topical courses in strategic management at the undergraduate, master's, and doctoral levels. He has taught topical courses in international strategy and strategic alliances and has made a number of specialized presentations on corporate governance, mergers and acquisitions, divestitures, strategy in emerging economies and corporate entrepreneurship, privatization, and cooperative strategy. These presentations were derived from his active research agenda in these topical areas. His teaching and research expertise in these areas has been recognized. For example, in 1998, he received an award for Outstanding Academic Contributions to Competitiveness, American Society for Competitiveness. He also received the William G. Dyer Distinguished Alumni Award given at the Marriott School of Management, Brigham Young University. He is a Fellow of the Academy of Management and a charter member of the Academy of Management Journals Hall of Fame. These recognitions come from his academic oriented publications in top peer-reviewed journals including the *Academy of Management Journal, Academy of Management Review, Strategic Management Journal, Organization Science, Journal of Management,* and *Journal of Management Studies.* Because of his interest in managerial practice and application, his advice has been published in journals that specialize in translating academic research into prescriptions for managerial practice, such as the *California Management Review, Academy of Management Executive, Long Range Planning,* and *Journal of World Business.* His research has been reviewed in the *MIT Sloan Management Review.* He has also coauthored a number of textbooks to foster instruction in Strategic Management including the 6th edition of *Strategic Management: Competitiveness and Globalization* and *Competing for Advantage* (1st edition). He has also coauthored *Downscoping: How to Tame the Diversified Firm* (Oxford University Press), a masters level text on restructuring large businesses. In serving the academic community, Hoskisson has served on several editorial boards for publications such as the *Academy of Management Journal* (including Consulting Editor and Guest Editor of a special issue), *Strategic Management Journal, Journal of Management* (including Associate Editor), *Journal of International Business Studies* (Consulting Editor), *Organization Science,* and *Journal of Management Studies* (Guest Editor). He completed three years of service as a representative-at-large on the Board of Governors of the Academy of Management and currently is on the Board of Directors of the Strategic Management Society.

Michael A. Hitt

Michael A. Hitt is a Distinguished Professor and holds the Joseph Foster Chair in Business Leadership and the C. W. and Dorothy Conn Chair in New Ventures at Texas A&M University. He received his Ph.D. from the University of Colorado. He has authored or coauthored over 120 journal articles and coauthored or coedited 25 separate books. Those books include: *Downscoping: How to Tame the Diversified Firm* (1994); *Mergers and Acquisitions: A Guide to Creating Value for Stakeholders* (2001); *Handbook of Strategic Management* (2001); *Strategic Entrepreneurship: Creating a New Integrated Mindset* (2002); *Managing Knowledge for Sustained Competitive Advantage* (2003); *Competing for Advantage* (2004); *The Blackwell Entrepreneurship Encyclopedia* (2005); *Strategic Management: Competitiveness and Globalization* (2005); and *Great Minds in Management: The Process of Theory Development* (2005). He has served on the editorial review boards of multiple journals and served as Consulting Editor (1988–1990) and Editor (1991–1993) of the *Academy of Management Journal*. He serves as President Elect of the Strategic Management Society and is a past president of the Academy of Management. He received the 1996 Award for Outstanding Academic Contributions to Competitiveness and the 1999 Award for Outstanding Intellectual Contributions to Competitiveness Research from the American Society for Competitiveness. He is a Fellow in the Academy of Management and a Research Fellow in the National Entrepreneurship Consortium, and received an honorary doctorate from the Universidad Carlos III de Madrid for his contributions to the field. He received the Irwin Outstanding Educator Award and the Distinguished Service Award from the Academy of Management.

Understanding Concepts of Business Strategy

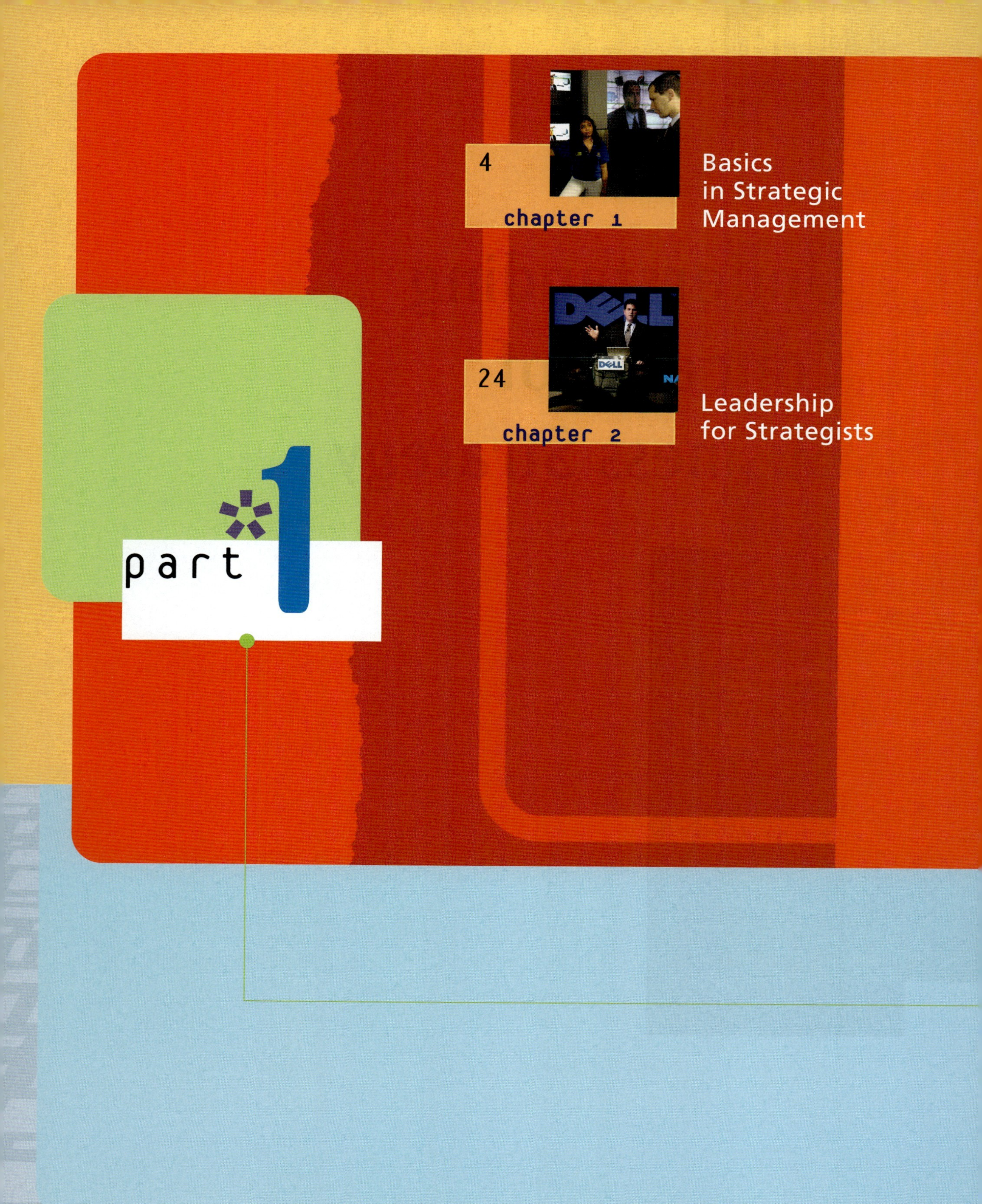

part 1

The Mission Statement, Vision and Strategy

Basics in Strategic Management

Reading and studying this chapter should enable you to:

*Knowledge Objectives

1_
Define strategic management.

2_
Discuss why firms use the industrial organization model to analyze their external environment.

3_
Discuss why firms use the resource-based view of the firm model to analyze their internal environment.

4_
Define stakeholders and understand their importance.

5_
Explain the work of strategic leaders.

© REUTERS/Heidi Schumann/Landov

Focusing on Strategy

Solidly Focusing on Customers: The Foundation for Best Buy's Success?

"We are in the midst of a strategic transformation to put the customer at the center of all that we do." (Brad Anderson, vice chairman and chief executive officer [CEO], Best Buy)

Consumer electronics is a highly competitive business. Just think of the options you have as a consumer when buying a LCD television, which is only one of many electronic products you could buy. First, you could use the Internet to learn more about LCD televisions made by Sony, Samsung, Hitachi, Panasonic, and a host of other firms. With some information about LCD televisions, you could then shop at retailers such as Circuit City and Best Buy, smaller retailers located in your city or region, or even specialized stores focusing on tailoring home theater systems that include a LCD television. You can even purchase a used LCD television through an eBay auction.

As a "big box retailer," Best Buy competes with all of these sellers (Circuit City, local retailers, specialized stores, and eBay) to serve customers shopping for a LCD television as well as many other electronic products. While Best Buy is fully aware of the competitors mentioned so far, the firm's leaders are increasingly concerned about new competitors from different sources. Dell and Gateway, for example, now sell their own LCD televisions (as well as other consumer electronic products) via the Internet. While Gateway's future remains cloudy, Dell's ability to produce high-quality products at a low cost and to use the Internet to sell directly to consumers presents a clear competitive threat to electronics retailers such as Best Buy. Perhaps even more daunting is the threat Wal-Mart poses as it moves further into electronics retailing. Given this threat, if you were the CEO of Best Buy, what actions would you think of taking to compete against Wal-Mart?

A transformation to what the firm calls *customer centricity* is Best Buy's answer to these competitive threats. According to the firm's CEO, Best Buy is "in the midst of a strategic transformation to put the customer at the center of all that it does." The firm is launching customer centricity as a preemptive strike to its new competitive threats and to continue competing successfully against current competitors.

In the initial stage of its efforts to put the customer at the center of all that it does, Best Buy developed five prototypical customers, each of whom was given a name. Over the next several years, Best Buy stores will be converted to concentrate on serving the needs of one, but no more than two of the firm's five customer segments. *Jill* is a busy suburban mom who wants to enrich her children's lives with technology and entertainment. *Buzz* is a focused, active, younger male seeking the latest technology in his entertainment purchases. *Ray* is a family man wanting to purchase electronics that improve his and his family's life. *BB4B* (short for Best Buy for Business) is a small-business customer who can use Best Buy's product solutions and services to increase productivity and profitability. Finally, *Barry* is an affluent professional who wants to buy the best technology and entertainment experience and demands superior customer service.

Is customer centricity a success at Best Buy? It's too early to tell. The firm may change aspects of the program as it is introduced across all stores. But Best Buy's same-store sales for the ending of the first quarter in 2004 increased 8.3 percent. *Same-store sales* compares the sales revenue for a store that has been open for one or more years on a similar basis (such as a full year to a full year or a specific quarter of the current year to a specific quarter of the previous year). *Same-store sales* is an important performance measure because it allows investors to understand the part of a firm's growth in sales revenue accounted for by stores that were opened in a given year as well as the part of growth in sales revenue accounted for by existing stores within a year.

In addition to sales revenue growth, profitability was also improving in 2004 at Best Buy. In fact, the firm estimated that its earnings from continuing operations during the fourth quarter of 2004 would jump by 55 percent. Best Buy's leaders will study the increases in the firm's sales revenue and profits to determine the degree to which the strong focus on the consumer contributed to them.

SOURCES: 2004, Best Buy accelerates customer centricity transformation, Best Buy Home Page, http://www.bestbuy.com, June 3; J. Freed, 2004, Marketing to "Jill," "Ray," and "Barry," *Richmond Times-Dispatch,* May 23: D1, D2; M. Higgins, 2004, New retail offering: Geeks on call, *Wall Street Journal Online,* http://www.wsj.com, May 20; J. Seward, 2004, Best Buy same-store sales rise, sees earnings in-line, *Wall Street Journal Online,* http://www.wsj.com, June 3.

Do you sometimes wonder why some firms are more successful than others? Why, for example, is Best Buy's sales revenue more than twice that of Circuit City, its closest competitor?[1] Why is Toyota, traditionally a marginal player in Europe, now becoming a significant force in European markets? (Hint: Some believe that Toyota's new design studio in southern France and its new highly efficient manufacturing facility in Valenciennes in northern France account for its recent European success.)[2]

Although the reasons for Best Buy's and Toyota's success as well as the successes of many other firms sometimes seem mysterious, they really aren't. As with Best Buy and Toyota, firms use strategic management to achieve success. The purpose of this book is to carefully explain each of the three parts of strategic management—*vision, analysis,* and *strategy.* We think you will enjoy learning about strategic management and know that you will benefit from doing so.

What Is Strategic Management?

Strategic management is the ongoing process companies use to form a *vision*, *analyze* their external environment and their internal environment, and select one or more *strategies* to use to create value for customers and other stakeholders, especially shareholders. Let's define the parts of the strategic management process so we can see the differences among them. We merely introduce you to the parts of strategic management in this chapter. You'll learn more about each part in the book's remaining chapters.

The **vision** contains at least two components—a mission that describes the firm's DNA and the "picture" of the firm as it hopes to exist in a future time period. DNA includes the core information and characteristics necessary for the firm to function. The vision is intended to inspire the firm's employees to realize or "picture" the future aspirations of what the firm can become. A **strategy** is an action plan designed to move an organization toward achievement of its vision. The mission of the firm is focused on the markets it serves and the products (either goods or services) it provides. Basically, the **mission** defines the firm's core intent and the business or businesses in which it intends to operate. The **external environment** is a set of conditions outside the firm that affect the firm's performance. Changes in population trends and income levels, competition between firms, and economic changes are examples of the many conditions in a firm's external environment that can affect its performance. For example, think of the effect of increases in mortgage rates (which are part of the *economic* external environment) on home builders. The **internal environment** is the set of conditions (such as strengths, resources, capabilities, and so forth) inside the firm affecting the choice and use of strategies.

Strengths are resources and capabilities that allow the firm to complete important tasks. Being able to effectively manage the flow of its inventory is one of Best Buy's strengths that help it complete the important task of having the right merchandise on its shelves for customers to buy. **Resources** are the tangible and intangible assets held by the firm. A strong balance sheet is one of Coca-Cola's tangible assets, while the knowledge held by its employees is one of Microsoft's intangible assets. **Capabilities** result when the firm integrates several different resources to complete a task or a series of related tasks.[3] 3M integrates the knowledge of its scientists (an intangible asset) with other resources, including its sophisticated scientific equipment (a tangible asset), to create its innovation capability. **Core competencies** are capabilities the firm emphasizes and performs especially well while pursuing its vision. The distribution and inventory competencies Dell uses to sell computers directly to customers are considered core competencies. Core competencies that differ from those held by competitors are called **distinctive competencies.** Dell's distribution and inventory competencies differ from those of its competitors (for example, HP and IBM) and thus are also distinctive competencies. When core competencies allow the firm to create value for customers by performing a key activity (such as Dell's distribution competencies) *better* than competitors, it has a **competitive advantage.** A firm can also have a competitive advantage when a distinctive competence allows it to perform an activity that creates value for customers that competitors can't perform.

Figure 1.1 is a diagram of strategic management, while Table 1.1 presents a set of strategic management's key characteristics. We continue our introduction of strategic management's parts in the next few sections.

FIGURE 1.1 The Strategic Management Process

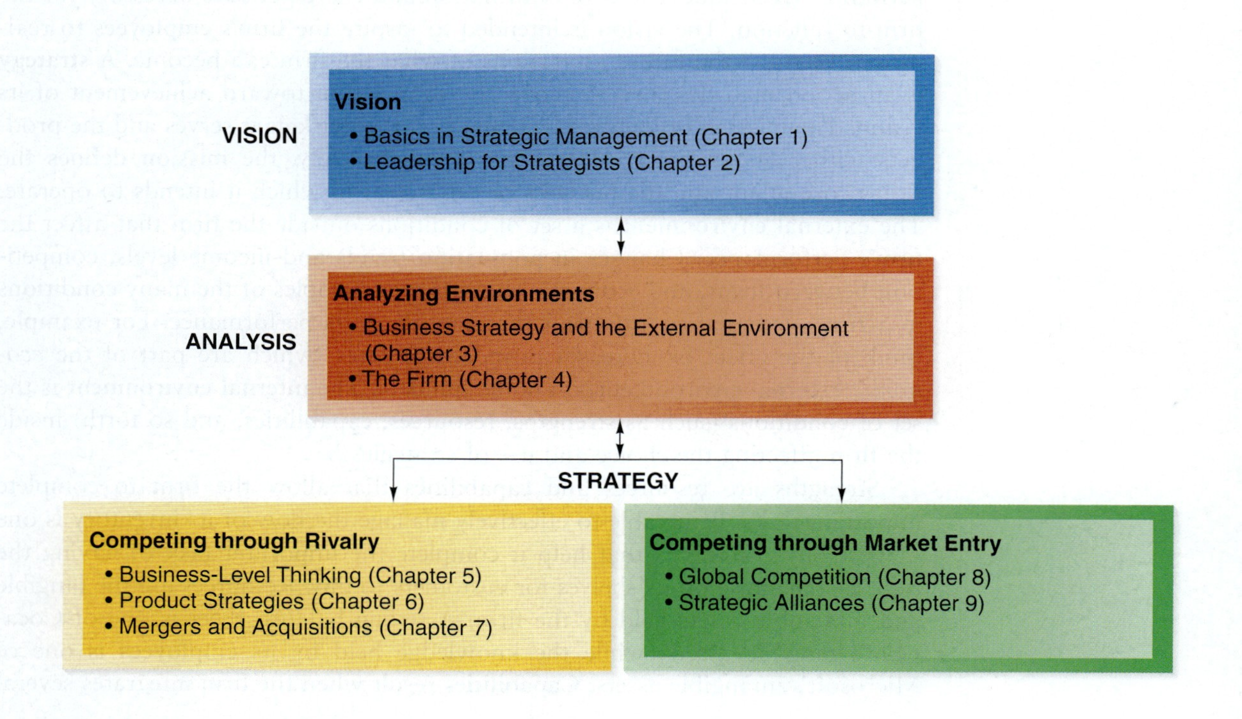

TABLE 1.1 Key Characteristics of Strategic Management

Strategic management is:
- Performance oriented
- Ongoing in nature
- Dynamic rather than static
- Oriented to the present and the future
- Concerned with conditions both outside and inside the firm
- Concerned with performing well and satisfying stakeholders

The Three Parts of the Strategic Management Process

As suggested in Figure 1.1, strategic leaders are responsible for forming a firm's vision and mission (we talk about this further in Chapter 2). As noted earlier, an effective mission provides direction to the firm while an effective vision "inspires people to subsequent efforts."[4] We present additional vision statements and mission statements from different types of organizations in Table 1.2. Which of the vision statements shown in Table 1.2 inspire you? Which of the mission statements does the best job of telling you about the direction a firm is taking? Would you make changes to any of the vision or mission statements shown in Table 1.2? If so, why, and what would those changes be?

Figure 1.1 also suggests that firms must *analyze* their external environment and their internal environment before strategies can be chosen and *implemented*. Here's how this worked at Best Buy. Following careful study, Best Buy spotted an opportunity in its external environment to group customers based on their different needs. After analyzing its internal environment, Best Buy decided to use its capabilities in supply chain management and customer relationship management systems to serve the unique needs of each customer group.

Rivals Coca-Cola and PepsiCo use various strategies to compete with each other. In what ways are their strategies unique?

As mentioned earlier, a strategy is an action plan designed to move an organization toward achievement of its vision. Strategy is about finding ways for the firm to be different from its competitors. The most effective companies avoid using "me-too" strategies—strategies that are the same as those of their competitors. A firm's strategy should allow it to deliver a unique mix of value to customers.[5]

As shown in Figure 1.1, firms use business-level strategies, multiproduct strategies, and international strategies to directly compete with rivals. With product names such as

TABLE 1.2 Vision and Mission Statements

Vision Statements

McDonald's

To give each customer, every time, an experience that sets new standards in value, service, friendliness, and quality.

NASDAQ

To build the world's first truly global securities market . . . A worldwide market of markets built on a worldwide network of networks . . . linking pools of liquidity and connecting investors from all over the world . . . assuring the best possible price for securities at the lowest possible cost.

Petsmart

To be the premier organization in nurturing and enriching the bond between people and animals.

Wachovia

Wachovia's vision is to be the best, most trusted and admired financial services company.

Mission Statements

Bristol-Myers Squibb

Our mission is to extend and enhance human life by providing the highest-quality pharmaceuticals and health care products.

GlaxoSmithKline

GSK's mission is to improve the quality of human life by enabling people to do more, feel better and live longer.

Merck

The mission of Merck is to provide society with superior products and services by developing innovations and solutions that improve the quality of life and satisfy customer needs, and to provide employees with meaningful work and advancement opportunities, and investors with a superior rate of return.

Wipro

The mission is to be a full-service, global outsourcing company.

Mastiff and Pitbull, Big Dog Motorcycles' strategy is to build premium, heavyweight motorcycles that are targeted for customers with needs for this unique product. Big Dog competes directly against Harley-Davidson with its business-level strategy, as do Coca-Cola and PepsiCo with their business-level, multiproduct, and international strategies. Companies also use certain strategies (such as mergers and acquisitions, alliances, and new ventures) to enter new markets. To expand into additional markets, for example, Aqua America, a water utility company, acquired more than 90 firms in the last several years. Beginning with locations in Pennsylvania, the firm now serves more than 800,000 customers in 13 states.[6] As the term implies, the firm uses market-entry strategies to begin competing in new markets.

Once chosen, strategies must be put into use. **Strategy implementation** is the set of actions firms take to use a strategy after it has been selected. PetMed Express is a pet pharmacy with a strategy of providing the largest selection of prescription and nonprescription pet medications to consumers at competitive prices. Part of how PetMed Express implements this strategy is by using the Internet and telemarketing to sell its products to customers.[7]

In "Understanding Strategy," we describe the initial success of Netflix. As you'll see, the firm has a vision and a strategy that it is successfully implementing. Thus, the strategic management process is being used effectively at Netflix. Indeed, the firm has experienced much success in its early years. Shareholders and employees hope that Netflix will continue to grow and will become a consistently profitable corporation. However, organizational success can be transitory, even for very famous companies. Levi Strauss, for example, was quite successful for many years. However, between 1996 and 2001, the firm's sales dropped from $7.1 billion to $4.3 billion.[8] When a firm such as Levi Strauss experiences trouble, some top-level managers become paranoid about their own company's future success. Patricia Sueltz, executive vice president of Salesforce.com, feels that she has to keep looking over her shoulder to see what competitors are doing to determine whether those actions are a threat to her firm's performance.[9] There are no guarantees that what currently works for any firm will work for it in the future. When used properly, though, the strategic management process contributes to a company's desire to reach its vision by competing successfully across time. Let's see how Netflix has used the strategic management process and learn about the challenges the firm faces to remain successful.

After reading about Netflix, what do you think? Will this firm continue to grow? On a long-term basis, will Netflix be able to compete against the likes of Wal-Mart and Blockbuster?[10] Given what you know, would you be willing to invest in Netflix? Why or why not?

We've now introduced you to the parts of strategic management, provided you with examples of vision statements and mission statements, and described how one firm—Netflix—is using the strategic management process. We'll use the remainder of this chapter to tell you a bit more about how firms analyze their external environment and their internal environment. Decision makers use the information gathered from the analyses of their firm's external environment and internal environment to select one or more strategies (see Figure 1.1). Before closing the chapter with a brief discussion of the contents of the book's remaining chapters, we'll introduce you to stakeholders and strategic leaders. In essence, stakeholders are the individuals and groups that firms try to satisfy when using the strategic management process, while strategic leaders are responsible for making certain their firm effectively uses the process.

The Industrial Organization Model

Firms use what is called the industrial organization (I/O) model to analyze their external environment. We introduce you to this model here and provide you with a fuller discussion of it and its use in Chapter 3. Using this model helps firms identify opportunities and threats. **Opportunities** are conditions in the firm's external environment that may help the firm reach its vision. **Threats** are conditions in the firm's external environment that may prevent the firm from reaching its vision. Performance often declines in firms that do not carefully study the threats and opportunities in their external environment. Firms use their resources to pursue environmental opportunities and to overcome environmental

learning from success

understanding strategy:

ONLINE RENTALS: USING STRATEGIC MANAGEMENT TO PIONEER A MARKET

Frustrated by recurring late fees, Reed Hastings developed the concept of an all-you-can-rent online movie business in 1997. Hastings established his firm, Netflix, after studying the external environment and concluding that "People love to rent movies, they hate late fees, and they like the Net." Netflix works like this: For a flat monthly fee beginning at $11.99 per month in January 2005, customers rent all the DVDs they want, three at a time, without incurring late fees. Viewed rentals are returned in prepaid mailing envelopes. Netflix then sends customers the next items on their own personalized list (called a "rental queue") that is retained for them on Netflix's Web site.

Netflix serves a niche in the movie rental market, and a growing number of analysts consider it "a brilliant idea (that) is well executed." In terms of strategic management, this comment suggests that as a strategic leader, Hastings worked with others to establish a vision for his company and then chose a strategy to reach it after analyzing the firm's external environment and its internal environment. Essentially, the vision is for Netflix to "provide superior service to movie buffs." "Well executed" means that the strategy is being effectively implemented. Carefully placed distribution centers and continuous efforts to understand and respond to customers' needs are examples of what Netflix does to implement its strategy.

What does the future hold for Netflix? Strong competition from Wal-Mart and Blockbuster is a significant challenge. Analysts warn that "Wal-Mart's brand name, in-store marketing and world-famous distribution system could eventually loom large" as a competitive threat similar to Blockbuster's Online rental service which was priced at $14.99 per month in January 2005. In addition, Blockbuster was still trying to acquire Hollywood Entertainment Corporation in the first part of 2005. If this effort succeeds, Blockbuster would become an even larger competitor for Netflix and Wal-Mart. In spite of the challenges from Blockbuster and Wal-Mart, Hastings is undeterred, believing that his firm has only "scratched the surface" of the value it can bring to customers. To continue delivering that value, Netflix should remain committed to using its strategic management process.

SOURCES: S. H. Meitner, 2004, Netflix flexes video rental muscle, *Richmond Times-Dispatch,* March 14: D9; D. Oestricher, 2004, Netflix won't match Blockbuster's price cut, CEO says, *Wall Street Journal Online,* http://www.wsj.com, December 22; E. J. Savitz, 2004, Netflix may be overvalued, *Wall Street Journal Online,* http://www.wsj.com, February 29; 2004, Netflix issues profit warning, citing subscriber growth costs, *Wall Street Journal Online,* http://www.wsj.com, February 24; 2004, Wrangling for rentals, *Barron's Online,* http://www.barrons.com, February 23.

threats. We demonstrate this point in "Understanding Strategy," which discusses Levi Strauss & Co.

The case of Levi Strauss shows how important it is for firms to understand the meaning of conditions in their external environment. As explained in "Understanding Strategy," Levi Strauss failed to detect changes in its external environment such as those in customers' preferences. Changing preferences among the firm's customers, which were threats to Levi Strauss, mandated that the firm begin to produce more fashionable jeans and related clothing items. Thus, firms must carefully analyze their external environment to anticipate its effects on their current strategy.

learning from failure

understanding strategy:

THE "501" JEAN: A CLOTHING ICON LOSES SOME OF ITS PANACHE

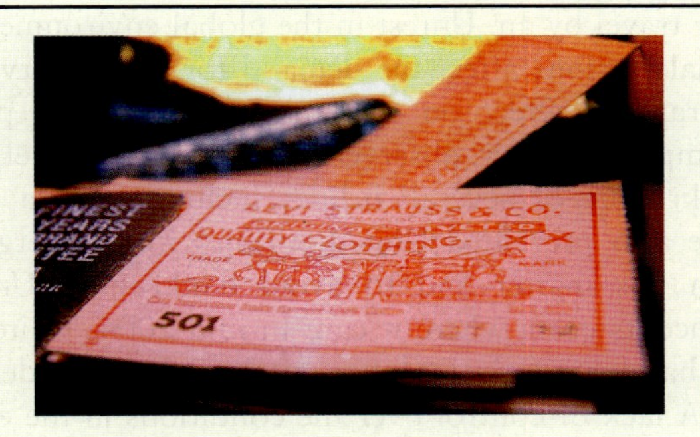

© GAMBARINI MAURIZIO/DPA/Landov

"One of America's most durable apparel brands is fighting for its life in the midst of a tough environment for apparel retailing." This comment by a business analyst suggests that difficult times are on hand for vulnerable jeans manufacturer Levi Strauss. Indeed, losses in market share and profit declines from the late 1990s into the early 2000s appear to demonstrate Levi's problems.

Established in 1873, Levi Strauss was the clear leader in the global jeans market as late as the 1970s. The famous 501 jean was the firm's flagship product and the foundation of its success. However, this product remained essentially unchanged through the 1970s, even though customers began to view jeans differently. Historically, jeans were generally thought to be a utilitarian, durable clothing item—something people could comfortably wear when working, especially for manual labor. By the end of the 1970s, though, jeans became fashionable as a result of the efforts of a number of firms such as Calvin Klein, Gloria Vanderbilt, Ralph Lauren, and Jordache. Indeed, these companies' stylish jeans revolutionized this product, damaging Levi Strauss's market share as a result. Soon, fickle customers were frequently changing their choice of jeans, moving from the current fashion trend to the next "hot" one on a regular basis. Jeans also were distributed more broadly, including through the channels of discounters such as Wal-Mart and Target. However, Levi Strauss chose not to sell through discounters' stores, preferring to remain focused on its traditional distribution channels (such as JCPenney and Sears, Roebuck). Thus, Levi Strauss's inability to handle threats in its external environment found the firm in a situation in which it was trying to sell items that customers didn't perceive as fashionable through distribution channels that were losing market share. Successful use of the strategic management process likely would have helped Levi Strauss deal more effectively with changes in its external environment (such as the changes in customers' preferences for jeans). In other words, if Levi had made a full-scale commitment to strategic management, it would have carefully studied its external environment in order to identify trends that might affect its operations.

Although it was slow to respond, Levi Strauss is now launching major product initiatives. "In late 2002," for example, "Levi Strauss overhauled its market strategy and, for the first time since the introduction of Dockers in 1986, rolled out a series of new brands," including the unusually cut Engineered Jeans, the Superlow for women, and the Type 1. Levi Strauss viewed the Type 1 as a product with truly innovative styling, as reflected by its exaggerated pocket details and superdark denim finishes. Levi promised that the Type 1 would be "the boldest, most provocative Levi's jeans in decades." However, early reaction was that the Type 1 was too cutting-edge for Levi's mainstream customer while it failed to appeal to other potential customers. Thus, only time will tell if Levi Strauss will return to its glory days as a top performer in its industry on the basis of the actions it is now taking.

SOURCES: S. Beatty, 2004, Levi Strauss plans to continue its sales strategy on jean styles, *Wall Street Journal Online*, http://www.wsj.com, March 3; D. K. Berman & S. Beatty, 2004, Levi to sell its Docker brand to Vestar for $800 million, *Wall Street Journal*, September 27: B6; D. Gross, 2004, Seams to be, *USAirways Attache*, March: 13–14; 2004, Levi Strauss & Co., *Hoover's*, http://www.hoovers.com, March 14; 2004, Levi Strauss & Co. Home Page, http://www.levistrauss.com, March 15.

Similar to Levi Strauss, the global airline industry illustrates the influence of the external environment on a firm's choice of strategy. Let's describe this influence.

Economic conditions, which as we said before are part of the firm's external environment, influence travel decisions. During poor economic times, for example, people might choose not to travel at all or to reduce the number of times they travel by air. Unrest in the global environment created by war and international tensions affect the demand for airline services. The cost of fuel can have a dramatic effect on each airline company's profitability; in mid-2004, for example, industry observers suggested that fuel costs could contribute to the bankruptcy of several airlines including Delta Airlines. Increasing fuel costs have also prevented United Airlines from emerging from bankruptcy. To deal with this matter and to avoid bankruptcy, United is aggressively trying to reduce its costs where it can. In mid-2004, United was studying the possibility of abandoning its employee pension plan in order to lower its costs.[11]

A lack of control over the conditions in the external environment reduces a firm's strategic options. A lack of options results in firms within an industry using similar strategies, such as is the case with airline companies. As a customer, think of your travel on airlines. The firms use the same planes to offer you essentially the same service at virtually the same price. While variances do exist, of course, do you think that customers can differentiate greatly among airline companies? If not, this could indicate that the external environment is influencing these companies to follow similar strategies.

In Figure 1.2, we diagram how firms use the I/O model to analyze their external environment. The information gained from this analysis is used to help decision makers choose one or more strategies. We'll explain the I/O model and its use in greater detail in Chapter 3.

The Resource-Based View of the Firm Model

While the I/O model focuses on the firm's external environment, the resource-based view (RBV) model describes what firms do to analyze their internal environment. The purpose of analyzing the internal environment is to identify the firm's strengths, resources, capabilities, core competencies, distinctive competencies, and competitive advantages. Thus, the I/O and RBV models complement each other; one (the I/O model) deals with conditions outside the firm and the other (the RBV model) deals with conditions inside the firm. We introduce you to the RBV model here and offer a fuller description of it in Chapter 4.

The RBV model suggests that effective management of the firm's operations creates resources and capabilities that are unique to that firm. This means that the bundle of productive resources across firms can vary quite substantially.[12] Louis Vuitton's resources and capabilities, for example, differ from those of competitors Prada, Gucci, Hermes, and Coach. With unique resources and capabilities, ones that are different from competitors', each of these firms has a chance to create competitive advantages that it can use to produce a product that creates value for a group of customers. Let's describe how Louis Vuitton uses its unique resources and capabilities to develop competitive advantages that in turn allow the firm to create value for a group of customers.

FIGURE 1.2 Using the Industrial Organization (I/O) Model to Analyze the External Environment

Studying
- Examining conditions in the firm's external environment to assess their effects on the firm

↓

Identifying
- Determining an attractive industry or segment of an industry

↓

Selecting
- Choosing the strategy called for by the influences of the firm's external environment

↓

Implementing
- Using the firm's resources to implement the chosen strategy

Customers of Louis Vuitton buy into the dream of owning luxury brand products.

The world's most profitable luxury brand, Vuitton has design skills and manufacturing efficiencies that are considered superior to those of its competitors. These capabilities allow Louis Vuitton to generate higher operating margins. In the words of an executive at competitor Coach, Vuitton's "operating metrics are second to none."[13] Because of Vuitton's superiority relative to its competitors, these capabilities are the foundation for the company's competitive advantages in product design and manufacturing.

Although expensive, the firm's products do create value for a group of customers. One customer sees this value as "buying into a dream." In this particular customer's words, "You buy into the dream of Louis Vuitton. We're part of a sect, and the more they put their prices up, the more we come back. They pull the wool over our eyes, but we love it."[14]

Unlike the external environment, firms have direct control over conditions in their internal environment. Each firm's decision makers make choices about the resources

FIGURE 1.3 Using the RBV Model to Analyze the Internal Environment

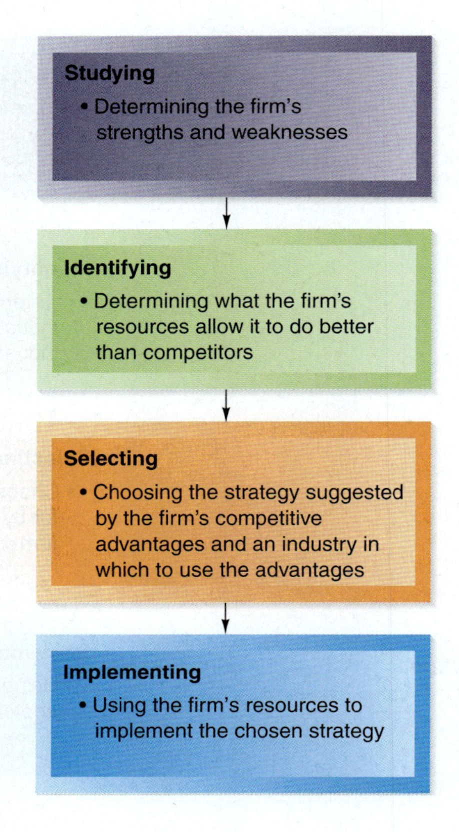

and capabilities the firm wants to control and about how they'll be nurtured and used. The ability to control the firm's resources and capabilities and to develop them in ways that differ from those of the competitors' increases the number of strategic options. Thus, from the RBV perspective, the uniqueness of the firm's resources and capabilities influences the choice of one or more strategies.

Figure 1.3 diagrams how firms use the RBV to analyze their internal environment. Notice how the firm's resources and capabilities influence the choice of a strategy.

Next, we discuss stakeholders—the individuals and groups the firm seeks to satisfy by using the strategy or strategies it has selected.

Stakeholders

Stakeholders are individuals and groups who have an interest in a firm's performance and an ability to influence its actions.[15] In essence, stakeholders influence firms by deciding the degree to which they will support the firm's strategy.

Shareholders, customers, and suppliers are stakeholders, as are a firm's employees and the communities in which the firm conducts business. Shareholders, for example, exercise their influence by deciding whether they will keep their shares in the firm or sell them. Employees decide whether they will remain with their employer or work for another firm, perhaps even a competitor. Not surprisingly, firms use strategic management to select and implement strategies that create value for stakeholders.[16]

As shown in Figure 1.4, firms have three major stakeholder groups—owners (shareholders), external stakeholders, and internal stakeholders. Each stakeholder wants the firm in which it has an interest to satisfy its needs. Generally speaking, stakeholders continue to support firms that satisfy their needs. However, stakeholders withdraw their support from firms failing to meet their needs.

Stakeholders' interest in performance, coupled with their ability to influence the firm through their decisions to support the firm or not, suggests that companies have important *relationships* with their stakeholders. These relationships must be managed in a way that keeps the stakeholders committed to the firm. Firms that can manage relationships with their stakeholders better than their competitors may gain a competitive advantage.[17] Firms that see stakeholders as their partners and keep them well informed about the company's actions provide an example.[18]

Firms and stakeholders have relationships because they need each other. To launch a company and operate it on a continuing basis, firms need capital (that is, money) provided by investors (such as stockholders) and financial institutions (such as banks), materials from suppliers that are used to produce a good or provide a service, and employees to complete necessary tasks. In addition and importantly, firms need customers to buy their good or service. Similarly, investors (individual stockholders and institutional stockholders such as pension funds) need to find viable businesses in which they can invest and earn a return on their capital. Employees need to work for organizations for income and at least some personal satisfaction. Customers want to buy goods and services from companies that will satisfy their various needs. Thus, firms need stakeholders, but stakeholders also need firms.

FIGURE 1.4 Stakeholder Groups

Owners
Shareholders
- Individual
- Institutional

External Stakeholders
- Customers
- Suppliers
- Local communities
- Governmental agencies
- General society

Internal Stakeholders
- Employees
- Managers

Managing relationships between the firm and its stakeholders is difficult because satisfying one stakeholder's needs may come at the expense of another stakeholder. Consider, for example, employees' desire to be paid more for their work. If wages are increased without an identical increase in productivity to offset the higher costs, the firm's cost of goods sold will increase, reducing the return on investment for shareholders. Alternatively, think of customers wanting to buy higher-quality products from a firm at ever-decreasing prices. The net result of the firm's lowering the price of its good or service without reducing the cost to produce it is fewer resources for wages and salaries and for returns to shareholders.

While other examples could be offered, the main point here is that firms must manage their relationships with stakeholders in ways that will keep all stakeholders at least minimally satisfied. In other words, the firm wants to retain quality suppliers, loyal customers, and satisfied employees while providing returns to shareholders that cause them to retain their investment in the firm. As these comments show, managing relationships among various stakeholders is a challenging, yet important task for the firm's strategic leaders.

Strategic Leaders

Strategic leaders are the individuals practicing strategic leadership. (We define and fully discuss strategic leadership in the next chapter.) Strategic leaders make certain that actions are being taken that will lead to their firm's success.[19] As CEO of Apple Computer, for example, Steve Jobs must make certain that his firm uses strategic management to continue benefiting from its highly successful iPod digital music player.[20] A firm's board of directors holds the CEO and her top management team responsible for ensuring that an effective strategic management process is developed and properly used throughout the organization. When doing their work, top-level managers concentrate on the "big picture" to envision their firm's future and the strategies necessary to achieve that vision.[21]

In small firms, the CEO may be the sole owner and may not report to a board of directors. In this instance, of course, she is responsible for both designing and using strategic management. Decisions that strategic leaders make when using the strategic management process include determining the resources acquired, the prices paid for those resources, and how to manage those resources.[22] Through the firm's vision statement, strategic leaders try to stimulate their employees' creativity to develop new products, new processes to produce the firm's products, and the administrative routines necessary to successfully implement the firm's strategies.[23]

The CEO and his top management team are also responsible for shaping and nurturing the firm's culture. **Organizational culture** is the set of values and beliefs that are shared throughout the firm. *Values* reflect what is important, while *beliefs* speak to how things should be done. In 3M's organizational culture, respecting the contribution of each employee and continuous innovation are important values.[24] The most effective organizational cultures let people know that they are appreciated. When this happens, culture can be a strong motivator of excellent performance by employees.[25]

Intangible in nature, culture can't be touched or seen but its presence is felt throughout every organization. Think of companies where you've worked, university classes you've attended, or other groups to which you've belonged. Consider the values and beliefs held by each of those groups. How did it feel to be a member of those groups? The groups you are thinking about are different in terms of their values and beliefs, aren't they? The same can be said of business organizations.

Increasingly, strategic management is becoming more decentralized in companies. The reason for this is to have the people who are "closest to the action" making decisions and taking actions.[26] Thus, the strategic management process is often shared among many people in an organization.[27] As a result, we need to be prepared to take on leadership roles regardless of our position in an organization. Additionally, frequent communication among all involved with the strategic management process helps ensure that changes are made when and where they are needed. Because of changing conditions, adjustments are often necessary when implementing strategies.

We should understand, though, that while many different people may be involved, the final responsibility for effective strategic management rests with the firm's strategic leaders. In addition, it is important to note that the best strategic leaders also act ethically in all that they do. *Ethics* are concerned with the standards for deciding what is good or bad, right or wrong[28] as defined by most members of a particular society.[29] In an organizational context, ethics reveal a value system that has been widely adopted by the firm's employees[30] and that other stakeholders recognize as an important driver of decisions and actions. Firms can record their ethics in documents such as a code of conduct. On a daily basis, however, ethics can be inferred by observing the actions of the firm's stakeholders, especially its employees.[31] Even a brief review of events in the business world shows that an organization's ethics are of interest to the general society as well as to other stakeholders whose interests can be negatively affected when a firm acts unethically. Thus, as explored further in Chapter 2, ethical practices are a vital part of effective strategic leadership and strategic management.[32]

How the Book Is Organized

The book has three major parts, corresponding to the three parts of the strategic management process. Part One of this book comprises two chapters. This first chapter introduces you to strategic management. In Chapter 2, we describe leadership from a strategic perspective. Strategic leadership is being effectively practiced when everyone in a firm is aware of the vision being pursued and the important role each person plays in pursuing that vision. We also describe the most important actions strategic leaders take to guide their organizations.

In Part Two, which also has two chapters, we focus on two analyses that firms use to obtain and evaluate the information needed to choose strategies for pursuing the firm's vision. Chapter 3 focuses on the external environment. A firm analyzes the external environment to identify factors outside the company that can affect the strategic actions the firm is taking to achieve its vision. Firms can influence but not control conditions in their external environment. The focus of Chapter 4 is inside the firm. Here, the purpose is to understand how the firm's unique resources and capabilities can be shaped to form competitive advantages (that is, create superior value for customers) and satisfy stakeholders' needs.

Part Three examines different types of strategies. The strategies the firm selects are a product of the vision and the conditions in its external environment and its internal environment. This means that the insights gained from the topics presented in the book's first four chapters strongly guide the selection of strategies. In Chapters 5, 6, and 7, our concern is with different strategies (business-level, multiproduct, and international) that firms use to successfully compete in different markets. Each chapter also provides guidelines for implementing different strategies. We follow these discussions with explanations in Chapters 8–9 of strategies (mergers and acquisitions, cooperative alliances, and new ventures) that firms use to enter new markets.

Summary

The primary purpose of this chapter is to introduce you to strategic management and to discuss how firms use this important organizational tool to continuously improve their performance for stakeholders. In doing so, we examined the following topics:

- **Strategic management** is the ongoing process that firms use to form a vision, analyze their external and internal environments, and select one or more strategies to create value for customers and satisfy other stakeholders. The external and internal environments are analyzed to determine which strategies should be used (and how to use them) to achieve the vision. Firms use the strategic management process to select one or more strategies to implement to reach their vision. Strategic management is concerned with both formulation (selection of one or more strategies) and implementation (actions taken to ensure that the chosen strategies are used as intended).
- Firms use the industrial organization model (the I/O model) to examine their **external environment** in order to identify opportunities and threats in that environment. Firms use the resource-based view of the firm model (the RBV model) to analyze their **internal environment** in order to identify their resources and competitive advantages. A firm must use both models to have all of the knowledge needed to select strategies that will enable it to achieve its vision.
- **Stakeholders** are individuals and groups who have an interest in how the firm performs and who can influence the firm's actions. Firms and their stakeholders are dependent on each other. Firms must operate in ways that satisfy the needs of each stakeholder (such as shareholders, customers, suppliers, and employees). Firms failing to do this lose a stakeholder's support. Owners, external stakeholders, and internal stakeholders are the three primary stakeholder groups with which firms are involved. But stakeholders need firms as well. Consider, for example, that owners want to invest in profitable firms, employees want to work for acceptable wages, and customers want to buy products that create value for them.
- **Strategic leaders** practice strategic leadership. When doing this, strategic leaders make certain that their firm is effectively using the strategic

management process. Increasingly, effective strategic management results when many people are involved with the strategic management process and when strategic leaders demand that everyone in the firm act responsibly and ethically in all that they do.

Key Terms

capabilities 7
competitive advantage 8
core competencies 8
distinctive competencies 8
external environment 7
internal environment 7
mission 7
opportunities 11
organizational culture 18
resources 7
stakeholders 16
strategic leaders 18
strategic management 7
strategy 7
strategy implementation 10
strengths 7
threats 11
vision 7

Discussion Questions

1. What is strategic management? Describe strategic management's importance to today's organizations.
2. What is the industrial organization (I/O) model? Why do firms use it to analyze their external environment?
3. What is the resource-based view of the firm model? Why do firms use this model to examine their internal environment?
4. Who are stakeholders? Why are stakeholders important to firms? What does it mean to say that the firm has relationships with its stakeholders?
5. What is the nature of the strategic leader's work?

Endnotes

1. J. Freed, 2004, Marketing to "Jill," "Ray" and "Barry," *Richmond Times-Dispatch,* May 23: D1, D2.
2. G. Edmondson & A. Bonnet, 2004, Toyota's new traction in Europe, *Business Week,* June 7, 64.
3. M. Byler & R. W. Coff, 2003, Dynamic capabilities, social capital and rent appropriation: Ties that split ties, *Strategic Management Journal,* 24: 677–686.
4. H. Mintzberg, 1990, The manager's job—folklore and fact: Retrospective commentary, *Harvard Business on Leadership,* Boston: Harvard Business School Press, 29–32.
5. M. E. Porter, 1996, What is strategy? *Harvard Business Review,* 74(6): 61–78.
6. P. Loftus, 2004, Aqua America CEO sees flood of water co. consolidation. *Wall Street Journal Online,* http://www.wsj.com, June 8.
7. 2004, Pets—PetMed Express Inc., *Fidelity Investments,* http://www.fidelity.com, June 9.
8. A. Kandybin & M. Kihn, 2004, Raising your return on innovation investment, *Strategy & Business Online,* http://www.strategyandbusiness.com, May 10.
9. J. Kerstetter, 2004, A long climb to Salesforce.com, *Business Week Online,* http://www.businessweek.com, May 12.
10. D. Oestricher, 2004, Netflix won't match Blockbuster's price cut, CEO says, *Wall Street Journal Online,* http://www.wsj.com, December 22.
11. A. Borrus, L. Woellert, & Nanette Byrnes, 2004, Pensions on a precipice, *Business Week,* September 6: 52.
12. E. T. Penrose, 1959, *The Theory of the Growth of the Firm,* New York: Wiley.
13. C. Matlack, R. Tiplady, D. Brady, R. Berner, & H. Tashiro, 2004, The Vuitton machine, *Business Week,* March 22: 98–102.
14. Ibid., 99.
15. S. L. Hart & S. Sharma, 2004, Engaging fringe stakeholders for competitive imagination, *Academy of Management Executive,* 18(1): 7–18.
16. M. Beer & R. A. Eisentat, 2004, How to have an honest conversation about your business strategy, *Harvard Business Review,* 82(2): 82–89.
17. A. J. Hillman & G. D. Keim, 2001, Shareholder value, stakeholder management, and social issues: What's the bottom line? *Strategic Management Journal,* 22: 125–139.
18. R. E. Freeman, A. C. Wicks, & B. Parmar, 2004, Stakeholder Theory and "The Corporate Objective Revisited,"

Organization Science, 15: 364–370; R. E. Freeman & J. S. Harrison, 2001, A stakeholder approach to strategic management, in M. A. Hitt, R. E. Freeman, & J. S. Harrison (eds.), *Handbook of Strategic Management,* Oxford, U.K.: Blackwell, 564–582.
19. P. F. Drucker, 2004, What makes an effective executive, *Harvard Business Review,* 82(6): 58–63.
20. P. Burrows, 2004, Rock on, iPod, *Business Week,* June 7, 130–131.
21. R. E. Kaplan & R. B. Kaiser, 2003, Developing versatile leadership, *MIT Sloan Management Review,* 44(4): 19–26.
22. D. G. Sirmon, M. A. Hitt, & R. D. Ireland, 2005, Managing resources in dynamic environments to create value: Looking inside the black box, *Academy of Management Review,* in press.
23. S. J. Shin & J. Zhou, 2003, Transformational leadership, conservation, and creativity: Evidence from Korea, *Academy of Management Journal,* 46: 703–714.
24. 2004, About 3M, 3M Home Page, http://www.3m.com, June 11.
25. R. Myers, 2004, The human capital vision, *NYSE Magazine,* January/February, 18–22.
26. C. L. Pearce, 2004, The future of leadership: Combining vertical and shared leadership to transform knowledge work, *Academy of Management Executive,* 18(1): 47–57.
27. H. M. Guttman & R. S. Hawkes, 2004, New rules for strategic management, *Journal of Business Strategy,* 25(1): 34–38.
28. E. Aronson, 2001, Integrating leadership styles and ethical perspectives, *Canadian Journal of Administrative Sciences,* 18: 244–256.
29. J. S. Harrison, 2004, Ethics in entrepreneurship, in M. A. Hitt & R. D. Ireland (eds.), *Entrepreneurship Encyclopedia,* Oxford, U.K.: Blackwell, 122–125.
30. J. S. Harrison & C. H. St. John, 2002, *Foundations in Strategic Management* (2nd ed.), Cincinnati, Ohio: South-Western College Publishing.
31. M. A. Hitt, R. D. Ireland, & G. W. Rowe, 2005, Strategic leadership: Strategy, resources, ethics and succession, in J. Doh & S. Stumpf (eds.), *Handbook on Responsible Leadership and Governance in Global Business,* New York: Edward Elgar Publishers.
32. S. Worden, 2003, The role of religious and nationalist ethics in strategic leadership: The case of J. N. Tata, *Journal of Business Ethics,* 47: 147–164.

Leadership for Strategists

Reading and studying this chapter should enable you to:

*Knowledge Objectives

1_
Define and explain strategic leadership.

2_
Explain how vision and mission create value.

3_
Define the meaning of a top management team and the value of having a heterogeneous top management team.

4_
Explain the importance of managerial succession.

5_
Define human capital and social capital and describe their value to the firm.

6_
Describe an entrepreneurial culture and its contribution to a firm.

7_
Explain the importance of managerial integrity and ethical behavior.

8_
Discuss why firms should have a control system that balances the use of strategic controls and financial controls.

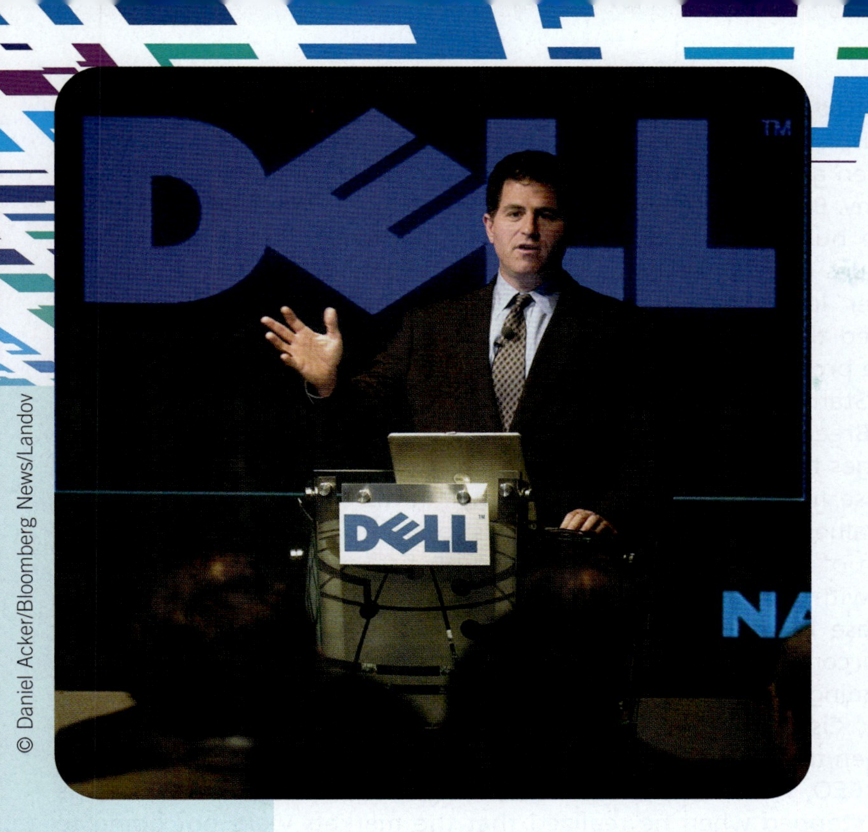

© Daniel Acker/Bloomberg News/Landov

Focusing on Strategy

Evolution and Revolution in Strategic Leadership

"Humility, service and lifting the human spirit work as well in the boardroom as they do in the classroom." (Ed Breen, CEO of Tyco)

Dell Inc. is known as one of the world's best-managed technology companies. Yet its CEO and founder, Michael Dell, recently decided to give up the CEO position and serve only as chairman of his company. Dell's then chief operating officer (COO), Kevin Rollins, was elevated to the CEO position. So while the leadership team was evolving, the primary leadership of Dell and Rollins remained intact. Why are they regarded as an excellent leadership team? There are several reasons. In 2001, for example, Dell and Rollins surveyed employees shortly after the firm's first large layoff. The survey showed that employees were unhappy and distrustful of Michael Dell and Kevin Rollins. Dell and Rollins took actions to turn the employees' attitudes around. Based on the survey's results, Dell met with his top 20 managers and presented a self-critique; he vowed to develop a stronger relationship with his management team, despite his shyness. He taped that session and showed it to every manager in the firm. Rollins placed a Curious George doll on his desk to remind him to obtain ideas from his management team before making important decisions.

Tyco has been one of the worst-managed firms in the United States. Former CEO Dennis Kozlowski made hundreds of acquisitions, building up huge debts and poorly managing the companies acquired. His successor, Ed Breen, is trying to create a revolutionary change in the company. Breen's leadership style is almost the opposite of Kozlowski's extravagant approach.

Breen stated in a recent talk at his alma mater that business leaders should display humility and provide service to the community. The quote from Breen at the beginning of this "Focusing on Strategy" illustrates his philosophy. Breen's comment suggests that strategic leaders should try to build the human spirit in the workforce and in society. He is applying these values in his attempt to reform Tyco after it was left in disarray by its former leadership team. His efforts appear to be working; Tyco announced that in the first quarter of 2004 it earned more than seven times the profit of the same quarter a year earlier.

Jack Stahl at Revlon and Daniel Carp at Kodak are trying to do the same as Breen. They are new CEOs and have to install almost revolutionary changes to ensure the survival of their firms. Both have to find a way to increase market share and return their firms to profitability to build market value for shareholders. Stahl has to develop a way to pay down a mountain of debt, and Carp must make his firm more innovative. Kodak is faced with significant changes as it moves from a chemical base to a digital base for its imaging products. Both new CEOs have only a little time to accomplish their revolutionary turnarounds, as their shareholders are becoming anxious for positive results.

Lastly, Cisco was once a Wall Street darling with a very high market value. Then the Internet boom busted and Cisco's fortunes tumbled. For a while its CEO, John Chambers, continued with the same practices, but he abruptly stopped when he realized that the markets were not going to return to the heady days of the 1990s. He analyzed the company and rebuilt its foundation. He began making fewer and more carefully planned acquisitions. Now, instead of having substantial individual autonomy, Cisco's managers work as a team to decide what markets to enter and how to enter them. Cisco also has become more efficient in its operations and more productive as well.

So continuing leaders (Dell, Chambers, and Rollins) have tried to create evolutionary changes, and new leaders (Breen, Stahl, and Carp) are working to implement revolutionary changes. Strategic leaders creating revolutionary change are likely to enjoy varying degrees of success because of the significant challenges involved in implementing such change. However, dealing with major strategic challenges underscores the importance of strategic leadership to a firm's success.

SOURCES: J. Thottam, 2004, Can this man save Tyco? *Time*, February 9: 48–50; Tyco basks in burst of profit, 2004, *Houston Chronicle*, May 5: B3; D. Brady, J. Carey, & A. Tsao, 2003, Putting a pretty face on Revlon, *Business Week*, November 3: 92–95; P. Burrows, 2003, Cisco's comeback, *Business Week*, November 24: 116–124; A. Park & P. Burrows, 2003, What you don't know about Dell, *Business Week*, November 3: 74–84; W. Symonds, 2003, The Kodak revolt is short-sighted, *Business Week*, November 3: 38.

Strategic leadership involves developing a vision for the firm, designing strategic actions to achieve this vision, and empowering others to carry out those strategic actions. As defined in Chapter 1, *strategic leaders* are the individuals practicing strategic leadership. Strategic leaders hold upper-level organizational positions. Remember from your reading of Chapter 1 that today's strategic leaders are involving people throughout the firm in strategic management. Thus, any person in the firm responsible for designing strategic actions and ensuring that they are carried out in ways that move the firm toward achievement of the vision is essentially playing the role of a strategic leader.

Is strategic leadership important? You bet it is![1] "Focusing on Strategy" shows major differences in the performance of companies due largely to the leaders. Michael Dell and Kevin Rollins have provided the leadership needed to build Dell into a major technology corporation. However, Tyco is suffering because of Dennis Kozlowski's prior leadership. Ed Breen is trying to build new values and return Tyco to profitability.

In this chapter, we examine important strategic leadership actions: establishing the firm's vision and mission, developing a management team and planning for succession, managing the resource portfolio, building and supporting an entrepreneurial culture, promoting integrity and ethical behavior, and using effective organizational controls. These strategic leadership actions are displayed in Figure 2.1. We begin with a discussion of how vision and mission are used to direct the firm's future.

FIGURE 2.1 Strategic Leadership Actions

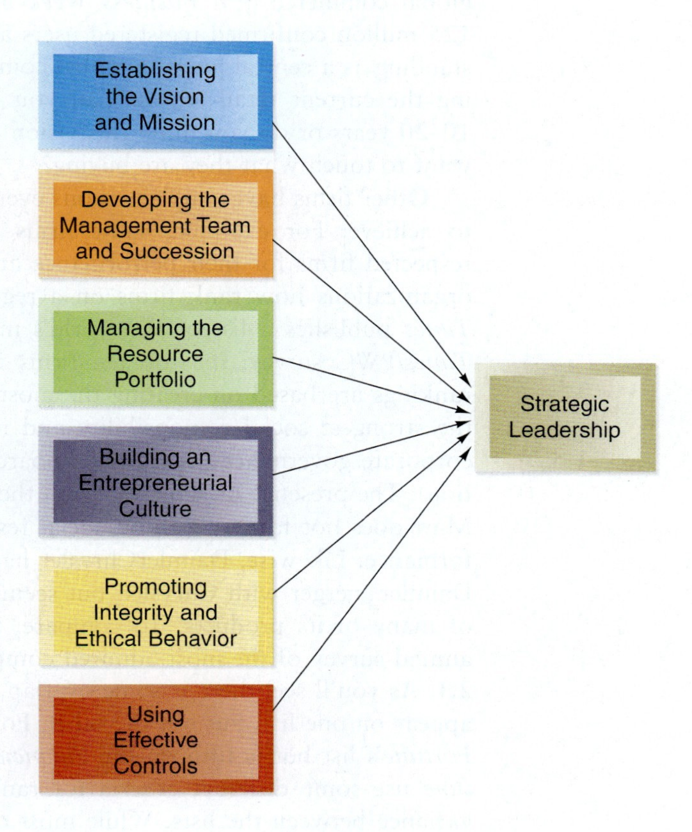

Establishing the Vision and Mission

While most strategic plans are designed for a 3-to-5-year time period, a vision is usually targeted for a longer time, say 10 to 20 years. As explained in Chapter 1, the *vision* contains at least two components—a statement describing the firm's DNA and the "picture" of the firm as it is hoped to exist in a future time period. The second part of the vision is *mission,* which defines the firm's core intent and the business or businesses in which it intends to operate. The mission flows from the vision and, compared to the vision, is more concrete in nature.

Visions can differ greatly across firms depending on the strategic leaders' intentions. For example, Steven Jobs, CEO of Apple, develops visions of new products and markets. He developed not only Apple but also Pixar, a hugely successful animation company that teamed with Disney to make *Finding Nemo.* He created the Mac revolution with the Apple Macintosh computer and more recently reshaped the music industry with Apple's iPod, which can store as many as 10,000 songs. Complementary to the iPod is Apple's iTunes online music venture, also a part of Jobs's vision to dramatically change this industry.[2]

In contrast, Meg Whitman, CEO of eBay, envisions her firm as a "dynamic self-regulating economy" using the eBay network to conduct all forms of transactions across the globe. While this seems almost crazy, 30 million people sold almost $22 billion in merchandise through eBay in 2003. More than 150,000 entrepreneurs sell all of their products using eBay, which also sells more automobiles than the largest U.S. auto dealer. eBay has been described as a hub for global commerce in a *Business Week* article.[3] Indeed, the fact that eBay had 125 million confirmed registered users as of September 2004 reflects the firm's standing as a central point in global commerce. Whitman's vision entails replacing the current retail stores. Can you imagine this happening over the next 10–20 years or do you think this vision is impossible to achieve because people want to touch what they are buying?

Other firms have simpler visions even though they still may be very difficult to achieve. For example, some firms may envision being among the most respected firms for their performance and effective management. A number of organizations now rank firms on a regular basis. For example, the *Financial Times* publishes a list of the world's most respected companies based on the *Times*/PWC survey; the top ten firms in 2003 are shown in Table 2.1. The rankings are based on creating the most shareholder value, but also exhibiting the strongest social responsibility and integrity and having the most effective corporate governance (such as the board of directors and executive compensation). The presence of some firms on the list is surprising. However, while Wal-Mart does not fare as well on social responsibility, it has strong financial performance. Likewise, DaimlerChrysler has had many publicized problems in the Daimler merger with Chrysler, but seems to rank highly because of the quality of many of its products. To compare, the top ten companies from *Fortune*'s annual survey of the most-admired companies for 2003 are also listed in Table 2.1. As you'll see, there is some overlap but the rankings differ and some firms appear on one list, but not the other. For example, Wal-Mart is ranked first on *Fortune*'s list but is fifth on the *Financial Times* list. *Financial Times* and *Fortune* use some different criteria for ranking the firms, thereby leading to the variance between the lists. While most of the firms on the *Financial Times* list

TABLE 2.1 Rankings of the Most Respected and Admired Firms

Financial Times Rankings	*Fortune* Rankings
1. General Electric	1. Wal-Mart
2. Microsoft	2. Berkshire Hathaway
3. Toyota	3. Southwest Airlines
4. IBM	4. General Electric
5. Wal-Mart	5. Dell
6. Coca-Cola	6. Microsoft
7. Dell	7. Johnson & Johnson
8. Berkshire Hathaway	8. Starbucks
9. DaimlerChrysler	9. Federal Express
10. Sony	10. IBM

Sources: M. Skapinker, 2004, Brand strength proves its worth, *Financial Times,* http://www.ft.com, January 19; A. Harrington, 2004, America's most admired companies, *Fortune,* March 8: 80–82.

are based in the United States, it is a world ranking, whereas *Fortune*'s ranking includes only U.S. firms.

An effective strategic leader not only can develop a vision of the future but also can inspire stakeholders' to commit to achieving it. It is especially important for the leader to gain the support of the company's shareholders and employees. If the shareholders do not support the vision, they may pressure the board of directors to change it or to find new strategic leaders. Similarly, employee commitment to the vision is needed because they must help implement the strategy designed to achieve the vision. Consider the case of Porsche. Company officials believe that they have a clear strategy in place to develop a group of new models through 2012. The firm's vision entails growth and maintaining its strong brand image by introducing these new products. One of the new models Porsche launched recently is a new, sporty SUV. In 2003, versions of this product were priced between $56,000 and $110,000. It is interesting to note that in 2004, Porsche was the most profitable automaker in the world; its shareholders probably support the firm's vision, while employees seem to be committed to helping achieve that vision through their work.[4]

Porsche's shareholders and employees seem committed to the firm's vision of launching new models, such as this Cayenne Turbo model in Germany.

As we mentioned earlier, strategic leaders often use their team of managers as well as others in the firm to help make major decisions, especially to define a vision for the firm. This team also helps formulate the firm's strategy. Next, we examine the teams of managers that strategic leaders use.

Developing the Top Management Team and Succession

Top Management Team

Because of the complexity of their roles, most strategic leaders form teams to help them complete their work. A **top management team** is the group of managers charged with the responsibility to develop and implement the firm's strategies. Generally, the top management team is composed of officers of the company with the title of vice president and higher.[5]

Typically, when people select individuals for a team to work with them, they prefer to choose people who think like them and are more likely to agree with them. While such a team can facilitate making fast decisions (because members of the team more easily agree), these teams are more prone to making mistakes. A team of people with similar backgrounds (a *homogeneous team*) may achieve a quick consensus about issues, but may lack all of the knowledge and information needed to make an effective decision. Additionally, because they "think alike," they may overlook important issues and make errors in judgment. Therefore, to be most effective, strategic leaders need a management team composed of members who see and think differently. This may mean that they have different types of education (such as engineering versus business) or varying amounts and types of experience (working in different functional areas, companies, or industries). We refer to this as a *heterogeneous team*. A heterogeneous team is likely to take more time to make decisions but also likely to make better decisions.[6]

Historically, Toyota included only Japanese employees in its management teams. However, as Toyota has begun to compete in more international markets, its managers have discovered the value of including other people in management teams to bring new perspectives to strategic management decisions. For example, Toyota's operations in the United States have many Americans on management teams. In fact, one author in *Fortune* described Toyota as "becoming more American." The CEO, Fujio Cho, has been making major changes in management teams to improve the design of Toyota vehicles as a complement to the firm's highly efficient manufacturing skills.[7] Someday, these changes may lead to succession of an American or a person from a country other than Japan to be Toyota's CEO, similar to the appointment of Sir Howard Stringer as CEO of Sony in 2005.

Management Succession

In addition to forming the management team, strategic leaders must develop people who can succeed them. In fact, having people with skills to take over a job when needed is very important to a firm's success. Some companies use sophisticated leadership screening systems to select people with the skills needed to perform well as a strategic leader.[8] The people selected then normally participate in an intensive management development program to further hone their leadership skills. The "ten-step talent" management development program at General Electric (GE) is considered one of the most effective programs for developing strategic leaders.[9]

Obviously, a change in CEO is a critical succession event in firms. The effects of CEO succession can be different based on whether the new CEO is from inside or outside the firm. The majority of CEO successions are from the inside, with a person groomed for the position by the former CEO or the board of directors. "Hiring from the inside" motivates employees because they believe that they have opportunities to receive promotions and better jobs if they perform well. Recent inside CEO successions were announced at Dell and Continental Airlines. In both cases, the COO was chosen to become the new CEO. As noted in "Focusing on Strategy," Kevin Rollins, COO of Dell, was selected to succeed Michael Dell as CEO. Likewise, the COO of Continental Airlines, Larry Kellner, was selected to succeed Gordon Bethune as CEO.[10] Both Michael Dell and Gordon Bethune had done a good job and the boards of the companies wanted to continue with the strategies they had put into place at each firm. Most new CEOs selected for the job in an inside succession are unlikely to change in any drastic way the strategies designed under the leadership of the former CEO.[11] However, when the firm is performing poorly, it is more common to select an outside successor.

When new CEOs are chosen from outside the organization, the board often does so with the desire to change the firm's strategies. A change in strategies may be desired because the firm is performing poorly or because opportunities and threats in the competitive landscape require adjustments to avoid performing poorly in the future.[12] For example, Motorola's board of directors chose Ed Zander as its new CEO in order to change the firm's strategy and turn around Motorola's poor performance in recent years. Zander was formerly president of Sun Microsystems, where he was highly regarded for his strategic leadership. Zander stated that he hoped to provide the value for Motorola that Lou Gerstner had for IBM when Gerstner was chosen to move from a consumer goods firm to become CEO of IBM. Gerstner transformed IBM into a successful performer again with a major change in its strategy.[13] Under Gerstner, IBM moved from a strategy based on selling separate pieces of hardware to a strategy calling for the firm to emphasize its service solutions and consulting services.

At times, it is more difficult to determine whether a succession is from the inside or outside. For example, in the 2004 CEO succession at Coca-Cola, the two major candidates were Steven Heyer, Coca-Cola's president and COO, and Neville Isdell, a former executive retired from Coca-Cola. Heyer was recruited to Coca-Cola in 2001 and many people felt he was the likely successor to Douglas Daft, the CEO at the time. However, Coca-Cola was not performing to the level desired by the board and they selected Isdell, who had the deep knowledge of the business and industry that was necessary to improve the firm's performance.[14]

Interestingly, industry analysts suggested that J. P. Morgan's acquisition of Bank One may have been partially motivated to find a good successor to William Harrison, CEO of J. P. Morgan. Harrison was scheduled to retire approximately two years after the merger was completed. Jamie Dimon, CEO of Bank One, is considered an excellent candidate to succeed Harrison. We can label this as an inside/outside succession.[15]

As discussed next, managing the firm's resource portfolio is another critical component of strategic leadership.

Managing the Resource Portfolio

Resources are the basis for a firm's competitive advantages and strategies (see Chapter 4). While we often think of physical resources such as buildings, manufacturing plants, offices, machinery, and computers as being important, intangible resources may be more important. Indeed, recent estimates suggest that as much as 75 percent of a firm's value may be contained in its intangible resources.[16] Intangible resources include human capital, social capital, and organizational capital (such as the organizational culture). Additionally, financial capital is a critically important resource.

Intellectual property can be an especially valuable intangible resource in high-technology companies. For example, Daniel Carp, Kodak's new CEO, discovered that the firm owned almost 600 patents on ink-jet technologies. However, for these patents to be of value, the technology had to be developed and introduced to the marketplace in the form of a product. As such, Kodak's patents (intellectual property) had not been properly managed. As an effective strategic leader, Carp set out to resolve this problem by commercializing the valuable technologies on which Kodak owned patents.[17]

A firm's intellectual property is developed by its human capital. **Human capital** includes the knowledge and skills of those working for the firm. Employees' knowledge and skills are critical for all organizations. According to Ed Breen, "Companies compete with their brains as well as their brawn. Organizations today must not only outgun and outhustle competitors, they must also outthink them. Companies win with ideas."[18] To outthink competitors, a firm must depend on the knowledge of its workforce (managers and nonmanagerial employees) and continuously invest in developing their knowledge and skills. Such organizations are focused on learning. Knowledge can be acquired in training programs or through experience on the job. Most experience is positive, but learning also usually occurs with failure. Unfortunately, learning through failure is difficult and can be costly. For example, Mark Mitchell, CEO of Mitchell & Company, an advertising agency, learned a valuable lesson. The company had 42 employees and approximately $4.5 million in annual revenue. But the revenue was highly dependent on one major customer, Owens Corning. Owens Corning had asbestos liability problems and filed for bankruptcy. To reduce its costs, Owens Corning decided to consolidate all of its advertising business with one agency and stopped doing business with Mitchell's firm. While Mitchell obtained some new business, it was not enough to pay his debts; he had to file for bankruptcy and close the firm. He said that he had been naïve to assume that his company was invaluable to Owens Corning. Mitchell is now the CEO of another advertising firm in Toledo, Ohio, and claims that he won't allow his new firm to become overly dependent on one customer again.[19] Not only must the CEO learn, however. It is the strategic leader's responsibility to help her firm learn faster than others. For example, if Mitchell & Company had been in a learning mode, it might have learned faster and spread its risk by obtaining more customers.

Effective strategic leaders base their strategies on the organization's human capital.[20] They do this because the human capital in the organization must have the skills and motivation needed to implement chosen strategies. As such, leaders must help develop skills throughout the firm's workforce, motivate employees to use their skills when working to implement strategies, and reward them for doing so.[21] Anne Mulcahy, the CEO who saved Xerox, credits much of her success to a talented and committed workforce. She suggests, "People always are the difference. That is why attracting them, motivating them, keeping them—making Xerox an employer of choice—is critical to our drive back to greatness."[22]

© Neal Hamberg/Bloomberg News/Landov

Anne Mulcahy, CEO of Xerox, believes human capital is the key to the success of an organization.

Another important resource is social capital. **Social capital** includes all internal and external relationships that help the firm provide value to customers and ultimately to its other stakeholders. *Internal social capital* refers to the relationships among people working inside the firm. These relationships help each organizational unit effectively complete its work while contributing to the overall value of the firm's human capital.

External social capital refers to relationships between those working within a firm and others (individuals and organizations) outside the firm. Such relationships are essential because they provide access to needed resources. Few firms have all of the resources they need. Furthermore, most firms cannot do everything well. It may be better to outsource some activities to partner companies who can perform those activities exceptionally well, thereby increasing the quality of the focal firm's ability to produce products. External social capital can also help firms enter new markets. New companies may seek the financial support and expertise of venture capitalists, whereas more established companies often develop alliances with reliable suppliers or joint ventures with highly competent partners. In a sense, strategic leaders serve as key points of effective linkages for their firm in a network of relationships with other organizations. Some relationships involve strong ties, where trust exists between the parties and reciprocity is expected, whereas other relationships represent weaker ties that serve more informational roles and allow strategic leaders to stay on top of the latest developments—even outside their industry—that may affect their firm (such as technology developments). So both strong and weak ties are important in strategic leaders' networks.[23]

The most effective social capital occurs when partners trust each other (strong ties). Effective strategic leaders have well-developed relational skills that help them establish trusting relationships with others inside and outside the organization. Andrea Jung, CEO of Avon Products, suggests that compassion is one of the key characteristics of effective leaders. As such, she believes that leaders should treat people fairly, with dignity and respect. In so doing, leaders are leading with their heart as well as their head.[24]

Other resources such as financial capital are also important. In fact, firms with strong human capital and social capital will more likely be able to build a good base of financial capital.[25] Some also believe that an organization's culture can be a valuable resource. We discuss this topic next.

Building an Entrepreneurial Culture

Strategic leaders are concerned about the organization's culture because it can have major effects on employees' actions. An organizational culture is based on the core values of an organization, largely espoused by its leaders. When these values support opportunities to innovate, an entrepreneurial culture may develop. An **entrepreneurial culture** encourages employees to identify and exploit new opportunities. It encourages creativity and risk taking but also tolerates failures.

Championing innovation is rewarded in this type of culture.[26] Building an entrepreneurial culture is of particular importance to strategic leaders, as explained in "Understanding Strategy."

Innovation is important in high-technology industries such as computers and in creative industries such as music and film animation, as shown in "Understanding Strategy." Thus, Steve Jobs is an appropriate strategic leader for Apple with his emphasis on creativity and innovation. However, 3M operates in several different industries with lower technology, such as adhesives (for example, Scotch tape, traffic signs, and sandpaper). Yet the firm has been a pioneer, being the first to introduce new products in its markets, such as the Post-it note. Therefore, an entrepreneurial culture is important in both firms.

Being innovative in high-technology industries is challenging and the payoff is often low. For example, innovations in the biotechnology industry require an average of 15–18 years to develop and introduce to the market (partly because of the time necessary for testing the product). A gene-therapy vaccine called Vical, for example, has been under development for 16 years with approximately $100 million invested, but the product is not ready for the market. Most venture capitalists are unwilling to wait even ten years to earn a return on their investments, much less 15–18 years. Therefore, some entrepreneurs seek to acquire firms that have products in which the development is 50 percent or more completed.[27]

Because of the pressure to be innovative yet profitable, many leaders try to focus their firm's innovation to increase the chances of success. For example, Scott Cook, founder and CEO of Intuit, tries to focus his firm's innovation activities on the customer. He strongly believes that profitable innovation is based on having an intimate understanding of the customer.[28] Similarly, Jim McNerney at 3M targets innovation by integrating the research scientists with marketing and manufacturing people. As a result, development is targeting new products requested by customers.[29]

The preceding discussions suggest the importance of innovation and strategic leadership. While the type and focus of innovation may vary, it is important in nearly all industries. As a result, building an entrepreneurial culture is a vital task for strategic leaders. Strategic leaders also must demonstrate ethical behavior. Next, we discuss the importance of integrity and ethical behavior for strategic leaders.

Promoting Integrity and Ethical Behavior

Strategic leaders not only develop standards for behavior among employees, but also serve as role models in meeting and exceeding those standards. While quality of performance is an important criterion, showing integrity and behaving ethically are also essential. So strategic leaders should determine the boundaries of acceptable behavior, establish the tone for organizational actions, and ensure that ethical behaviors are expected, praised, and rewarded. Lack of integrity and unethical behavior can be serious and highly costly for a firm and for the person lacking integrity and behaving unethically. In fact, extraordinary unethical behavior can even lead to a firm's demise; Enron is a well-known example.

Recently, cases in which strategic leaders acted opportunistically in managing their firms have been a major concern. Acting opportunistically means that managers are making decisions that are in their own best interests rather than

learning from success

understanding strategy:

RESTORING INNOVATION THROUGH LEADERSHIP

Jim McNerney became 3M's CEO in 2001, the first CEO selected from outside the firm. The reason for selecting an outsider as CEO was the perceived need by 3M's board to restore the firm's orientation to innovation. At one time, 3M was considered one of the most entrepreneurial firms in the United States. However, its innovative capability and innovations have decreased over time. 3M devotes considerable resources to produce innovation. The company invests $1.1 billion annually in research and development (R&D) and has almost 1,000 scientists and engineers doing research to develop innovative products.

Rebuilding an entrepreneurial culture has been a challenge for McNerney. First, he acquired some firms with strong R&D operations. He is also trying to increase innovation by building a culture that expects and rewards entrepreneurial actions. He is investing in 3M's human capital. He also operates as a team leader. He has high expectations of those working with him but also rewards high performance. He emphasizes his people rather than himself, exemplifying a strategic leader who values teamwork.

Similarly, Steve Jobs is credited with restoring the entrepreneurial culture at Apple. He did it largely through leadership and exhibiting creativity himself. There is little doubt that he expects people working for Apple to create innovative products. Apple first restored innovation by developing creative new designs for the PC. However, Jobs has gone beyond computers and has developed new product lines that he sees as the future of Apple. Before returning to Apple, Jobs started Pixar, now the leader in animated films. He is now leading Apple into a new segment in the music industry with iTunes online music access and the iPod, which can store and play a large number of songs.

SOURCES: M. Arndt & J. Brady, 2004, 3M's rising star, *Business Week Online*, http://www.businessweek.com, April 12; R. Grover, 2004, Pixar twists the mouse's tail, *Business Week Online*, http://www.businessweek.com, January 30; C. Hawn, 2004, If he's so smart . . . : Steve Jobs, Apple, and the limits of innovation, *Fast Company*, http://www.fastcompany.com, January; P. T. Larsen, 2004, Pixar head Jobs slams Disney over split, *Financial Times*, http://www.ft.com, February 5.

in the firm's best interests. Enron and Tyco are examples of firms in which opportunistic behavior likely occurred.

Because of opportunistic behavior in a number of companies, significant emphasis has been placed on how firms govern themselves (*corporate governance*). Corporate governance begins with the board of directors, whose members are responsible for overseeing managerial activities and approving (or disapproving) managerial decisions and actions. The outcry from shareholders and the public in general has placed pressure on board members to be more diligent in examining managerial behavior. Legislation (such as the Sarbanes-Oxley Act of 2002) has even been passed in the United States requiring more managerial responsibility for the firm's activities and outcomes. Institutional owners in particular have pressured boards to enact better governance practices. For example, they generally want to have more independent outsiders than inside officers on the board. They believe that independent outside board members will be more objective and are less likely to agree with the CEO if he is taking actions that appear not to be in the firm's best interests. In this way, managers' opportunistic actions can be curtailed.[30]

One form of potential opportunism, **related-party transactions,** involves paying a person who has a relationship with the firm extra money for reasons other than his or her normal activities on the firm's behalf. For example, Apple CEO Steve Jobs was reimbursed $1.2 million for costs he incurred while using his personal jet on company business. Two directors for Ford Motor Company, William Clay Ford and Edsel Ford, receive hundreds of thousands of dollars in consulting fees in addition to their compensation for serving as directors. Many of these transactions are legitimate, but some can be for questionable purposes as well. The Securities and Exchange Commission has begun carefully scrutinizing related-party deals because of the opportunity for unethical behavior. Related-party deals were curtailed in the United States by the Sarbanes-Oxley Act.[31]

As explained in "Understanding Strategy," Michael Eisner was once a highly successful CEO at Disney. However, his strategies in recent years have been ineffective and Disney's performance has suffered. Worse, Eisner seems to have deliberately avoided developing a successor for his job. He appointed a number of friends and associates to Disney's board, which has approved extraordinarily high compensation for Eisner at a time when the company's performance was poor. Thus, Eisner has been criticized for managerial opportunism and ineffective strategic leadership, and, at the same time, the firm has been criticized for weak corporate governance.

Often worse than opportunistic actions by managers are fraudulent and other unlawful activities in which managers and companies' representatives engage. The costs of white-collar fraud are substantial, with estimates as high as $600 billion in losses by U.S. firms annually. White-collar crime is the reason for at least 30 percent of new-venture failures as well.[32] In 2002, the board of Peregrine Systems requested the resignation of the CEO and chief financial officer (CFO) because of an alleged falsification of $100 million in revenues. Eventually, three former Peregrine executives were convicted of criminal fraud. The investigations showed that as much as $500 million was nonexistent, more than half of which was because of fraud. These actions caused the firm to file for Chapter 11 bankruptcy protection. While Peregrine has partially recovered from these terrible actions, it still has significant problems and more work to do before it can achieve a level of stability.[33]

Only leaders who demonstrate integrity and values respected by all constituents of the company will be able to sustain effective outcomes over time. Those who engage in unethical or unlawful activities may go unrecognized or undetected for a time, but eventually they will fail. People working under the leader often demonstrate the same values in their actions that are evident in the leader's behavior. Thus, if the leader engages in unethical activities, the followers are likely to do the same. Therefore, the leader will suffer from the poor performance that results from their own and others' unethical behaviors. However, when the leader displays integrity and strong positive ethical values, the firm's performance will be enhanced over time because the followers will do the same. Opportunism and unethical activities evident in several companies in recent times clearly show the importance of having effective control systems, which are discussed next.

learning from failure

understanding strategy: BREAKDOWNS IN GOVERNANCE AND MANAGERIAL OPPORTUNISM

Michael Eisner saved the Walt Disney Company when he became the CEO in 1984. He implemented many creative and insightful strategic actions that turned around Disney's fortunes. However, Eisner's leadership has been criticized in recent years because of a multitude of problems culminating in the firm's weak financial performance. Eisner has been criticized for exceptionally high levels of compensation, especially at times of weak firm performance, and for not developing a person to succeed him as CEO. His last five or more years as CEO have been controversial.

© REUTERS/Tim Shaffer/Landov

Disney (and Eisner) has been criticized for having a weak board with many members having ties to Eisner. In fact, the board has awarded Eisner compensation at levels highly criticized in the media and has also taken no action against Eisner for his ineffective decisions, strategies, and actions.

However, the situation at Disney changed in 2004. Powerful shareholders such as Roy Disney and the California Public Employees Retirement System (CalPERS), a large institutional investor, stated they would vote against reappointing Eisner as CEO. CalPERS representatives said, "We have lost complete confidence in Mr. Eisner's strategic vision and leadership in creating shareholder value in the company."

The vote of no confidence for Eisner as CEO was supported by 43 percent of the shareholders. Such a vote is almost unprecedented. While the board did not oust Eisner as CEO, they withdrew his position as chairman of the board and gave it to George Mitchell, a former U.S. senator. While some feel that Eisner has "nine lives," he may have used all of them. The board reported that it is developing a detailed succession plan and is working to increase its independence from the CEO. Of course, a critical issue is the need for improvement in Disney's performance. All of these actions may have influenced Eisner to state in late 2004 that he would step down as CEO in September 2006. However, critics were not quieted until the board announced that it would hire a search firm no later than June 2005 to move forward with the succession plan.

SOURCES: H. Yeager, 2004, Disney board taking the right steps, *Financial Times*, http://www.ft.com, May 21; L. M. Wilson, 2004, Eisner vote forces Disney to catch up, *New York Times*, http://www.nytimes.com, March 10; B. Orwall & J. S. Lublin, 2004, Disney shareholders' revolt widens, *Wall Street Journal Online*, http://www.wsj.com, February 27; P. T. Larsen, 2004, CalPERS turns against Disney's Eisner, *Financial Times*, http://www.ft.com, February 26; B. Orwall & J. S. Lublin, 2004, Eisner's critics now like the script: Roy Disney, Stanley Gold suspend bid to oust CEO after board pledges action, *Wall Street Journal*, September 29: B3.

Using Effective Controls

Controls are necessary to ensure that standards are met and that employees do not misuse the firm's resources. Control failures are evident in such dismal outcomes as exemplified by Enron and Tyco. Unfortunately, in both of these cases, the strategic leaders with responsibility for implementing the controls violated them, and the governance in both firms was weak and unable to identify and correct the problems until they became excessive and external entities expressed concern about them. However, the potential value of controls goes beyond preventing fraud and managerial opportunism. Properly formed and used controls guide managerial decisions, including strategic decisions. Effective strategic leaders ensure that their firms create and use both financial controls and strategic controls to guide the use of the strategic management process.

Financial controls focus on shorter-term financial outcomes. These controls help the firm stay on the right path in terms of generating sales revenue, maintaining expenses within reason, and remaining financially solvent. Of course, a prime reason for financial controls is to generate an adequate profit. However, if financial controls are overly emphasized to increase current profits, managers are likely to limit their expenditures more than is necessary. Too many expense reductions in certain categories (such as R&D) can damage the firm's ability to perform successfully in the future. Money spent on R&D helps the firm develop products that customers will want to buy.

Alternatively, **strategic controls** focus on the content of strategic actions rather than on their outcomes. Strategic controls are best employed under conditions of uncertainty. For example, a firm may employ the correct strategy but the financial results may be poor because of a recession or unexpected natural disasters or political actions (such as the 9/11 terrorist attacks). To use strategic controls, the strategic leader or board must have a good understanding of the industry and markets in which the firm or its units operate in order to evaluate the accuracy of the strategy. Using strategic controls encourages managers to adopt longer-term strategies and to take acceptable risks while maintaining the firm's profitability in the current time period.

The most effective system of controls is balanced using strategic *and* financial controls. Controlling financial outcomes is important while simultaneously looking to the longer term and evaluating the content of the strategies used. To obtain the desired balance in control systems, many firms use a **balanced scorecard,**[34] which provides a framework for evaluating the simultaneous use of financial controls and strategic controls.

Four foci are used in the balanced scorecard—*financial* (profit, growth, and shareholder risk), *customers* (value received from the firm's products), *internal business processes* (asset utilization, inventory turnover) and *learning and growth* (a culture that supports innovation and change). In addition to helping implement a balanced control system, the balanced scorecard allows leaders to view the firm from the eyes of stakeholders such as shareholders, customers, and employees.

Summary

The primary purpose of this chapter is to explain strategic leadership and emphasize its value to an organization. In doing so, we examined the following topics:

- **Strategic leadership** involves developing a vision for the firm, designing strategic actions to achieve this vision, and empowering others to carry out those strategic actions. Establishing the firm's vision (and mission), developing a management team and planning for succession, managing the resource portfolio, building and supporting an entrepreneurial culture, promoting integrity and ethical behavior, and using effective organizational controls are the actions of strategic leadership.

- Strategic leaders, those practicing strategic leadership, develop a firm's vision and mission. The vision contains at least two components—a statement describing the firm's DNA and the "picture" of the firm as it is hoped to exist in the future. The mission of the firm focuses on the markets it serves and the goods and services it provides, and defines the firm's core intent and the business or businesses in which it intends to operate.
- A **top management team** is the group of managers responsible for developing and implementing the firm's strategies. A heterogeneous team usually develops more-effective strategies than a homogeneous team because it holds a greater diversity of knowledge, considers more issues, and evaluates more alternatives.
- Managerial succession is important for the maintenance of the firm's health. Individuals should be developed and prepared to undertake managerial roles all up and down the firm's hierarchy.
- **Human capital** includes the knowledge and skills of those working for the firm. Employees' knowledge and skills are an important resource to all organizations. Another important resource is social capital. **Social capital** includes all internal and external relationships that help the organization provide value to customers and ultimately to its other stakeholders. Strategic leaders must help develop the skills within the firm's workforce, motivate employees to use those skills to implement strategies, and reward them when they successfully use their skills.
- Strategic leaders shape an organization's culture. In the current competitive environment, all firms need to be innovative to remain competitive. Therefore, building an entrepreneurial culture is of particular importance to strategic leaders. An **entrepreneurial culture** encourages employees to identify and exploit new opportunities. It encourages creativity and risk taking and tolerates failures as a result.
- Strategic leaders develop standards for behavior among employees and also serve as role models for meeting these standards. Integrity and ethical behavior are essential in today's business environment. Lack of integrity and unethical behavior can be serious and highly costly—to the firm and to individuals lacking integrity and behaving unethically. Ethical strategic leaders guard against managerial opportunism and fraudulent actions.
- Effective controls guide managerial decisions, including strategic decisions. **Financial controls** focus on shorter-term financial outcomes, whereas **strategic controls** focus on the content of the strategic actions rather than their outcomes. An effective control system balances the use of financial controls and strategic controls. The balanced-scorecard approach is a useful technique that can help balance these two types of control.

Key Terms

Discussion Questions

1. What is strategic leadership? Describe the major actions involved in strategic leadership.
2. How do a vision and a mission create value for a company?
3. What is a top management team? Why does a heterogeneous top management team usually formulate more effective strategies?
4. Why is it important to develop managers for succession to other managerial jobs?
5. What do the terms human capital and social capital mean? What is the importance of human capital and social capital to a firm?

6. How can a strategic leader foster an entrepreneurial culture and why is such a culture valuable to a firm?
7. Why are managerial integrity and ethical behavior important to a firm?
8. Why should strategic leaders develop a control system that balances strategic controls and financial controls?

Endnotes

1. J. E. Post, L. E. Preston, & S. Sachs, 2002, Managing the extended enterprise: The new stakeholder view, *California Management Review,* 45(1): 6–28; D. Sirmon & M. A. Hitt, 2003, Managing resources: Linking unique resources, management and wealth creation in family firms, *Entrepreneurship Theory and Practice,* 27: 339–358.
2. P. Burrows, R. Grover, & T. Lowry, 2004, Showtime, *Business Week,* February 2: 56–64.
3. R. D. Hof, 2003, The eBay economy, *Business Week,* August 25: 125–128.
4. G. Edmondson, 2004, Porsche's CEO talks shop, *Business Week Online,* http://www.businessweek.com, January 19.
5. I. Goll, R. Sambharya, & C. L. Tucci, 2001, Top management team composition, corporate ideology and firm performance, *Management International Review,* 41(2): 109–129.
6. M. Jensen & E. Zajac, 2004, Corporate elites and corporate strategy: How demographic preferences and structural position shape the scope of the firm, *Strategic Management Journal,* 25: 507–524; L. Markoczy, 2001, Consensus formation during strategic change, *Strategic Management Journal,* 22: 1013–1031.
7. A. Taylor III, 2004, The Americanization of Toyota, *Fortune,* http://www.fortune.com, February 29.
8. W. Shen & A. Cannella, 2002, Revisiting the performance consequences of CEO succession: The impacts of successor type, post succession, senior executive turnover and departing CEO tenure, *Academy of Management Journal,* 45: 717–734.
9. R. Charan, 2000, GE's ten-step talent plan, *Fortune,* April 17: 232.
10. E. Souder, 2004, Continental's Bethune leaves Co in good hands, *Wall Street Journal Online,* http://www.wsj.com, January 19.
11. W. Shen & A. Cannella, 2003, Will succession planning increase shareholder wealth? Evidence from investor reactions to relay CEO successions, *Strategic Management Journal,* 24: 191–198.
12. L. Greiner, T. Cummings, & A. Bhambri, 2002, When new CEOs succeed and fail: 4-D theory of strategic transformation, *Organizational Dynamics,* 32: 1–16.
13. T. Foremski, 2004, Motorola's new boss aims for Zanderdu, *Financial Times,* http://www.ft.com, May 9.
14. B. Liu & N. Buckley, 2004, Coca-Cola veteran named new chief, *Financial Times,* http://www.ft.com, May 5.
15. S. Tully, 2004, The dealmaker and the dynamo, *Fortune,* February 9: 77–82; E. Thornton & J. Weber, 2004, A made-to-order megamerger, *Business Week Online,* http://www.businessweek.com, January 15.
16. M. Reitzig, 2004, Strategic management of intellectual property, *MIT Sloan Management Review,* 45(3): 35–40.
17. A. Perez, 2003, What it boils down to for Kodak, *Business Week Online,* http://www.businessweek.com, November 24.
18. B. Breen, 2004, Hidden asset, *Fast Company,* March: 93.
19. L. Randall, 2004, Lessons learned the hardest way, by going belly-up, *New York Times,* http://www.nytimes.com, February 29.
20. B. C. Skaggs & M. Youndt, 2004, Strategic positioning, human capital and performance in service organizations: A customer interactionist approach, *Strategic Management Journal,* 25: 85–99.
21. J. Champ, 2003, The hidden qualities of great leaders, *Fast Company,* November: 139.
22. A. M. Mulcahy, 2003, From survival to success: Leading in turbulent times, speech in the U.S. Chamber of Commerce Leadership Series, Washington, D.C., http://www.uschamber.com, April 2.
23. J. Nahapiet & S. Ghoshal, 1998, Social capital, intellectual capital and the organizational advantage, *Academy of Management Review,* 23: 242–266; R. D. Ireland, M. A. Hitt, & D. Vaidyanath, 2002, Alliance management as a source of competitive advantage, *Journal of Management,* 28: 413–446.
24. A. Jung, 2004, You will stand on our shoulders, keynote address at the WWIB Conference, Knowledge @ Wharton, http://knowledge.wharton.upenn.edu, November 5.
25. R. A. Baron & G. D. Markman, 2003, Beyond social capital: The role of entrepreneurs' social competence in their financial success, *Journal of Business Venturing,* 18: 41–60.
26. R. D. Ireland, M. A. Hitt, & D. Sirmon, 2003, A model of strategic entrepreneurship: The construct and its dimensions, *Journal of Management,* 29: 963–989.
27. A. Pollack, 2004, Is biotechnology losing its nerve? *New York Times,* http://www.nytimes.com, February 29.
28. D. Lidsky & D. Whitford, 2004, Cook's recipe, *Fortune,* http://www.fortune.com, February 15.
29. M. Arndt & D. Brady, 2004, 3M's rising star, *Business Week Online,* http://www.businessweek.com, April 12.
30. R. E. Hoskisson, M. A. Hitt, R. A. Johnson, & W. Grossman, 2002, Conflicting voices: The effects of ownership heterogeneity and internal governance on corporate strategy, *Academy of Management Journal,* 45: 697–716.
31. J. R. Emshwiller, 2003, Many companies report transactions with top officers, *Wall Street Journal Online,* http://www.wsj.com, December 29.
32. K. Schnatterly, 2003, Increasing firm value through detection and prevention of white-collar crime, *Strategic Management Journal,* 24: 587–614.
33. C. Hawn, 2004, Surviving a corporate death, *Fast Company,* http://www.fastcompany.com, February.
34. R. S. Kaplan & D. P. Norton, 2001, Transforming the balanced scorecard from performance measurement to strategic management: Part I, *Accounting Horizons,* 15(1): 87–104.

part 2
44
chapter 3
Business Strategy and the External Environment
68
chapter 4
The Firm

Strategic Analysis

Business Strategy and the External Environment

Reading and studying this chapter should enable you to:

*Knowledge Objectives

1_
Explain the importance of analyzing the firm's external environment.

2_
Identify the categories of trends in the general environment that create opportunities or threats for the firm.

3_
Describe the five forces of an industry analysis.

4_
Understand how to complete a competitor analysis.

5_
Identify potential reactions to significant strategic moves by competitors.

6_
Understand how complementors support value creation for the firm in a competitive situation.

© Ann Johansson/CORBIS

Focusing on Strategy

Changing Population Bases in the United States Lead Businesses to Change Their Focus

"$700 billion a year is spent by U.S. Hispanic consumers, a figure that is growing by eight percent per year (three times as fast as the overall U.S. rate)." (Joel Millman, *Wall Street Journal*)

Hispanic demographics are influencing the strategies firms are using to serve the needs of the growing Hispanic population in the United States. Almost half of all new workers to the workforce in the 1990s were Hispanic, and Hispanics are expected to account for nearly 25 percent of the workforce by 2010, up from 12 percent in 2004. This growth is likely to significantly increase the buying power of Hispanics in the United States. Furthermore, Spanish-speaking members of society are experiencing increasing political power. It is expected that both Texas and California will become Hispanic-majority states over the next decade. This growth in the Hispanic population suggests that Spanish could become a second accepted language in the United States, similar to French in Canada. Interestingly, Hispanics often retain more of their cultural and language heritage than other U.S. immigrants from Europe.

Given its increasing size, firms will likely see the Hispanic segment as one that is changing from a niche market to a major independent market in the United States. For instance, ad revenues for Spanish-language TV climbed 16 percent in 2004. Revenues of Univision, the number one Spanish-language media firm in the United States, soared 44 percent between 2001 and 2003, with a 146 percent increase in the 18–34 age segment. Clear Channel Communications, a vast network of radio stations based in San Antonio, Texas, has formed a partnership with Group Televisa, Mexico's leading broadcaster and media company. Clear Channel is interested in making a bigger push in to Spanish programs and advertising. Most Hispanics (63 percent) speak both Spanish and English, and this is expected to increase to 67 percent by 2010. In comparison, Hispanics are four times as likely to keep their native language relative to immigrants from the Philippines, Vietnam, and China.

With this significant growth, new businesses will likely be launched to cater to Hispanics' needs. As such, the number of firms using Spanish as their language to communicate with customers will probably increase. For instance, Procter & Gamble spent $90 million on advertising directed at Latinos for 12 products, including Crest and Tide. This was ten percent of its ad budget for the 12 brands and represented a 28 percent hike over the previous year (2002).

Citigroup is also seeking to serve the needs of a larger Hispanic population. Because more than half of the Hispanic community in the United States is Mexican, Citigroup is introducing a binational credit card that can be used by Mexican citizens living the United States and by members of their family living in Mexico. As we'll explain in this chapter, one of the outcomes the firm seeks when analyzing its external environment is to understand demographic trends such as those we are describing about the growing Hispanic population in the United States.

SOURCES: R. O. Crockett, 2004, Why are Latinos leading Blacks in the job market?, *Business Week,* March 15: 70; Dow Jones Newswire, 2004, Citigroup eyes Hispanic market, *Wall Street Journal,* June 16: D12; B. Grow, R. Grover, A. Weintraub, C. Palmeri, M. Der Hovanesian, and M. Eidam, 2004, Hispanic nation, *Business Week,* March 15: 59–70; M. Jordan, 2004, The economy: Latinos take the lead in job gains, *Wall Street Journal,* February 24: A2; J. Millman, 2004, "El gringo malo" wins fans airing Spanish baseball, *Wall Street Journal,* September 14: B1; G. Smith, 2004, Can Televisa conquer the U.S.? *Business Week,* October 4: 79.

Recall from Chapter 1 that the external environment is the set of conditions outside the firm that affect the firm's performance. As "Focusing on Strategy" suggests, the external environment can indeed affect the firm's choice and use of strategy. External events, such as the war in Iraq and changes in demographics (such as the growing number of Hispanics), illustrate how changes can create opportunities as well as threats for firms. To pursue an opportunity or to protect itself against a threat, the firm might choose to change how it is implementing a current strategy or may even change to a different strategy.

In this chapter, we examine the three parts of a firm's external environment—the general environment, the industry environment, and the competitor environment (see Figure 3.1). Firms analyze their external environment to collect information that will help them select a strategy. The conditions in the external environment influence what the firm might choose to do. In other words, the firm might choose to pursue a certain opportunity or it might choose to take action to avoid an impending threat. The firm's decisions about these choices are affected by conditions inside the firm itself. We will discuss the conditions inside the firm in the next chapter. The actual choice of a strategy is a function of conditions in the firm's external environment and the conditions in its internal environment.

As mentioned in Chapter 1, being able to identify opportunities and threats is an important reason why firms study their external environment. *Opportunities* are conditions in the firm's general, industry, and competitor environments

FIGURE 3.1 External Environment Analysis

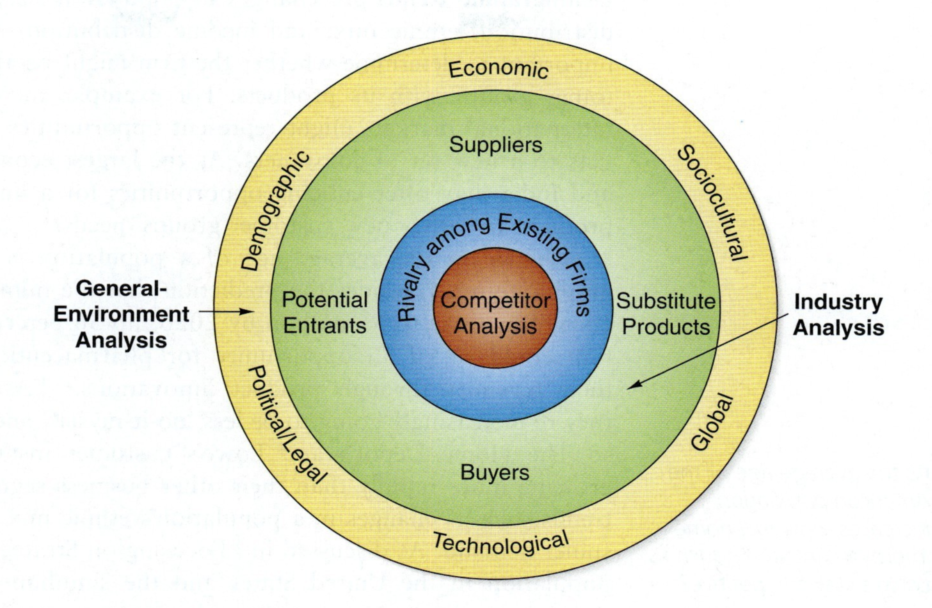

that enable the firm to use its core competencies to achieve its vision. *Threats,* on the other hand, are conditions in the firm's general, industry, and competitor environments with the potential to prevent the firm from successfully using its core competencies. Evaluating trends in the firm's general environment, evaluating the effects of competitive forces in the industry in which the firm intends to compete, and studying competitors are actions the firm takes to recognize the opportunities and threats it faces.

Firms should not rely on personal opinions and casual observations to study their external environment. In-depth study is required, and it is important to ask the right questions. There is no substitute for continually studying all parts of the firm's external environment—the general, industry, and competitor environments. In addition, complements to industry competition should be examined. Beginning with the general environment, we discuss each analysis the firm performs to fully understand the conditions in its external environment.

Analyzing the General Environment

The **general environment** is composed of trends in the broader society that influence an industry and the firms in it. Firms must pay attention to six trends in the general environment: demographic, economic, political/legal, sociocultural, technological, and global. Each category has conditions that affect the firm's choice of strategy. Conditions in the general environment are outside the firm's direct control; no firm can control demographic trends, for example.

Keep this in mind while reading about each category and while thinking about how conditions that are part of each trend could influence different types of firms.

Demographic Trends

Demographic trends are changes in population size, age structure, geographic distribution, ethnic mix, and income distribution. Analysis of these trends is important to determine whether the firm might be able to serve additional customer groups with its products. For example, increasing population rates in international markets might represent opportunities for a firm to sell its products to a new set of consumers. As the largest economies in the world, China and India may offer enticing opportunities for a number of firms to use their products to satisfy new customer groups' needs.

Change in the average age of a population is another important demographic trend. Consider the prediction that the number of Americans over age 65 will increase to 55 million by 2020, up 56 percent from 2000. This prediction could signal an opportunity for pharmaceuticals companies to increase their revenues through product innovations.[1] "As baby boomers get older, they're increasingly going to be less 'do-it-myself' and more 'do-it-for-me,'" and so The Home Depot's and Lowe's customer installation service business is growing more rapidly than their other business segments.[2] Other demographic trends such as changes in a population's ethnic mix can affect patterns of consumer demand. As discussed in "Focusing on Strategy," the increasing Hispanic population in the United States and the simultaneous increase in these customers' purchasing power will influence firms' decisions about the customers they seek to serve and the types of products they sell to serve those needs.

As the average age of the American population increases, how will home improvement stores such as Lowe's stay competitive?

© WENN/Landov

Shifts in the geographic distribution of a population can also affect firms. For example, the U.S. population continues to migrate from north and east to west and south. This trend may reduce the number of customers for some firms in the north and east while increasing the number of customers for firms offering similar products in the west and south.

Economic Trends

Economic trends concern the direction of the economy in which a firm competes or may choose to compete. Gross national product, interest and inflation rates, income growth or decline, savings rates, and currency exchange rates in companies across the globe are examples of economic factors that firms examine to understand current economic trends and to predict future economic trends. Of course, economic trends also affect customers' purchasing decisions. Isn't that true for you? Doesn't your current and expected income influence what you decide to buy and from whom? In addition, economic trends affect the broader society, such as when there is a recession. A recession in 2001 that extended into 2002 in the

United States began to turn to expansion toward the end of 2003 and through 2004. The Federal Reserve reduced interest rates to record lows during this time period to help bring the economy out of recession.[3] The recessionary conditions have significant effects on firms in most industries. When facing less-than-favorable economic trends, firms must decide how to allocate their resources so they will be positioned to grow when domestic and/or global economies improve.

Political/Legal Trends

Political/legal trends pertain to changes in organizations and interest groups that compete for a voice in developing and overseeing the body of laws and regulations that guide interactions among firms and nations. Because political conditions affect how business is conducted, firms try to influence legislation in ways that benefit them through political strategy.[4] The means used to influence political and legal trends must be ethical, moral, and consistent with the laws of the land.

Increasingly, privatization of government-owned and government-regulated businesses has transformed many state-owned enterprises to private firms (as in eastern Europe) and has deregulated formerly regulated businesses (such as U.S. utility firms); consequently, the global competitive landscape is increasingly dynamic (open to competition) and deregulated. This trend is being fostered by countries such as China's admittance to the World Trade Organization (WTO). The Geneva-based WTO helps establish trade rules in the global environment. China's recent entry into the WTO signaled a significant trend in emerging countries regarding the reduction in trade barriers across multiple industries such as telecommunications, banking, airlines, automobiles, movies, and professional services.

Managers must carefully examine political trends in antitrust, taxation, and industry regulations as well as labor laws because of their potential importance to the implementation of strategies. Often, firms develop political strategies before establishing competitive positions within an industry.

Specific regulatory bodies frequently oversee industry activities. The airline industry is greatly affected by the Federal Aviation Administration (FAA) and the food and drug industries are strongly influenced by the Food and Drug Administration (FDA). The influence of regulations and antitrust laws on a firm's strategy is shown in the example of Microsoft.

Microsoft is a highly successful company with a market capitalization of $279 billion, second only to General Electric, and approximately $1 billion per month in cash flow. Accordingly, it is the most profitable company in the technology sector. On March 25, 2004, the European Commission announced a judgment that Microsoft was abusing its power in technology markets. In particular, Microsoft's linking of computers and players of music and video clips concerned European regulators. Accordingly, the company was ordered to reveal code from its "dominant Windows desktop operating system to help rivals' competing in similar software." The commission fined Microsoft $612.7 million, a single-company record in Europe. Because Microsoft at the time of the fine had $50 billion in cash and short-term liquidity investments, the fine was less important than the order to modify its business model.[5] Similar fines were also levied against Microsoft in the United States. After these judgments, Microsoft also settled a longtime dispute with Sun Microsystems subsequent to the European fine and injunction against Microsoft. These descriptions of Microsoft's experiences show how political trends in the general environment can affect a firm and how it will implement its chosen strategy or strategies.[6]

Sociocultural Trends

Sociocultural trends deal with changes in a society's attitudes and cultural values. These trends often differ across countries. For example, the emphasis on saving the environment is relatively strong in Europe and throughout the developed world; however, these issues are less important in emerging economies such as Russia, India, China, and Latin America. Health consciousness is also a trend that has increasingly been important in many countries around the world. Especially in the United States, women have been increasingly entering the workforce rather than remaining in traditional family roles. Additional talented workers, such as women, represent human capital that a firm might hire to pursue an opportunity. Do you see any sociocultural trends on the horizon that you believe are important for U.S. businesses to understand? What are they? What should firms do to be prepared to successfully deal with these trends?

Technological Trends

Technological trends concern changes in the activities involved with creating new knowledge and translating that knowledge into new products, processes, and materials. Some firms require a thorough examination of technological trends because of swift technological changes and shortened product life cycles in their industries. In particular, Internet technology has played an increasingly important role in domestic and global technological change. Furthermore, the Internet is an excellent source of data to help understand the three parts of the external environment. Significant changes in communications technology, especially wireless communications technology, have provided opportunities for many firms. For example, new industries have been created by combining handheld devices and wireless communications equipment in a variety of network-based services. This technology enables individuals to use their handheld computers for scheduling, as mobile phones, and to send e-mail or conduct Web-based transactions (such as online purchases of stock and other investments).

As our discussion is suggesting, firms must study technological trends to identify opportunities and threats. In "Understanding Strategy," we describe how Nokia lost market share to competitors because it failed to effectively deal with changes in the cell phone industry regarding flip-top or "clamshell" phones.

Global Trends

Global trends concern changes in relevant emerging and developed country global markets, important international political events, and critical changes in cultural and institutional characteristics of global markets. Table 3.1 lists five important global trends that some expect to significantly influence global markets in future years. Examining trends such as the ones shown in Table 3.1 helps the firm identify opportunities and threats outside its domestic market. Being able to do this is important, because firms are sometimes able to grow by pursuing opportunities in other countries. Furthermore, moving production overseas through global outsourcing enables some firms to increase productivity.

learning from failure

understanding strategy:

NOKIA MISSES A SIGNIFICANT TREND IN CELL PHONES

Nokia was the leader in cell phones with 35 percent of the market in 2003. However, by the end of the first quarter of 2004, Nokia had lost three percentage points of market share since the last quarter of 2003. At the same time, Samsung, which ranks third by sales volume after Nokia and Motorola, gained significant ground. Samsung has a goal of obtaining 40 percent of worldwide mobile phone sales, from its current approximate ten percent. Nokia's first-quarter 2004 profits dropped two percent, while first-quarter 2004 profits for Samsung rose 178 percent with sales up more than 50 percent for the quarter. How did this change in market share and profits occur? Nokia indicated that it was "not satisfied with our sales development during the first quarter," which seems to be an understatement. What happened to Nokia?

While Samsung focused on high-end products such as "clamshell" cell phones, Nokia has yet to launch a set of clamshell products. Also, Nokia has emphasized sales in emerging economies that require low-end phones rather than in richer markets such as the United States and Europe. Although Nokia introduced five new models in mid-2004, including the clamshell-type products, Samsung and Motorola have been quick to offer innovative products with improved features such as color screens and digital camera capabilities.

As Nokia has grown in size, it has encountered difficulties in responding quickly to changing trends such as the clamshell-type phone. As a result, Nokia's stock price has fallen while other companies such as Ericsson and Siemens in Europe have experienced positive changes in market value. While sales of cell phones increased 25 percent on an annual basis in the first quarter of 2004, Nokia's shipments rose only by 19 percent. As a result, its mobile phone division profits fell considerably relative to competitors' financial performances. This illustrates the importance of keeping abreast of important technological trends and consumer fashions in the marketplace. Making adjustments to successfully respond to trends in the general environment can greatly affect firm performance.

SOURCES: K. Belson, 2004, As Nokia falters, Motorola rides strong sales to higher profits, *New York Times,* http://www.nytimes.com, April 21; A. Cowell, 2004, Slow to adapt, Nokia loses market share in latest cell phones, *New York Times,* http://www.nytimes.com, April 14; N. Fildes, 2004, Nokia forecasts growth in handsets; maker of mobile phones launches five new models to halt market-share loss, *Wall Street Journal,* June 15, B6; T. Hanrahan and J. Fry, 2004, Catch me if you webcam; Nokia flips its phone strategy, *Wall Street Journal Online,* http://www.wsj.com, April 19; M. Hansson, 2004, Sony Ericsson swings to profit on strong camera-phone sales, *Wall Street Journal Online,* http://www.wsj.com, April 20.

Consider the variety of purposes for which you use the Internet. The many ways most of us, likely including you as well, use the Internet demonstrate its power. From a global trends perspective, it is interesting to understand that to date, the Internet has had the greatest impact on firms competing in the United States. However, this is predicted to change. China, for example, has the potential to become the second major business power on the Internet. In fact, by 2006, it is expected that more people from China will use the Internet than any other nation on earth. For this reason, Nortel Networks decided to invest $200 million in a research-and-development facility in Beijing that will manufacture networking and wireless equipment. One reason why Nortel made this decision is the prediction that China will have more broadband users than the United

TABLE 3.1 Five Important Global Trends

1. **The advent of nanotechnology.** Advances in manipulating organic and inorganic material at the atomic and molecular levels will lead to the ability to create smaller, stronger products. Michael D. Mehta, a sociology professor at the University of Saskatchewan, says, "Nanotechnology will usher in a new industrial revolution, have impacts on global trade and intellectual property, and will ultimately shape how we view the world and our place in it." Recently, the U.S. government earmarked $3.7 billion over four years for nanotech research.
2. **Globalization.** One of the consequences of globalization is an increasing gulf between rich and poor countries. Steven M. Kates, an associate professor of marketing at Simon Fraser University in Burnaby, British Columbia, predicts that many corporations may play an increasingly paternalistic role in third-world countries, developing infrastructure and stepping in where governments have failed.
3. **Global warming.** Earth's average surface temperature has risen by about 1°F in the past century, with accelerated warming during the past two decades, largely due to the buildup of greenhouse gases. Climate change will affect everything from human health and agriculture to forests and water supplies.
4. **Water shortages.** Population growth will increase pressure on water supplies. "Blue gold" is in short supply throughout much of the world. The management and conservation of potable water will become increasingly important.
5. **The employment power shift.** By 2006, two North Americans will be leaving jobs for every one available to refill those positions. Two years after that, projections show a worker deficit of 10 million people. This will shift the balance of power between employees and companies, and firms will have to compete to acquire talent.

SOURCE: "The 5 Most Important Global Trends" by Laura Pratt as appeared in *Profit,* December 2003, p. 24. Reprinted by permission of Laura Pratt.

States by 2006. The opportunities suggested by this expectation are contributing to the launch of many startup firms in Internet retailing, mobile services, and gaming services in China.[7]

Although the Chinese Internet market represents a significant opportunity, global trends can also present significant threats both from foreign competitors and in regard to the complexity in competing in different countries. Companies must understand the sociocultural and institutional differences in global markets in order to be successful. Significant changes in currency and political risks because of war and nationalization of assets also need to be considered.

As you have seen, firms focus on the future when studying the general environment. However, that future must take place within a particular context. An **industry,** which is a group of firms producing similar products, is the context within which a firm's future is experienced. Firms analyze the industry environment to understand the profitability potential of a particular industry or of a segment within an industry. We discuss how firms study an industry in the next section.

Analyzing the Industry Environment

Michael Porter developed a framework for classifying and analyzing the characteristics of an industry's environment.[8] His five-forces model of competition examines competitive forces that influence the profitability potential in an

FIGURE 3.2 The Five-Forces Model

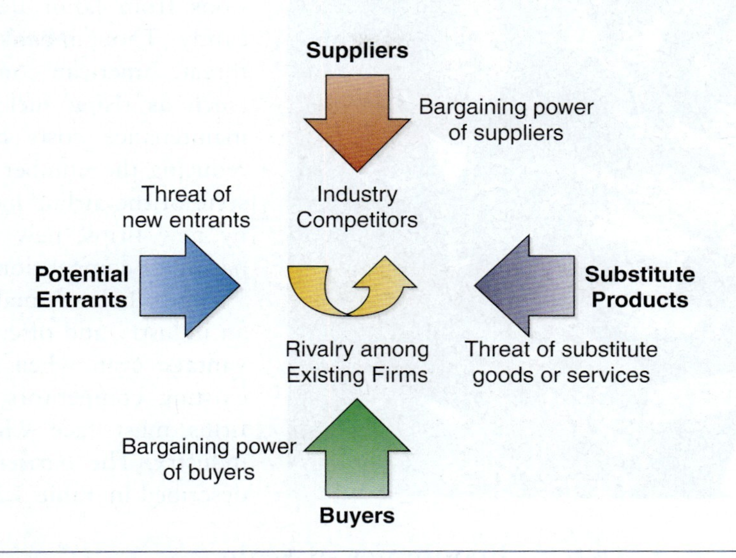

SOURCE: Adapted with the permission of The Free Press, an imprint of Simon & Schuster Adult Publishing Group, from *Competitive Advantage: Creating and Sustaining Superior Performance* by Michael E. Porter, p. 5.

industry or of a segment within an industry. Each force can reduce the probability that a firm can earn profits while competing in an industry. You'll see how this is the case while reading the following descriptions of each force. As shown in Figure 3.2, potential entrants, substitute products, suppliers, buyers, and rivalry among existing firms are the five forces that affect the profitability potential of an industry. Firms competing in an industry want to understand these forces so they can position themselves in the industry to maximize their ability to earn profits. Firms thinking of entering an industry want to understand these forces to decide whether the industry profitability potential is sufficient to support a decision to enter that industry.

Potential Entrants

Potential entrants can be a threat to firms already competing in an industry; by entering that industry, new firms may take market share away from current competitors. Potential entrants also pose a threat to existing competitors because they bring additional production capacity, which can lead to overcapacity in the industry. Overcapacity reduces prices for consumers, but results in lower returns for industry firms. On the positive side, new entrants may force incumbent firms to learn new ways to compete. For example, initiating a new Internet-based distribution channel has been important for established pharmacy competitors such as Walgreen's, given new Internet drug distributors in the United States and Canada.

In the highly competitive airline industry, American Airlines has been weakened by new entrants such as JetBlue. As smaller, more nimble, and more focused competitors such as Southwest Airlines and JetBlue have increased market share,

© Noah Berger/Bloomberg News/Landov

The entrance of lower-cost airlines such as Southwest into the industry has forced veteran competitors to rethink their strategies.

old-guard airlines with traditionally high cost structures have had to dramatically change their strategies and their implementation or fail. American, unlike United, barely managed to avoid bankruptcy by bargaining for concessions from labor unions and by cutting costs significantly. Though bankruptcy is no longer an immediate threat, American continues to face numerous challenges (such as rising fuel costs). American has trimmed its maintenance costs by finding new suppliers and by reducing the number of different aircraft in its fleet.[9] In spite of the airline industry's significant barriers to entry by new firms, new market entrants have changed the nature of competition in the airline industry.

Entry barriers make it difficult for new firms to enter an industry and often place them at a competitive disadvantage even when they are able to enter. Therefore, existing competitors try to develop barriers that new firms must face when deciding whether to enter an industry. The barriers we will discuss next are briefly described in Table 3.2.

Economies of Scale

Economies of scale are the improvements in efficiency a firm experiences as it incrementally increases its size. Economies of scale can be realized through increased efficiencies in almost all business functions such as marketing, manufacturing, research and development, and purchasing. The important point about economies of scale is that they reduce the costs the firm incurs to produce additional units of its products. Without economies of scale, new entrants are at a cost disadvantage trying to compete against established competitors.

Capital Requirements

A significant amount of financial capital is often needed for a firm to establish operations in an industry. Financial capital enables the entering firm to build or lease physical facilities, purchase supplies, support marketing activities, and hire talented workers (human capital) who know how to compete in a particular industry. If the amount of financial capital needed isn't available, a firm may not be able to enter an industry at all, or it may do so at a competitive disadvantage (because it lacked the capital to build or acquire what is needed to successfully compete against established competitors).

Switching Costs

Switching costs are the one-time costs customers incur when they decide to buy a product from a different supplier. Switching costs can be low, high, or anywhere in between. Think of the costs you would incur to fly with one airline instead of a competing airline. Assuming the ticket costs are about the same, it costs you essentially nothing to check in at a different ticket counter after arriving at the airport and to land at a different terminal or a different part of a terminal at your destination city. On the other hand, deciding to transfer as a last-

TABLE 3.2 Barriers to Entry into an Industry

Barrier	Description
Economies of scale	Without economies of scale, potential new entrants are likely to be at a cost disadvantage relative to established competitors with economies of scale.
Capital requirements	If the amount of financial capital needed isn't available, a firm may not be able to enter an industry at all or may lack the resources to compete against an established competitor.
Switching costs	A firm thinking of entering an industry would want to determine how costly it would be for an industry's customers to buy from a new firm compared to continue buying from an established competitor.
Differentiation	If customers decide that an established firm's product uniquely meets their needs, then it may be difficult for a new firm to enter that segment of the market.
Access to distribution channels	If established firms have developed relationships with the majority of distribution channels, potential entrants may find it difficult to gain access because a change may create switching costs for a distributor.
Government policy	Some industries are more regulated than others and require a government license or permit before business can be conducted; entry then becomes more difficult.

semester senior in college to another university or college could be quite costly because most educational institutions require students to complete the last 60 or so hours of course work on site. So the cost to switch to another university or college as a last-semester senior is quite substantial. Existing competitors try to create switching costs for customers. Airline frequent-flyer plans are an example of this. A firm thinking of entering an industry would want to determine how costly it would be for an industry's customers to buy from a new firm compared to continue buying from an established competitor.

Differentiation

Over time, customers may decide that an established firm's product uniquely meets their needs. Such perceptions of uniqueness are defined as *differentiation* (see Chapter 5 for a more formal definition). Even in a commodity-type business such as soft drinks, firms such as Coca-Cola and PepsiCo have been effective at establishing customer loyalty through strong marketing programs. In these circumstances, a potential entrant must invest significant resources to overcome existing customer loyalties. Often this means entering with low-end products that compete on price rather than brand image. However, low-end products often require lower prices because of incumbent firms' economies of scale. New entrants may have difficulty in matching the low prices because realizing similar economies of scale without experiencing losses is difficult.

Access to Distribution Channels

Over time, established firms learn how to build and use effective distribution channels. Often relationships develop between firms and their distributors, creating switching costs for the distributors. Thus, potential entrants frequently find it difficult to gain access to distribution channels. Price breaks and cooperative-advertising allowances might be proposed by a potential entrant. But, if taken, these actions can be expected to reduce the new entrant's profit. Beyond this, there is no reason to believe that firms already competing in the industry wouldn't be able to match these actions.

Government Policy

Entry can also be limited by government policy through licensing and permit requirements. Some industries are more regulated than others. Liquor retailing, banking, and trucking, for example, are highly regulated. Substantial regulations limit entry by new firms. The Federal Communications Commission (FCC) grants licenses to radio and television stations. In 1997, the FCC took bids on licenses for satellite radio and only two licenses were granted to bidders. From these licenses only two competing companies were formed: XM Radio and Sirius Radio. XM has an agreement with General Motors, while Sirius has agreements with Ford and DaimlerChrysler.[10] In early 2005, rumors began circulating that XM Radio and Sirius Radio might try to merge. Government regulations, in terms of antitrust policies, would have a significant bearing on this possible transaction. So while regulations may protect established competitors from the challenges of new entrants, excessive regulations generate costs that reduce the industry's profitability potential.

Substitute Products

Substitute products also have the potential to influence an industry's profitability potential. **Substitute products** are goods or services that perform similar functions to an existing product. Consider the music industry as an example of an industry that has experienced a number of substitute products over the years. Cassette tapes became substitutes for phonograph records, and compact discs (CDs) became substitutes for tapes. Currently, MP3 and other digital formats are being substituted for CDs. In general, product substitutes present a strong threat to an incumbent firm when the substitutes are more effective and sold at a lower price. Thus, the product performance relative to the price is the relevant concern, especially if the incumbent firms' products lack switching costs. However, if the incumbent firms can differentiate the existing product in ways that customers value (such as after-sales service), a substitute product's attractiveness will be lower.

Bargaining Power of Suppliers

Suppliers' actions can also reduce the ability of firms to earn profits while competing in an industry. Think of it this way: If a supplier can either increase the price of its product or reduce the quality while selling it at the same price, the effect on established firms' profitability is negative. A supplier that can do one of these things is said to be a powerful supplier. Suppliers tend to be powerful when:

- There are a few large suppliers and the buying firms' industry is not concentrated.
- Substitute products are not available to the buying firms.
- The buying firms are not a significant customer for the suppliers.

- The suppliers' goods are essential to the buyers' marketplace success.
- The suppliers' products have high switching costs for the buyers.
- The suppliers pose a credible threat to integrate forward into the buyers' industry.

As illustrated in "Understanding Strategy" focused on Nokia, there are many cell phone suppliers such as Nokia and its competitors who are competing against one another to supply wireless phone service companies such as Sprint. Thus, in this industry, suppliers do not have much power and therefore do not negatively affect the profitability potential of cell phone service companies.[11] However, Electronic Arts (EA) has power as a supplier. Because EA has done an excellent job of developing high-quality, innovative games, electronic game box manufacturers such as Sony (Playstation), Nintendo (GameCube), and Microsoft (Xbox) are willing to pay a premium to contract for EA's products. EA's best-selling titles—MVP Baseball, Madden NFL, FIFA Soccer, Harry Potter, Lord of the Rings, and James Bond—have all been hits on these game platforms.[12] As a powerful supplier, EA's actions have the potential to reduce the profits that Sony, Nintendo, and Microsoft can earn while competing in the electronic game box industry.

Bargaining Power of Buyers

Firms selling a product want to increase their profitability, while their customers (buyers) want to buy high-quality products at a low price. These goals mean that buyers try to reduce their costs by bargaining with selling firms for lower prices, higher quality, and greater levels of service. In contrast, firms try to offer value to customers at prices that clearly exceed the costs of providing that value. Of course, powerful customers have the potential to reduce the profitability potential of an industry. Buyers or customers tend to be powerful when:

- They buy a large portion of the selling firm's total output.
- The selling firm is dependent on the buyers for a significant portion of its sales revenue.
- They can switch to another seller's product with few switching costs.
- The selling industry's products are undifferentiated or similar to a commodity.
- They present a credible threat to integrate backward into the sellers' industry.

As buyers, cell phone carriers such as Verizon and Sprint in the United States and DoCoMo in Japan have been gaining power over cell phone manufacturers such as Nokia, Motorola, Sony, and Samsung. The buyers' power is increasing in this case because the average consumer does not have a strong preference to buy, for example, a Nokia phone instead of a Motorola phone. Phone service companies often lure customers with cell phone giveaway programs; customers' indifference to cell phone brand makes this possible. Unless cell phone manufacturers have sufficient market share to maintain the scale of their operation and keep costs low, their ability to earn profits likely will be reduced because of the power of their main customers.[13]

Rivalry among Existing Firms

Competitive rivalry is the set of actions and reactions between competitors as they compete for an advantageous market position. For example, competitive rivalry is highly visible and intense in the airline industry. When one airline lowers its prices in a market, that action is likely to affect a competitor's business in that market; so the tactical action of reducing prices by one airline invites a competitive response by one or more of its competitors. Competitive rivalry is likely to be based on dimensions such as price, quality, and innovation. Next, we discuss conditions that influence competitive rivalry in an industry.

Degree of Differentiation

Industries with many companies that have successfully differentiated their products have less rivalry, resulting in lower competition for individual firms and less of a negative effect on the industry's profitability potential. This usually results because competing companies have established brand loyalty by offering differentiated products to their customers. Differentiated products to which customers are loyal cannot be easily imitated and often earn higher profits.[14] However, when buyers view products as undifferentiated or as commodities, rivalry intensifies. Intense rivalry finds buyers making their purchasing decisions mainly on the basis of price. In turn, intense price competition negatively affects an industry's profitability potential.

Switching Costs

The lower the buyers' switching costs, the easier it is for competitors to attract them. High switching costs partially protect firms from rivals' efforts to attract customers. Interestingly, the government has lowered the switching costs of cell phone carriers by reducing regulation of phone numbers. Consumers can now transport their old cell phone number to a new cell phone service provider, which reduces the switching cost for the customer. However, lower switching costs for customers are likely to increase rivalry among cell phone service providers.[15]

Numerous or Equally Balanced Competitors

Intense rivalries are common in industries in which competing firms are of similar size and have similar competitive capabilities. An intense rivalry is evolving between SABMiller and Anheuser-Busch (AB).[16] These large competitors are battling to gain a dominant position in the global beer market. In China, one of the hotly contested markets, AB recently outbid SABMiller to acquire Harbin Brewery Group. This acquisition gives AB ownership of the fourth-largest Chinese brewer and serves as a platform for selling AB's own products in China.[17] Because of their intense rivalry, though, AB can anticipate that SABMiller will react to its acquisition of Harbin.

Slow Industry Growth

Growing markets reduce the pressure to attract competitors' customers. However, when sales growth declines, the only way to increase sales for current products is to take market share from competitors. Therefore, rivalry usually increases in no-growth or slow-growth markets. The battle often intensifies as firms react to actions by competitors to protect their market shares. One of the worst downturns in the information and communication technology industry occurred between 2000 and 2003. In 2004, the industry began to recover, but firms vary in their financial conditions. Lucent Technologies, for instance, cut R&D very deeply, while network giant Cisco invested considerable amounts in

R&D to retool its product line. As John Chambers, CEO of Cisco noted in 2004, "We have never invested more, looking out three years plus, than we are at the present, and that is at a time when almost all of our global peers did the exact opposite."[18] As the recovery continues, firms with abundant resources are able to take advantage of the weaker firms.

High Strategic Stakes

Competitive rivalry tends to be high when it is important for competitors to perform well in their chosen market(s). For example, the competition for global market share between SABMiller and Anheuser-Busch represents high strategic stakes for both firms. Similarly, as airlines compete with lower demand for their services and with the growth of low-cost airlines, many larger carriers are not as competitive as they once were. Alitalia, the flagship Italian airline, has been struggling and seeking to restructure even though Italy is a leading tourist destination.[19] Besides mismanagement and political problems due to government involvement, Alitalia is facing a number of low-cost carriers such as Ryanair. Ryanair handles about 9,000 passengers per employee, while the ratio at Alitalia is about 1,100 passengers per employee; the cost structure differences are significant.[20] Because of the importance of the Italian market to Alitalia and its competitors, increased competitive rivalry can be expected.

High Fixed Costs or High Storage Costs

When fixed or storage costs are a large part of total costs, companies try to spread costs across a larger volume of output. However, when many firms attempt to better utilize their capacity, excess capacity often results in the industry. Therefore, firms try to reduce their inventory by cutting the price of their product. Alternatively, they may offer rebates and other special discounts. This practice is quite common in the automobile industry and leads to more-intense competition. This pattern is also often found in perishable-goods industries; as perishable-goods inventory grows, intense competition follows, with price cutting used to sell products and avoid spoilage. When this happens, rivalry increases.

High Exit Barriers

Firms facing high exit barriers often continue competing in industries even when their performance is less than desired. In such industries, there is intense competition because firms often make desperate choices to survive. Barriers to exiting from an industry include the following:

- Specialized assets (assets with values linked to a particular business or location)
- Fixed costs of exit (such as labor agreements)
- Strategic interrelationships (relationships of mutual dependence, such as those between one business and other parts of the company's operations, including shared facilities and access to financial markets)
- Emotional barriers (aversion to economically justified business decisions because of fear for one's own career, loyalty to employees, and so forth)
- Government and social restrictions (more common outside the United States; often based on government concerns for job losses and regional economic effects)

© BLOOMBERG NEWS/Landov

For what reasons might satellite radio companies such as Sirius have high exit barriers?

The airline industry has high exit barriers because of the specialized assets associated with air travel, agreements with airports and other partners, government restrictions, and unions. Satellite radio rivals XM and Sirius, who are in a battle to gain customers, have high exit barriers as well. Sirius recently signed Howard Stern, a talk-show host who often uses colorful language. XM, the industry subscriber leader, is trying to sign other celebrities to counter this move.[21]

With an understanding of the potential of each of the five competitive forces to influence an industry's profitability, the firm can determine the attractiveness of competing in that industry. In general, the stronger the competitive forces, the less attractive the industry. An industry characterized by low barriers to entry, strong suppliers, strong buyers, the potential of product substitutes, and intense rivalry among competitors suggests little potential for firms to generate significant profits while competing in that industry. On the other hand, an industry characterized by high entry barriers, suppliers and buyers with little bargaining power, few potential substitutes, and moderate rivalry suggests that the profitability potential of that industry is strong.[22]

A competitor analysis is the final part of the external environment that firms must evaluate to fully recognize their opportunities and threats. The purpose of the competitor analysis is to fully understand the firm's competitors.

Competitor Analysis

Studying competitors is often the most important part of the external environment analysis (see Figure 3.1). Answering the questions in Table 3.3 can help a firm recognize its most important current and future competitors.

Armed with a list of critical competitors, the firm is prepared to conduct a thorough analysis of each, focusing on the competitor's strategic intent, current strategy, and major strengths and weaknesses.

Recently, Airbus seems to be winning in its continuing competitive battles with Boeing, its main rival.[23] We describe the intense competition between these competitors in "Understanding Strategy." After reading about these two firms, decide which of them you believe will be more successful over the next ten years or so.

Competitor Strategic Intent

Strategic intent is the firm's motivation to leverage its resources and capabilities to reach its vision. Understanding a competitor's strategic intent increases

learning from success

understanding strategy:

AIRBUS SURPASSES BOEING AS THE LEADING MAKER OF COMMERCIAL JETS

Historically, Boeing has been the global leader in manufacturing commercial airplanes. Today, though, Airbus is outperforming Boeing—for several reasons. First, Airbus's intermediate-sized A330, which carries approximately the same number of passengers as the Boeing 767, is more fuel-efficient and has a greater flying range than the 767. Additionally, because Airbus cockpits share a similar design across planes, buyers experience lower costs to train their pilots. Although Boeing is trying to undercut the success of the A330 with its new fuel efficient 7E7 Dreamliner, it is concerned about Airbus underpricing this aircraft. If Airbus moves substantially ahead in the current economic cycle, Boeing will face significant hurdles in its effort to regain the largest share of the global market for commercial airplanes.

Airbus's CEO, Noel Forgeard, suggests that Airbus's planned superjumbo jetliner, the A380, has the potential to widen the gap between the two firms. The A380 has about 35 percent more seats than Boeing's largest jetliner, the 747–400. The size of the A380 could also work in Airbus's favor because of the chronic shortage of departure slots in airports such as London Heathrow. Moreover, Airbus believes that the fuel efficiency of the A380 will result in a fuel-consumption reduction of about 20 percent per passenger on most routes. However, reaching this goal means that the plane's weight must be reduced—a technological challenge. Increasing the percentage of the A380 that is made of composite materials is one action Airbus is taking to reduce the plane's weight.

As we expect, Boeing is trying to become more competitive in its battles with Airbus. Currently, Boeing is seeking support from the U.S. government to develop a "blended-wing design." Boeing believes that this technology has the potential to dramatically increase the efficiency of airplanes such as the military tanker plane Boeing wants to build for the U.S. government. If successful in an application to military aircraft, Boeing intends to use the blended-wing design technology to produce commercial planes as well.

SOURCES: S. Holmes, 2004, A silver lining for Boeing: The loss of a big contract could help its blended-wing tanker get off the ground, *Business Week,* May 24: 44; D. Michaels, 2004, Jumbo bet: For Airbus, making huge jet requires new juggling acts, *Wall Street Journal,* May 27: A1; C. Matlack & S. Holmes, 2003, Mega Plane: Airbus' A380 is the biggest superjumbo ever, and airlines have ordered more than 120 already, *Business Week,* November 10: 88.

a firm's ability to predict how that competitor will react to a competitive action.

The strength of strategic intent can be gauged by examining important competitor characteristics such as the competitor's market dependence. *Market dependence* is the extent to which a firm's revenues or profits are derived from a particular market. Competitors with high market dependence are likely to respond strongly to attacks threatening their market position.[24] Boeing is not as dependent on the commercial aircraft business as it once was;

TABLE 3.3 Basic Questions for Conducting an Industry Analysis to Screen Key Competitors

Threat of new entrants:

- Which firms have developed economies of scale and how strong are they?
- How differentiated are the industry's products and services?
- Would buyers encounter switching costs to purchase from a new entrant?
- Which firms pose the most significant threat of potential new entry?

Substitute products:

- What product functionalities can be duplicated in some other fashion?
- Are there lower-cost alternatives to current products?

Bargaining power of suppliers:

- Is the supply chain dominated by only a few companies?
- How important is the industry to its suppliers?
- How differentiated are suppliers' products?
- Do suppliers pose a threat of forward integration into the industry?

Bargaining power of buyers:

- Are there large concentrations of buyers in the industry?
- Are products a high percentage of buyers' costs?
- Do buyers pose a threat of backward integration into the industry?

Rivalry among existing competitors:

- How many competitors are there?
- How differentiated are they?
- What are the exit barriers?
- Which competitors are most likely to respond to a specific competitive move?

the firm has diversified into military aircraft and other defense-related equipment, as well as a space and satellite-launching business, to reduce its dependence on commercial aircraft production. Understanding Boeing's strategic intent in the commercial aircraft business can help Airbus in formulating its strategy to compete with Boeing. Understanding the strategic intent and actions of competitors clearly contributes to the firm's ability to compete successfully.[25]

Current Competitor Strategy

Gathering data and information to understand a competitor's current strategy is critical to conducting an effective competitor analysis. Meaningful information about a competitor's current strategy helps the firm predict that competitor's behavior. Despite the importance of studying competitors, evidence suggests that only a relatively small percentage of firms use formal processes to collect and disseminate such information. Some firms forget to analyze competitors' future objectives as they try to understand their current strategies, thereby yielding incomplete insights about those competitors.[26] Even if research is inadequate, appropriate interpretation of that information is important. "Research found that how accurate senior executives are about their competitive environments is indeed less important for strategy and corresponding organizational changes than the way in which they interpret information about their environments."[27] Thus, although competitor scanning is important, investing money to appropriately interpret that information may be just as important as gathering and organizing it. Therefore, assessing whether a competitor represents an opportunity or a threat and what that competitor's strengths and weaknesses are is extremely important.

Strengths and Weaknesses of the Competitor

Assessing a competitor's strengths and weaknesses is the final component of a competitor analysis. Firms with few or competitively unimportant strengths may not be able to successfully respond to a competitor's actions. Boeing has a number of strengths and resources that have enabled it to respond to Airbus's introduction of the A380 jumbo jet. But smaller jet producers such as Bombardier may be unable to respond to this action. Basic areas that firms study to understand where a competitor is strong and where it is weak are financial resources, marketing capability, human resource management, and innovation capability. A firm will want to avoid attacking a competitor where it is strong, and instead attack where it is weak.

Complements to Competitive Interaction

When a product is sold, complementary products may be necessary to facilitate the sale or to increase the functionality of the product as it is used.[28] **Complementors** are the network of companies that sell goods or services that are complementary to another firm's good or service. If a complementor's good or service adds value to the sale of a firm's good or service, it is likely to create value for that firm. For example, a range of complements are necessary to sell automobiles, such as financial services to arrange credit and luxury options (stereo equipment, extended warranties, and so on). Personal computers are complemented by peripheral devices and services such as printers, scanners, personal digital assistants, operating systems, software and games, and Internet service providers. Digital cameras are complemented by digital storage disks, software that creates usable and storable digital images, and printers and services for printing digital photographs.

As illustrated in Figure 3.3, complementors are a part of understanding the nature of value creation in an industry. A firm can increase its chances of achieving value creation by paying attention to customers, suppliers, competitors, and complementors.

FIGURE 3.3 Value Creation in an Industry

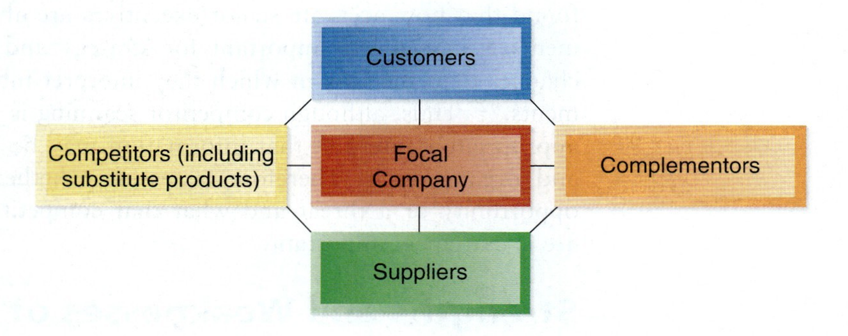

SOURCE: From *Co-opetition* by Adam M. Brandenburger and Barry J. Nalebuff, copyright © 1996 by Adam M. Brandenburger and Barry J. Nalebuff. Used by permission of Doubleday, a division of Random House, Inc., and Barry Nalebuff, Adam Brandenburger, and Helen Rees Literary Agency, Boston, Mass.

Summary

The primary purpose of this chapter is to describe what firms do to analyze the three parts of their external environment—the general, industry, and competitor environments. In doing so, we examined the following topics:

- Although the firm's external environment is challenging and complex, examining it is important. Careful analysis of the external environment enables a firm to identify opportunities and threats. The firm cannot directly control its external environment; however, the firm can use information about the external environment when choosing strategies to implement.
- The external environment has three major parts: (1) the **general environment** (trends in the broader society that affect industries and their firms), (2) the industry environment (forces that influence a firm in relationship to its buyers and suppliers and current and potential competitors), and (3) the competitor environment (in which the firm analyzes each major competitor's current and potential strategic actions).
- The general environment has six categories of trends that need to be analyzed: demographic, economic, political/legal, sociocultural, technological, and global.
- The five-forces model of competition examines the threat of entry, the power of suppliers, the power of buyers, product substitutes, and the intensity of rivalry among competitors. By studying these forces, the firm tries to find an attractive position in an industry. Compared to the general environment, the industry environment has a more direct effect on the firm's strategic actions.
- Competitor analysis informs the firm about the strategic intent, current strategies, and strengths and weaknesses of its major competitors. Competitor analysis helps the firm understand how its competitors likely will compete in its chosen industry.
- Understanding how complementors' products or services add value to the sale of the focal firm's product or service will help the focal firm improve its competitive position.

Key Terms

competitive rivalry 57
complementors 63
demographic trends 48
economic trends 48
economies of scale 54
general environment 47
global trends 50
industry 52
political/legal trends 49
sociocultural trends 50
strategic intent 60
substitute products 56
switching costs 54
technological trends 50

Discussion Questions

1. Why is it important for a firm to study and understand the external environment?
2. What are the six segments of the general environment that are important to study? Explain the relationships and differences among them.
3. How do the five forces of competition in an industry affect its attractiveness?
4. What three components are necessary to conduct a competitor analysis?
5. When would a competitor likely respond to a strategic competitive move?
6. How can complementors add value to a firm's competitive situation?

Endnotes

1. D. Armstrong, 2004, Sale of Eckerd to CVS, Coutu appears close, *Wall Street Journal,* April 1: B1.
2. D. J. Hanford, 2004, Installation help is growing market for home retailers, *Wall Street Journal,* December 28: B6.
3. G. Ip, 2003, Federal Reserve maintains interest-rate target at 1%, *Wall Street Journal Online,* http://www.wsj.com, August 13.
4. A. J. Hillman, G. D. Keim, & D. Schuler, 2004, Corporate political activity: A review and research agenda, *Journal of Management,* 30: 837–857.
5. J. Kanter, D. Clark, & J. R. Wilke, 2004, EU imposes sanctions on Microsoft, *Wall Street Journal,* March 25: A2.
6. J. Greene, J. Kerstetter, P. Burrows, S. Hamm, & S. E. Ante, 2004, Microsoft's midlife crisis, *Business Week Online,* http://www.businessweek.com, April 19.
7. B. Einhorn, 2004, The Net's second superpower, *Business Week,* March 15: 54–56.
8. M. E. Porter, 1980, *Competitive Strategy,* New York: Free Press.
9. M. Maynard, 2004, No longer on the brink, American Air is still in peril, *New York Times,* http://www.nytimes.com, March 18.
10. C. DeLeon, 2004, Daimler-Chrysler to bundle 1-yr Sirius subscription, *Wall Street Journal Online,* http://www.wsj.com, April 6.
11. T. Hanrahan & J. Fry, 2004, Catch me if you webcam: Nokia flips its phone strategy, *Wall Street Journal Online,* http://www.wsj.com, April 19.
12. C. Edward, 2004, Keeping you glued to the couch: In video games, top developer Electronic Arts zaps the competition, *Business Week,* May 27: 58–59.
13. R. O. Crockett, A. Reinhardt, & M. Ihlwan, 2004, Cell phones: Who's calling the shots? *Business Week,* April 26: 48–49.
14. D. M. De Carolis, 2003, Competencies and imitability in the pharmaceutical industry: An analysis of their relationship with firm performance, *Journal of Management,* 29: 27–50.
15. B. Stone, 2003, Cutting the (phone) cord, *Newsweek,* December 8: 103.
16. J. Ewing & J. Weber, 2004, The beer wars come to a head, *Business Week,* May 24: 68.
17. C. Lawton, 2004, Anheuser, with Harbin in tow, sorts through China options, *Wall Street Journal Online,* http://www.wsj.com, October 12.
18. D. Pringle, 2004, Top tech firms to boost R&D spending, *Wall Street Journal,* January 29: B6.
19. K. Johnson & L. DiLeo, 2004, Alitalia can't stanch red ink, *Wall Street Journal,* April 21: A16.
20. J. Spencer, 2004, The discount jet-set: Europe's budget airlines, *Wall Street Journal,* April 27: D1.

21. J. Helyar, 2004, Radio's Stern Challenge, *Fortune,* November 1: 123–127.
22. Porter, *Competitive Strategy.*
23. J. L. Lunsford, 2004, Dog Fight—Behind Slide in Boeing Orders: Weak Sales Team or Firm Prices? *Wall Street Journal,* December 23: A1.
24. K. G. Smith, W. J. Ferrier, & C. M. Grimm, 2001, King of the hill: Dethroning the industry leader, *Academy of Management Executive,* 15(2): 59–70.
25. G. McNamara, R. A. Luce, & G. H. Thompson, 2002, Examining the effect of complexity in strategic group knowledge structures on firm performance, *Strategic Management Journal,* 23: 153–170.
26. L. Fahey, 1999, Competitor scenarios: Projecting a rival's marketplace strategy, *Competitive Intelligence Review,* 10(2): 65–85.
27. K. M. Sutcliffe & K. Weber, 2003, The high cost of accurate knowledge, *Harvard Business Review,* 81(5): 74–82.
28. A. Brandenburger & B. Nalebuff, 1996, *Co-opetition,* New York: Currency Doubleday.

The Firm

Reading and studying this chapter should enable you to:

*Knowledge Objectives

1_
Explain how to identify the firm's strengths and weaknesses through an internal analysis.

2_
Define resources, capabilities, and core competencies and explain their relationships.

3_
Describe the four characteristics that core competencies must have to be competitive advantages.

4_
Explain the value chain and describe the differences between primary and support activities.

5_
Describe the advantages and disadvantages of outsourcing.

6_
Explain the relationship between a firm's resources and its performance.

© AP Photo/David Kohl

Focusing on Strategy

Building Resources for Innovation

"The consumer is boss; Reframe the Brands [defining P&G's brands more broadly]; Connect and develop; 360 degree innovation [differentiating products not just by formulating but also by design]. There is a lot of jargon. But we have to find things that are simple for 100,000 people to understand. And more than half my organization doesn't have English as a first language. So it's intentional." (A. G. Lafley, CEO of Procter & Gamble, speaking about what he is doing to make P&G more innovative)

Innovation's importance is no longer limited to high-technology industries. Indeed, innovation has become highly important for firms striving to be competitive in almost all types of industries. For example, Procter & Gamble (P&G), once considered a staid and bureaucratic company, has introduced many new innovative products since 2000. With new CEO A. G. Lafley emphasizing innovation, P&G has regained an image as a growth company. According to Lafley, P&G lost its market-leading positions in toothpaste and diapers because of competitors' superior innovation capabilities. Lafley is taking many actions to enhance innovation at P&G, including partnering with and acquiring other firms with innovation skills. Focusing on creating synergy by combining the skills of acquired firms with those already inside P&G has resulted in several innovative products such as Iams Dental Defense (a tartar-fighting pet food), developed after P&G acquired Iams. The same objective of combining synergy as a source of product innovations was the reason for P&G's intention to acquire Gillette for $57 billion (this intended transaction became public in January 2005). Other actions Lafley has taken to build his firm's innovation capabilities include expanding P&G's one-on-one consumer research, encouraging expansions of each brand, reaching outside the firm for new product ideas, and delegating more authority to product designers. These efforts seem successful, in that some believe that under Lafley's leadership, P&G now "takes mundane products and make[s] them so glamorous and distinctive that the world's largest retailer [Wal-Mart] won't be able to resist them."

Jeffrey Immelt, GE's CEO, is intent on building a culture of innovation at GE. One of the actions Immelt took was to appoint an outsider to head a new business, which was created by merging GE's health-care business unit with Amersham PLC, a U.K.-based firm that GE had acquired. Rather than appoint one of GE's homegrown managers to head the new unit, Immelt named Sir William Castell, CEO of Amersham, to be in charge of the new business. Castell is charged with fostering a new concept called *personalized medicine* that refocuses the level of research and diagnosis. Immelt believes that the personalized-medicine concept will create many innovations in this new business unit as well as provide a testing ground for applying versions of the concept in other GE units in the future. Immelt's interest in this new unit and its use of the personalized-medicine concept is high because of his conviction that innovation is the only way to truly jump-start GE growth. Immelt also strongly believes that innovation is the entry price that firms must pay to be able to effectively compete in the global economy.

Evidence shows that innovation also characterizes most "hot growth companies," firms that are growing rapidly. Currently, though, hot growth company Amgen is changing the way it operates. It is moving from being a pure biotechnology firm focused on basic and creative innovation to integrate its innovation skills with the more traditional R&D activities of large, established pharmaceutical firms. Large pharmaceutical firms are interested in gaining access to the innovation skills of firms such as Amgen primarily because during the last decade, R&D spending by large pharmaceutical firms doubled, but the number of new products decreased. Firms such as Sony have gone to external parties and even to consumers to foster development of new computer games. The retailer Sharper Image has its own R&D staff developing new product ideas. Both of these approaches are quite different from those of competitors in their industry. Regardless of whether the ideas come from inside or outside the firm, the capability to be innovative and create superior value for consumers is critical for a company to be competitive.

SOURCES: S. Ellison, A. Zimmerman, C. Forelle, 2005, P&G's Gillette edge: The playbook it honed at Wal-Mart, *Wall Street Journal,* January 31, A1, A12; M. Boyle, 2004, Growing against the grain, *Fortune,* May 3: 148–156; D. Brady & K. Capell, 2004, GE breaks the mold to spur innovation, *Business Week,* April 26: 88–89; P. O'Connell, 2004, Sharper Image's broader, richer focus, *Business Week Online,* http://www.businessweek.com, May 23; A. Overholt, 2004, Smart strategies: Putting ideas to work, *Fast Company,* April: 63–70; P. Sellers, 2004, P&G: Teaching an old dog new tricks, *Fortune,* May 31: 167–174.

As we discussed in Chapter 3, firms must be concerned with their competitors' actions as well as with other conditions in the external environment. At the same time, though, there must be concerns about the *internal environment,* which we defined in Chapter 1 as the set of conditions inside the firm affecting the choice and use of strategies. The reason managers must devote attention to understanding their firm's internal environment is that any strategy a firm chooses must be based on its resources. This means, for example, that Procter & Gamble's objective of becoming more innovative won't be reached if it lacks the resources needed. In "Focusing on Strategy," we explained some of the actions being taken at P&G to increase the firm's ability to innovate. GE's CEO, Jeffrey Immelt, is trying to do the same in his company. Sharper Image and Sony each have different approaches to increase innovation. Both focus on the use of human capital. However, Sharper Image uses internal human capital (people already working for the company) for new product ideas, while Sony additionally relies on external human capital (people outside the firm such as customers and suppliers) to identify and sometimes develop ideas for new products such as computer games.

In Chapter 1, we defined *resources* as the tangible and intangible assets held by a firm. To implement a strategy, managers integrate or combine different resources so the firm will be able to complete different work-related tasks. We also defined capabilities in Chapter 1. As we noted, *capabilities* result when the firm integrates several different resources so it will be able to complete a task or a series of related tasks. As we described in "Focusing on Strategy," P&G is combining resources between its former health-care business unit and a firm it acquired to form capabilities as the foundation for improving its ability to innovate.

We described how to conduct an external analysis (analysis of the firm's external environment) in Chapter 3. In this chapter, we discuss how to complete an internal analysis of the firm. To discuss this topic, we first describe how resources are integrated to create capabilities and how some capabilities are then developed into core competencies. Core competencies that satisfy certain conditions help the firm achieve a competitive advantage. We describe these important conditions in this chapter as well. Finally, we end the chapter with discussions of managing the firm's value chain and outsourcing. All of these terms, such as *core competencies, competitive advantages, value chain,* and *outsourcing,* are defined in this chapter.

Conducting an Internal Analysis

To develop and implement the best strategy, managers need to understand what the firm's resources and capabilities make possible. Indeed, as we noted earlier, a firm cannot successfully implement any strategy without being able to use the appropriate set of resources and capabilities. Think of it this way: A U.S.-based firm that wants to begin selling its products in Mexico won't be able to do so unless it has the resources and capabilities needed to properly distribute its products in Mexico, the financial capital to support the new distribution channel, the manufacturing capacity to produce additional quantities of its products, the capability to sell its products in a market outside the United States, and so on.

Therefore, because of the importance of resources and capabilities to the effectiveness of all strategies, managers conduct an internal analysis to identify and understand them as a precursor to selecting a strategy.[1] Through an internal analysis, the firm discovers many things, including its strengths and weaknesses.

As defined in Chapter 1, *strengths* are resources and capabilities that allow the firm to complete important tasks. **Weaknesses** are the firm's resource and capability deficiencies that make it difficult for the firm to complete important tasks. In general terms, *strengths* suggest possibilities while *weaknesses* suggest constraints. Think of a firm in your local community. What do you think are its strengths and weaknesses? Do you think the owners are aware of their firm's strengths and weaknesses?

The analysis of a firm's internal environment focuses on resources, capabilities, core competencies, and competitive advantages. We discuss these important concepts next.

Resources, Capabilities, and Core Competencies

Resources

There are two kinds of resources—tangible and intangible. **Tangible resources** are valuable assets that can be seen or quantified, such as manufacturing equipment and financial capital. **Intangible resources** are assets that contribute to creating value for customers but are not physically identifiable. They often accumulate and become more useful over time. Reputation, brand name, know-how, and organizational culture are examples of intangible resources. Both tangible and intangible resources play an important role in creating value for customers. **Value** is judged in terms of the satisfaction a firm's product creates for customers and can be measured by the price customers are willing to pay for the firm's product.[2]

Tangible resources such as financial capital are important for acquiring other physical assets (such as technology). Financial capital is also necessary for obtaining human capital. Tangible resources alone, however, will not create value for customers. Intangible resources play a critical role in the value creation process. For example, manufacturing equipment must be operated by employees (human capital) or by computers programmed by and using software developed by human capital. In fact, human capital is likely the most valuable intangible resource for most firms,[3] because of the importance of human knowledge in gaining and maintaining a competitive advantage.[4]

Human capital at upper managerial levels can have a strong influence on a firm's performance, as demonstrated by Coca-Cola. Although Coca-Cola is a well-known global brand name with much potential value for customers, the firm's stock has performed poorly in the market in recent years. This poor performance has been attributed largely to the firm's human capital in the form of its CEO and top management team. Analysts have been highly critical of the two successive CEOs and management teams that governed the firm after the unfortunate death of former CEO Roberto Goizueta. Articles detailing the poor strategies, indecisiveness, and political infighting among Coca-Cola's top executives and board of directors leave little doubt that the firm suffered from a weakness of strategic leadership for a number of years.[5]

Managers constantly take action to acquire resources, including human capital. The full set of resources a firm holds is called a *resource portfolio*. The need for managers to acquire resources and to develop an effective resource portfolio applies to organizations of all types, including professional sports teams. For example, the owners of the Boston Red Sox acquired the rights to two new pitchers, Curt Schilling and Keith Foulke (see "Understanding Strategy"). These pitchers represent specific human capital in the Red Sox resource portfolio, just as Magic Johnson and Larry Bird were human capital in the Los Angeles Lakers and Boston Celtics resource portfolios in the 1980s. Because they are pitchers, Schilling and Foulke do not play in every game. Their ultimate value to the team is affected by the decisions of the team's manager (another source of human capital) regarding against which teams each pitcher should pitch. Likewise, Johnson & Johnson acquired firms with resources the firm needed to compete. The managers making these acquisitions were filling out the firm's resource portfolio. The Home Depot acquired White Cap to gain access to an important share of a new market. In order to capitalize on White Cap's positive reputation in the commercial builders and tradesmen industry, a valuable resource, The Home Depot did not change the name of the firm.

The firms described in "Understanding Strategy" hope that their actions have shaped an effective resource portfolio—an important move, because failing to do so can limit a firm's strategy or its ability to implement a particular strategy. For example, Danone's expansion plans into China were constrained by its lack of qualified managers. Peng Qin, chairman of Danone's Chinese operations, stated that his company did not have the necessary caliber of human capital to expand at the pace desired by Danone, especially in the wealthy Guangdong province.[6]

Intangible assets require constant attention to retain and extend their value. For example, employees' skills should be continuously updated so that the firm's human capital can perform at peak levels. Intangible resources such as brand names also must be reinforced with customers or their value will diminish. That is why Coca-Cola continuously advertises the Coca-Cola brand, even though it is well known globally.[7] Additionally, negative events can harm a firm's reputation. For example, investigations by the Securities and Exchange Commission and the Department of Justice into Computer Associates' accounting practices have harmed the firm's reputation. As a result of these concerns, the CEO resigned and the company restated its financial results for 2000 and 2001. The new interim CEO had to address these problems at the firm's annual customer conference in 2004, but emphasized positive actions that were being taken to minimize harm to the firm's reputation.[8]

While it may seem easy to identify a firm's strengths and weaknesses, this generally isn't the case for several reasons. First, managers need full information about the firm's resources and capabilities to accurately evaluate them. Tangible resources (such as plants and equipment) aren't hard to identify, but intangible resources (such as organizational culture and brand name) are more challenging for managers to identify and evaluate. Tangible resources—financial resources, for example—are usually identified in the firm's accounting system and audited and certified by an external accounting firm (however, given recent problems identified in some firms' financial reports, we recognize that they are not always accurate). Physical resources can be visually identified and values placed on them by standard (accepted) practices. Yet a firm's intangible

learning from success

understanding strategy:

ACQUIRING AND MAINTAINING VALUABLE RESOURCES

The value of human capital is clearly evident in professional service firms and in professional sports teams. For example, major accounting firms, management consulting firms, and law firms base how they operate on two major resources: human capital and the firm's reputation. The reputation is based on the quality of the services that clients have received over time. These services are provided mainly by the firm's human capital. Likewise, professional sports teams also provide value to customers primarily with the human capital held by the organization. The Boston Red Sox, for example, satisfy their fans (customers) by winning baseball games, especially when they beat their traditional rival, the New York Yankees. While highly successful in 2003, the Red Sox lost the American League championship to the New York Yankees in the seventh game of the series. Because of this, the owners decided to change some key personnel. For example, they fired the team's manager and hired a new one. They also acquired new players, such as Curt Schilling and Keith Foulke, two all-star pitchers, and made other strategic moves as well. Their intent is to win future championship games and to become world champions. They know that they can do so only with the best human capital. The New York Yankees have been world champions 26 times since 1920, the most of any professional baseball team. The Yankees are also widely regarded to have the strongest human capital in the major leagues. However, the Red Sox's decisions about human capital brought dividends in the 2004 American League championship series. Schilling pitched an excellent game to win Game Six for the Red Sox, who then beat the Yankees 10–3 in the seventh and deciding game of the series. This was the first time since 1986 that the Red Sox had advanced to the World Series, and they went on to win it. So it seems that the changes in human capital paid off handsomely for the team and for the Red Sox organization.

© (MLB)(Kyodo)/Landov

Johnson & Johnson (J&J) has been a highly successful firm operating in health-care products industries. However, due to increasing competition, J&J decided to acquire other businesses to gain access to resources needed to compete effectively. It also invested more money into its drug development activities because drugs generate 60 percent of the firm's profits. Likewise, Nissan has developed value-creating resources in its manufacturing activities. In fact, its manufacturing flexibility gives it a competitive advantage over its competitors—not because of high-quality output but because of its ability to manufacture a variety of vehicles at lower costs. Nissan has also integrated external suppliers into its manufacturing process more effectively than its competitors have.

Use of a more intangible resource is exemplified by an acquisition made by The Home

Depot. The firm has been trying to use its reputation to move into related markets such as sales to commercial builders, but has had limited success. The Home Depot then chose a different approach and acquired White Cap, a firm with $500 million in annual sales to commercial builders and tradesmen. Because of the strength of White Cap's reputation with its customers, The Home Depot decided to continue using that name for its newly acquired stores.

SOURCES: F. Arner & A. Weintraub, 2004, J&J: Toughing out the drought, *Business Week,* January 26: 84–85; D. Fonda, 2004, Revenge of the bean counters, *Time,* March 29: 38–39; D. Morse, 2004, Home Depot looks to lure builders, buys supply firm, *Wall Street Journal Online,* http://www.wsj.com, May 7; W. C. Symonds, 2004, Breaking the curse, *Business Week,* April 26: 75–82; D. Welch, 2003, How Nissan laps Detroit, *Business Week,* December 22: 58–59.

resources, such as human capital, brand names, and reputation, are harder to evaluate. Ultimately, the judgment of either a tangible or intangible resource is made in terms of its ability to help create value for customers.

Resources as Options

Resources may be acquired or developed to use at a future time. When this happens, resources are thought of as *options.* For example, a firm may purchase a piece of land and hold it for future expansion. The land can be used as a location for a future plant or store. Thus, in this instance, the firm holds the purchased land as an *option* to expand. Some refer to these as *real options* because without the land, for example, the firm could not expand in that particular location if it decided to do so. By buying the land now and holding it, managers can always decide to use the land later to expand. The thought is that the land will be more expensive later, which is why the firm took out an option on the land by buying it at a lower price today. Real options create strategic flexibility for firms. Effectively executed options normally hold their value or may even increase in value. Therefore, if the firm decides not to use the resource being held as an option, it can be sold to recoup the original investment and possibly additional returns. In this way, real options represent investments having value and also provide options to support future strategies.[9]

Resources acquired as real options can be especially useful for firms competing in highly uncertain environments. This is the case for pharmaceutical companies. These firms (such as Pfizer, Merck, and Johnson & Johnson) invest large sums of money in R&D and develop a number of new drug compounds, some of which are used as real options. In other words, they invest to develop a variety of drugs that are intended to treat different illnesses, even though the firms know that many of the drugs they develop won't succeed. Also, although some of the new drugs will succeed, this will be true only in the long run. These firms do not focus on only one or a few drugs because of the uncertain success of new products (drugs) and the highly competitive nature of their industry. Each firm's competitors are also investing heavily to discover the next "blockbuster" drug. Investing to develop a variety of drugs provides the firm with a portfolio of potential drugs that can be developed and marketed.[10]

Many firms in high-technology industries also use their resources to create options. They invest in the development of a variety of technologies to provide flexibility to use if needed, given conditions in their highly competitive environments.[11] Some firms that compete in highly uncertain industries even invest in resources that provide options to move into totally new industries. Firms take these actions to maintain flexibility in case the industry changes dramatically and they find themselves lacking the resources needed to adapt to those changes.[12] This was the case with U.S. Steel. Once only a steel manufacturer, the firm now uses its resource portfolio to compete in a range of other businesses such as coal mining, transportation, real estate development, and mineral resource management. U.S. Steel initially took options in these different fields because of the intense competition facing it as a steel manufacturer.

However, regardless of whether resources are held as options or are designed for current use only, simply having them is not enough to build a competitive advantage.[13] The true value of a firm's resources emerges when they are integrated to form capabilities.[14] Another way of saying this is that Boston Red Sox pitcher Curt Schilling can't win a ball game alone, even if he pitches a strong game. Fielders must catch balls that are hit to them, and Schilling's teammates must get hits and score runs. This is how it is in companies as well. Individual resources must be integrated into capabilities to complete work-related tasks. The capabilities then must be leveraged with a strategy to satisfy customer needs. Some capabilities are developed into core competencies. We show how resources are managed to develop capabilities and competencies in Figure 4.1.

Capabilities

Many of the companies mentioned in "Focusing on Strategy" have developed capabilities that help them produce innovation, which means that they have successfully integrated some of their resources to form capabilities. For example, the capabilities of P&G and GE that we described are in each firm's research and development (R&D) unit. Each firm's R&D unit is composed of human capital (such as research scientists and engineers, a resource) and scientific research equipment (another resource). These resources have been combined to form R&D capabilities at P&G and GE. Apple is known as a highly innovative company. In fact, according to an article in *Fast Company,* "since its earliest days, Apple has been hands down the most innovative company in its industry—and easily one of the most innovative in all of corporate America."[15] In 2003, Apple introduced the new iTunes digital music store and the iPod digital music player. These products resulted from Apple's innovation capabilities.

FIGURE 4.1 Managing Resources to Develop Capabilities and Core Competencies

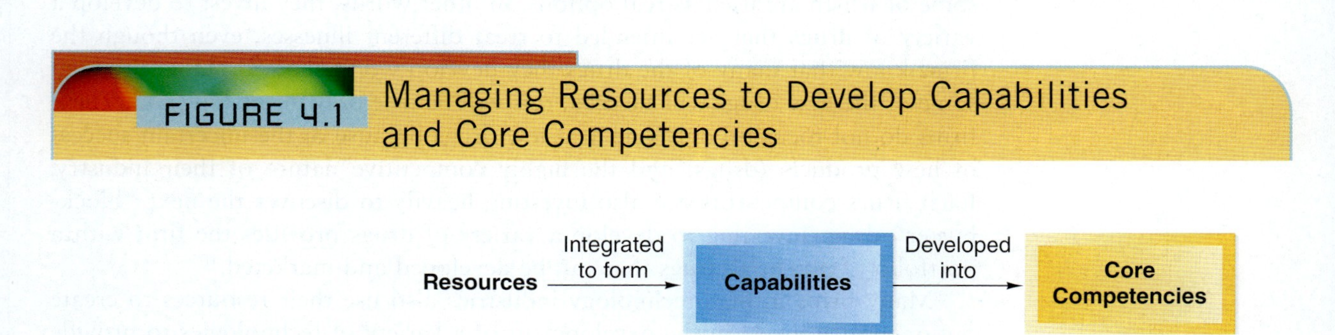

© Royalty-Free/CORBIS

According to some sources, as many as 20 million Americans own iPods—clearly a successful product innovation for Apple.

One of the "hot growth companies" identified by *Business Week* in 2004, Shuffle Master, invests 12 percent of its annual revenues in R&D to support its capability in this area. The percentage that Shuffle Master allocates to R&D exceeds the percentages allocated to R&D by the firm's competitors. But the money is well spent; Shuffle Master continues to be the leader in its industry in product innovations. One of its newest machines can rapidly shuffle through a deck of cards and determine whether the deck is complete. This new machine saves casinos money by allowing them to open fewer new decks of cards. Shuffle Master's R&D capability also has produced new proprietary card games such as Let It Ride and Crazy 4 Poker.[16]

Other firms try to build their capabilities to successfully manage their operations in international markets. In recent times, superior customer service has become a capability many firms want to develop. For example, Rackspace, a Web-hosting company based in San Antonio, recognizes an employee each month with the "Straightjacket Award" for providing fanatical customer support. In fact, Rackspace has trademarked the term "Fanatical Support" to highlight what it believes is the unique service it provides to customers throughout the world.[17] So Rackspace has integrated some of its tangible (such as financial) and intangible (such as people) resources to develop a capability in customer and product service.

Capabilities are normally based on the knowledge held by the firm's employees (its human capital).[18] For example, Apple's new products are developed based on ideas from the software engineers and designers in its R&D function. The same is true for Shuffle Master, a firm in a significantly different industry. Employees of Rackspace are trained to provide superior customer service. They then apply this knowledge and develop relationships with the customers that eventually result in social capital (explained in Chapter 2). Capabilities are often formed in functional areas such as marketing, R&D, and manufacturing. As noted earlier, some capabilities may be developed into core competencies.

Core Competencies

As defined in Chapter 1, *core competencies* are capabilities that the firm emphasizes and performs especially well while pursuing its vision. When the firm's core competencies are different from those held by competitors, they may be referred to as *distinctive competencies*,[19] another term we defined in Chapter 1. When core competencies enable a firm to complete activities effectively and thereby provide products to customers that are superior to those provided by competitors, the core competencies help the firm achieve a *competitive advantage*.

So what causes core competencies to produce competitive advantages? As you will see in the following materials, core competencies must have four characteristics to help a firm achieve a competitive advantage for the firm. These characteristics are summarized in Table 4.1.

Characteristics of Core Competencies That Lead to a Competitive Advantage

Valuable	Contribute to value creation for customers by exploiting new opportunities or neutralizing threats
Rare	Held by few if any competitors
Difficult to imitate	Difficult to recreate because intangible resources or their specific contribution to the capability cannot be easily identified
Nonsubstitutable	No resources/capabilities exist that can complete the tasks and provide the same value to customers

1. Competencies must be *valuable*. Valuable competencies help the firm create value for the customer, exploit market opportunities, or neutralize threats from competitors. For example, firms with core competencies in R&D develop new products that exploit opportunities in the external environment. These opportunities represent customer needs that haven't been satisfied. Apple's iTunes digital music store provides a substantial selection of music at reasonable prices with easy access for customers, satisfying their need to listen to the music they prefer at a time that is convenient for them. Likewise, Shuffle Master's new machine that rapidly shuffles decks and counts the cards satisfies casinos' need to keep games moving along quickly. Rackspace's competence in customer service neutralizes threats from competitors by keeping customers satisfied while building social capital with them and, ultimately, customer loyalty.
2. Competencies must be *rare*. Rarity means that few if any competitors can perform an activity with the same quality. If many firms hold a valuable capability that isn't also rare, it can only contribute to competitive parity.[20] Earlier, we noted that Nissan is highly efficient and productive with its manufacturing activities, much more so than many of its global competitors. However, most major Japanese car manufacturers have developed a capability to build a common vehicle architecture or platform that can be used for several different cars. For example, Honda builds four different vehicles on the Civic platform. Because the major Japanese firms have this manufacturing capability, it leads to competitive parity among them. However, because some of their global competitors lack this capability, it gives them an advantage over non-Japanese rivals.[21] General Motors (GM) is trying to develop the capability of a common platform. If developed, GM hopes to quickly use its common platform to produce its products.[22] If GM is able to develop and successfully use a common platform, its Japanese competitors would no longer have a capability that is rare compared to GM.
3. Competencies must be *difficult to imitate*. Competitors want to imitate another firm's valuable and rare capabilities. However, some of a competitor's capabilities, such as an R&D capability, are not simple to identify or to imitate. An R&D capability results from combining some of the firm's

resources, such as integrating its engineers and scientists with laboratories and providing appropriate financial support to R&D activities. When these resources are effectively integrated, a positive and productive culture evolves. Because it is a tangible, visible resource, a firm's laboratory is the easiest resource for competitors to imitate. However, as intangible resources, the skills and knowledge of the engineers and scientists along with a supportive, productive culture are much more difficult for competitors to understand and certainly to imitate.

4. Competencies must be *nonsubstitutable.* This means that for a core competence to be a competitive advantage there cannot be equivalent competencies possessed by a competitor that can perform the same function. Customer service may be performed in a variety of ways, but the most valuable usually varies with the type of product sold. With some products, before-sales service is most important. Usually service before or with the sale is more important with simpler products. However, with complex products such as computers or automobiles, after-sales service is often the most important. When customers have problems with their computers or automobiles, they expect to receive fast and courteous service. Dell is known to provide quality service after the sale of its computers for its corporate accounts. This characteristic is often acknowledged by analysts as one of the factors contributing to Dell's competitive advantages of speed and an unrelenting sense of urgency to constantly do better.[23] No competitor has been able to duplicate or substitute Dell's service competence applied to its corporate customers or direct-sales ability. These two competencies have contributed significantly to a competitive advantage for the firm.[24] Yet, some have criticized Dell's service quality for individual customers; Dell outsources much of this service to IT operations in India.

Competitive Advantages

Firms with valuable and rare core competencies are able to achieve competitive advantages over their rivals. Competencies that are difficult to imitate and nonsubstitutable as well as being valuable and rare often produce competitive advantages that last for a relatively long time. But no competitive advantage can be sustained forever; competitors eventually learn how to imitate another firm's core competencies or how to use their own capabilities to produce products that create more value for customers.

Competitive advantages are important because they enable firms to capture larger shares of the market and to increase their returns. When they do so, they also create value for their owners and other stakeholders. As a result, managers are continuously searching for ways to develop competencies that are valuable, rare, difficult to imitate, and nonsubstitutable. Alternatively, if a competitor holds a competitive advantage, firms try to imitate it or substitute for it. Firms can try to imitate a core competence in many ways. For example, while a productive R&D capability is difficult to imitate, firms might acquire a company with an identified capability in R&D. Similarly, a firm could develop an alliance with companies having complementary capabilities that, when integrated with their own, form a unique and valuable core competence. As described in "Focusing on Strategy," Procter & Gamble acquired firms with strong R&D capabilities. Integrating P&G's own capabilities with the acquired firms' capabilities helps it create core competencies that it can use to develop innovative products. As we noted earlier, Johnson & Johnson is also acquiring firms so it can integrate their capabilities with its own to build new and valuable core competencies.

Next, we examine how firms use value-chain activities to develop a competitive advantage.

The Value Chain

The **value chain** consists of the structure of activities that firms use to implement their business-level strategy. Firms analyze their value chain to better understand the activities that contribute the most strongly to creating value for customers and the cost incurred to complete each activity. Of course, to succeed, the firm must create value that exceeds the costs incurred to produce, distribute, and service products for customers.[25] Based on the firm's analysis of its value-chain activities, it can compare them to those of its competitors. One common means of making these comparisons is through benchmarking. **Benchmarking** is the process of identifying the best practices of competitors and other high-performing firms, analyzing them, and comparing them with the organization's own practices.[26] Through these comparisons, firms sometimes identify better ways to complete activities that create greater value for customers. FedEx studied the activities and best practices of transportation companies to invent the overnight-delivery business. Other firms may develop means of handling the value-chain activities differently from competitors because they could not complete the activity in a comparable way. For example, Dell decided to handle distribution activities differently from its competitors. As we know, Dell decided to sell its computers directly to customers rather than through retail outlets. It would have been highly difficult for Dell to obtain the needed retail agreements to market its computers and outsell its competitors. The growth and popularity of the Internet greatly enhanced Dell's ability to reach customers and sell its products using the direct-sales approach.

The focus of value-chain analysis is on primary and secondary activities. **Primary activities** include inbound logistics (such as sources of parts), operations (such as manufacturing, if dealing with a physical product), sales and distribution of products, and after-sales service. Therefore, primary activities are directly involved in creating value for the customer. **Support activities** provide support to the primary activities so that they can be completed effectively. Support activities, then, are only indirectly involved in creating value for the customer as they support the primary activities. Below we examine primary and support activities to more fully explain the value chain.

Focusing on the primary activities, the product moves from raw-material suppliers to operations, to finished-goods inventory, to marketing and distribution, and finally to after-sales service. These activities are shown in Figure 4.2. Each stage of the value chain's primary activities adds costs, but hopefully cre-

FIGURE 4.2 The Value Chain

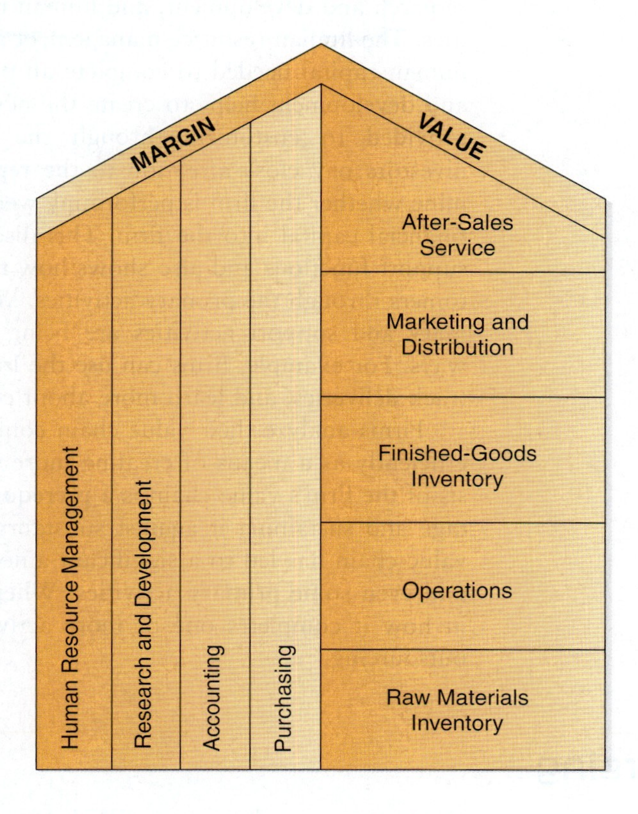

ates value as well. Some firms are especially effective in managing the *supply chain* and relationships with suppliers. In this way, they know where and when to buy specific supplies and usually have developed good working relationships with suppliers. In so doing, they can obtain high-quality goods when needed and at an appropriate price.[27]

A critical component of the value chain is knowledge of the customer.[28] This knowledge must be injected into each stage of activities to ensure that all activities are intended to create value for the customer. For example, using knowledge about customers, the firm ensures that its raw materials are of appropriate quality to build a product that meets or exceeds customer needs. These materials should be delivered in a timely matter so that the firm can provide the finished product on the dates required by the customer. Of course, the firm must be able to transform the raw materials into a high-quality finished product. These products are then sent to inventory so that marketing can distribute them to the customer when needed and at the lowest possible distribution cost. Marketing develops sales and promotion campaigns to attract customers and to ensure that they understand the value provided by the product. Finally, after-sales service helps customers use the product and makes certain that the product meets the customers' standards. The value provided is reflected in the size of the margin shown in Figure 4.2.

Support activities are important even though their effect on creating customer value is indirect. As shown in Figure 4.2, purchasing, accounting, research and development, and human resource management are support activities. The human resource management function is responsible for recruiting the human capital needed to complete all primary and support activities. Research and development helps to create the new products that then are produced and provided to customers through the primary activities. Shareholders and investors pay close attention to the reports provided by accounting to determine whether the firm is performing well and whether they want to invest more financial capital into the firm. This discussion emphasizes the necessity of the support functions and also shows how they affect the creation of value for customers through the primary activities. With today's new technologies, some primary and support activities are being performed in new and more efficient ways. For example, firms can use the Internet to communicate with customers, track deliveries, and learn more about customers' needs.[29]

Firms analyze their value chain continuously to find ways to operate more efficiently as a means of creating more value for customers. Continuous analysis of the firm's value chain is a prerequisite to developing a competitive advantage and sustaining it against substantial competition. In fact, analysis of the value chain has led to a significant amount of outsourcing of support activities and even some primary activities. When a firm identifies serious inefficiencies in how it completes one or more activities, they then become candidates for outsourcing.

Outsourcing

Outsourcing has become a popular and yet controversial activity among U.S. firms. **Outsourcing** involves acquiring a capability from an external supplier that contributes to creating value for the customer. Outsourcing is being used more frequently because of the increased capabilities in global markets by firms specializing in specific activities. An external supplier can often provide output of the same quality or better at a lower cost.[30] It can provide the higher quality because of supplier specialization that cannot be achieved by the acquiring firm and the economies of scale that the specialization produces. Therefore, by outsourcing, a firm benefits from the value created by another company's use of its core competence in a primary or support activity. Outsourcing of a support activity is depicted in Figure 4.3.

In spite of these benefits, outsourcing is controversial because of the job losses that some critics suggest result from decisions to outsource work to firms in other nations.[31] This controversy may exist for a while, in that companies in countries to which a great deal of low level work is being outsourced, such as China and India, are developing core competencies in higher value activities (such as an aspect of R&D, a support activity) of the value chain.[32]

In addition to the value provided by the external supplier, firms that outsource increase their flexibility, reduce their risks, and decrease their capital

FIGURE 4.3 Outsourcing the HRM Function

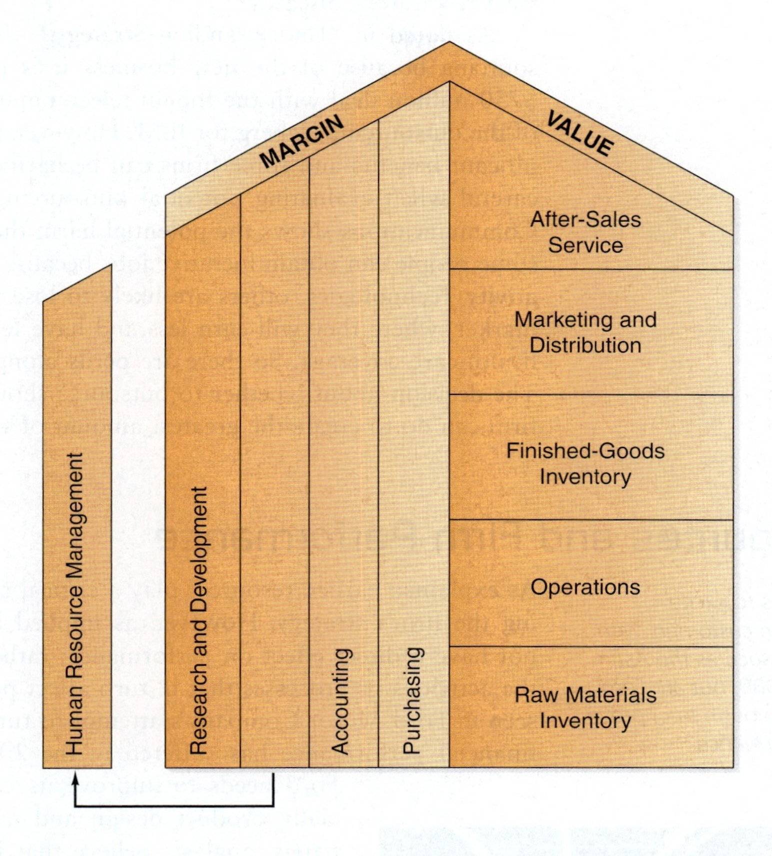

investments. Firms that outsource one or more primary or support activities have more flexibility because they can change suppliers, reduce the number of activities performed (if those activities become less important to producing value for customers), and more easily change their strategies and make other capital investments when needed. Outsourcing also allows the firm to focus on properly nurturing the core competencies it possesses.

Outsourcing, however, is not a panacea. In fact, firms must carefully evaluate outsourcing decisions because they are difficult to reverse.[33] The firm doesn't want to outsource an activity in which it has a capability that could become a core competence. Developing a capability that has been outsourced requires the firm to obtain the necessary human capital and to organize a new structure and internal mechanisms to insert it into the value-chain activities of the firm. This process is often time-consuming and costly. Some firms respond to this threat by outsourcing only part of an activity. For example, a firm such as Merck would likely never outsource its complete R&D function, given R&D's critical contribution to creating value for customers and its importance for competitive advantage in the pharmaceutical industry. However, Merck has begun to undertake alliances with small high-potential research-intensive firms that have promising drugs under development. In 2003, Merck paid $5 million for an exclusive license and a multiyear collaboration with Amrad Corporation, a small Australian biotech firm with a promising drug under development to treat respiratory diseases.[34]

As noted in "Understanding Strategy," IBM's CEO is delighted with outsourcing because of the new business it is generating for his company. The $750 million deal with the Indian telecommunications company is only the tip of the outsourcing iceberg for IBM. However, not all companies will receive significant benefits and some firms can be harmed by outsourcing if they are not careful when evaluating potential outsourcing activities. The example of AM Communications shows the potential harm that can accrue. Additionally, while some people can obtain lucrative jobs because of outsourcing, such as with Relativity Technologies, others are likely to lose jobs and enter the contract labor market, where they will earn less and have fewer or no fringe benefits such as health-care coverage. So there are perils along with benefits from outsourcing. The decision about whether to outsource should be made in terms of what the firm can do to create the greatest amount of value for customers.

Resources and Firm Performance

Ford tries to excite European customers with vehicles such as the Astin Martin DB9, but are Ford's efforts enough to improve its performance?

As explained earlier, resources play a critical role in developing and implementing the firm's strategy. However, as implied by this statement, resources may not have a direct effect on performance; rather, they may affect the quality of the activities or processes that in turn affect performance.[35] An example can be seen in Ford Motor Company's attempt to turn its performance around. Ford's financial performance has suffered in the 2000s. To deal with this problem, Ford needs to improve its capabilities in several areas, especially product design and manufacturing efficiency. Unfortunately, analysts believe that Ford's efforts have not been successful. For example, some analysts argue that the firm continues to design vehicles that are boring to European customers. Analysts also suggest that because the company hasn't produced competitively designed and manufactured vehicles for several years, the Ford brand image has been tarnished. Therefore, its weak capabilities in design and manufacturing are having a negative effect on its brand image,[36] an important intangible resource. A tarnished brand image is likely to hurt the sales of Ford vehicles; in turn, weak sales lead to poor financial performance.

© Andrew Fox/Alamy

It is important for Ford and all other companies to have strong resources, because strong resources support the use of value-chain activities and are the foundation for a strategy that can produce positive performance. For example, firms desiring to enter China need a partner for access to local markets. Many firms are interested in China because of the current large and growing markets (see Chapter 8). However, to

understanding strategy:

THE PROS AND CONS OF OUTSOURCING

Very few primary and support activities are not subject to outsourcing. Staffing customer service help lines, installing expensive and sophisticated medical equipment, interpreting medical X rays, servicing computers, and providing software and design services are examples of activities firms can outsource to other companies.

There are positive stories about the use of outsourcing. One of these stories concerns Relativity Technologies. Currently, this firm employs approximately 50 Russian programmers. If the firm were unable to outsource the programming function, the CEO, Vivek Wadhwa, claims that the firm and its 100 jobs in the United States, paying an average of about $100,000 annually, would not exist. Additionally, CEOs such as IBM's Samuel Palmisano argue that outsourcing provides major benefits to firms. Besides allowing the firm doing the outsourcing to focus on what it does best, the firm receiving the outsourcing business benefits by offering the outsourcing service. In recent years, IBM has generated significant revenues by completing activities (such as data-processing tasks) that firms have outsourced to it.

However, outsourcing also has negative aspects. For example, outsourcing has produced an explosion in temporary employment (often referred to as casual labor), even for highly professional jobs. Unfortunately, this "contract labor" is largely unregulated by U.S. labor laws. Additionally, some firms have learned that outsourcing can produce a form of brain drain. By outsourcing, firms can lose their capabilities to create value for the customers. For example, AM Communications outsourced a number of activities and then experienced some difficult times due to an economy in recession. When the original owners sought investors to revive the firm, they experienced problems because the investors felt that the firm's manufacturing, development services, and software and engineering know-how existed primarily in its external suppliers (firms to which AM had outsourced activities). The investors did not want to invest in the firm, which eventually filed for bankruptcy.

Some argue that outsourcing is being used primarily because of efficiencies that involve transfers to low-wage contexts. This scenario certainly exists in many services provided by Indian companies and contract manufacturing provided by Chinese companies. However, a critical component is whether they are also providing the quality of service needed. It should also be noted that outsourcing activities are not only in one direction. For example, IBM's CEO is excited about outsourcing because he expects his company to be a major supplier. In 2004, IBM obtained a new ten-year contract with Bharti Tele-Ventures to provide computing and information technology services. The contract is worth approximately $750 million over its life. Thus, while outsourcing has a rough edge, some firms can benefit but should realize that they are living on "the razor's edge"; the service they provide must be cost-efficient for the customer or they may be replaced by other firms that specialize in producing the outsourced service.

SOURCES: W. M. Bulkeley, 2004, IBM's Palmisano sees huge gains in outsourcing, *Wall Street Journal Online,* http://www.wsj.com, May 20; D. Gumpert, 2004, An unseen peril of outsourcing, *Business Week Online,* http://www.businessweek.com, March 3; C. Salter, 2004, Surprise package, *Fast Company,* February: 62–66; P. Taylor & R. Marcelo, 2004, IBM wins Indian telecoms outsourcing deal, *Financial Times,* http://www.ft.com, March 26; V. Wadhwa, 2004, My son, it's time to talk of outsourcing . . . , *Business Week Online,* http://www.businessweek.com, March 12; B. Grow, 2003, A day's pay for a day's work—maybe, *Business Week,* December 8: 100–103.

find a good local partner, they may need to provide something that partner needs in exchange, as General Electric (GE) discovered in its quest to sell power equipment in China. GE had to agree to transfer technology for building the equipment to its new partners; therefore, its resources allowed it to have access to a huge new international market. Similarly, Motorola invested more than $300 million in 19 different technology research centers in China to gain better access to markets there. Microsoft and Siemens AG have also made significant investments in China as one step to gaining access to Chinese markets.[37]

Firms should understand, though, that resources can constrain their strategy as well. For example, Volkswagen has a "middle-class" brand image. Because of this brand image, VW's recent attempt to develop and market high-priced luxury autos has been largely unsuccessful. However, its brand image is facilitating VW's efforts to reach the growing middle class in China, a potentially huge market. Chinese firms are simultaneously trying to develop the capabilities to compete in international markets. One resource needed is an international brand image. A few Chinese firms have already developed an international brand. For example, Haier manufactures small refrigerators in South Carolina and has about 50 percent of the U.S. mini-refrigerator market. As a way to develop their image, many other Chinese firms are venturing into other Asian countries to develop their competitive capabilities before they enter Western markets.[38]

Summary

The primary purpose of this chapter is to explain how a firm's resources can be managed to develop one or more competitive advantages. In doing so, we examined the following topics:

- To develop and implement the best strategy, managers need to understand the firm's resources and capabilities. Therefore, managers need to conduct an internal analysis to identify the firm's strengths and weaknesses. Strengths are resources and capabilities that allow the firm to complete important tasks. **Weaknesses** are the firm's resource and capability deficiencies that make it difficult for the firm to complete important tasks.
- Resources are either tangible or intangible. **Tangible resources** are valuable assets that can be seen or quantified, such as manufacturing equipment and financial capital. **Intangible resources** are assets that contribute to creating value for customers but are not physically identifiable.
- Resources may be acquired or developed to use in the future. These resources are considered *options*. Resource options provide firms with strategic flexibility. These options normally hold their value and may even increase in value.
- Capabilities are formed by integrating several resources with the intent of accomplishing a major task or series of related tasks. Capabilities are normally based on the knowledge held by the firm's employees (its human capital).
- Core competencies are capabilities that are performed especially well and are emphasized by the organization in its quest for a competitive advantage. If these core competencies are different from those held by competitors, they may be referred to as distinctive competencies. To be a competitive advantage for the firm, a core

competence must be valuable, rare, difficult to imitate, and nonsubstitutable.

- The **value chain** is the structure of activities the firm uses to implement its business-level strategy. Firms analyze their value chain to better understand the activities that contribute the most strongly to creating value for customers and the costs of each of them in order to understand how to ensure efficient operations. A firm examines its primary and support activities when studying the value chain.
- **Outsourcing** involves acquiring a capability from an external supplier that contributes to creating value for the customer. Outsourcing has become common because of increased capabilities in global markets by firms specializing in specific activities.
- Without adequate resources, a firm will be unable to compete effectively. In fact, competitive advantages are based on valuable and rare resources. Therefore, managers must seek to obtain and manage superior resources effectively to achieve firm success.

Key Terms

benchmarking 80
intangible resources 72
outsourcing 82
primary activities 80
support activities 80
tangible resources 72
value 72
value chain 80
weaknesses 72

Discussion Questions

1. What are strengths and weaknesses and how does the firm identify them?
2. What are resources, capabilities, and core competencies? How are these concepts related?
3. What four characteristics of core competencies are necessary for them to become a competitive advantage?
4. How would you explain the value chain to a classmate? What are primary and support activities?
5. What is outsourcing? How does outsourcing create value for the firm? What are the potential problems with outsourcing?
6. How do resources contribute to a firm's performance?

Endnotes

1. C. M. Christiansen, 2001, The past and future of competitive advantage, *Sloan Management Review,* 42(2): 105–109; C. M. Christiansen & M. E. Raynor, 2003, Why hard-nosed executives should care about management theory, *Harvard Business Review,* 81(9): 66–74.
2. D. G. Sirmon, M. A. Hitt, & R. D. Ireland, 2005, Managing firm resources in dynamic environments to create value: Looking inside the black box, *Academy of Management Review* (in press).
3. M. A. Hitt, L. Bierman, K. Shimizu, & R. Kochhar, 2001, Direct and moderating effects of human capital on strategy and firm performance in professional service firms, *Academy of Management Journal,* 44: 13–28.
4. S. K. McEviley & B. Chakravarthy, 2002, The persistence of a knowledge-based advantage: An empirical test for product performance and technological knowledge, *Strategic Management Journal,* 23: 285–305.
5. B. Morris, 2004, The real story: How did Coca-Cola's management go from first-rate to farcical in six short years? *Fortune,* May 31: 84–98.
6. L. Chang, 2004, Groupe Danone builds a major market in China, *Wall Street Journal Online,* http://www.wsj.com, March 4.
7. D. G. Sirmon & M.A. Hitt, 2003, Managing resources: Linking unique resources, management and wealth creation in family firms, *Entrepreneurship Theory & Practice,* 27:

339–358; M. Maynard, 2004, Wrapping a familiar name around a new product, *New York Times,* http://www.nytimes.com, May 22.
8. M. LaMonica, 2004, CA shifts focus to product strategy, *New York Times,* http://www.nytimes.com, May 23.
9. R. G. McGrath & A. Nerkar, 2004, Real options reasoning and a new look at R&D investment strategies of pharmaceutical firms, *Strategic Management Journal,* 25: 1–21.
10. Ibid.
11. K. D. Miller & A. T. Arikan, 2004, Technology search investments: Evolutionary, option reasoning, and option pricing approaches, *Strategic Management Journal,* 25: 473–485.
12. T. B. Folta & J. P. O'Brien, 2004, Entry in the presence of dueling options, *Strategic Management Journal,* 25: 121–138; D. Harding & S. Rovit, 2004, Building deals on bedrock, *Harvard Business Review,* 82(9): 121–128.
13. Sirmon, Hitt, & Ireland, Managing firm resources; D. L. Deeds, D. De Carolis, & J. Coombs, 2000, Dynamic capabilities and new product development in high-technology ventures: An empirical analysis of new biotechnology firms, *Journal of Business Venturing,* 15: 211–229.
14. M. Blyler & R. W. Coff, 2003, Dynamic capabilities, social capital and rent appropriation: Ties that split pies, *Strategic Management Journal,* 24: 677–686.
15. C. Hawn, 2004, If he's so smart . . . : Steve Jobs, Apple, and the limits of innovation, *Fast Company,* January: 68–74.
16. A. Barrett, C. Palmeri, & S. A. Forest, 2004, Hot growth companies: The 100 best small companies, *Business Week Online,* http//:www.businessweek.com, June 7.
17. A. Overholt, 2004, Cuckoo for customers, *Fast Company,* January: 86–93.
18. S. E. Jackson, M. A. Hitt, & A. DeNisi, 2003, *Managing Knowledge for Sustained Competitive Advantage,* San Francisco: Jossey-Bass.
19. M. A. Hitt & R. D. Ireland, 1985, Corporate distinctive competence, strategy, industry and performance, *Strategic Management Journal,* 6: 273–293.
20. J. Barney, 2001, Is the resource-based view a useful perspective for strategic management research? Yes, *Academy of Management Review,* 26: 41–56.
21. D. Welch & K. Kerwin, 2004, Detroit tries it the Japanese way, *Business Week Online,* http://www.businessweek.com, January 20.
22. Ibid.
23. B. Breen, 2004, Dell time, *Fast Company,* November: 86–95.
24. A. Serwer, 2002, Dell does domination, *Fortune,* January 21: 70–75.
25. M. A. Hitt, R. D. Ireland, & R. E. Hoskisson, 2005, *Strategic Management: Competitiveness and Globalization,* Cincinnati, Ohio: South-Western; M. Porter, 1985, *Competitive Advantage,* New York: Free Press.
26. M. A. Hitt, J. S. Black, & L. W. Porter, 2005, *Management,* Upper Saddle River, N.J.: Pearson Prentice Hall.
27. L.-Y. Li & G. O. Ogunmokun, 2001, Effect of export financing, resources and supply-chain skills on export competitive advantages: Implications for superior export performance, *Journal of World Business,* 36(3): 260–279.
28. J. W. Boudreau, 2003, Strategic knowledge measurement and management, in S. E. Jackson, M. A. Hitt, and A. DeNisi (eds.), *Managing Knowledge for Sustained Competitive Advantage,* San Francisco: Jossey-Bass, 330–359.
29. R. Amit & C. Zott, 2001, Creating value in e-business, *Strategic Management Journal,* 22(Special Issue): 493–520.
30. F. T. Rothaermel, M. A. Hitt, & L. Jobe, 2004, Organizing for innovation: Product portfolios, new product success, and firm performance, paper presented at the Strategic Management Society, November: San Juan, Puerto Rico.
31. M. Forney, 2003, Tug-of-war over trade, *Time,* December 22: 42–43; K. Madigan & M. J. Mandel, 2003, Outsourcing jobs: Is it bad? *Business Week,* August 25: 36–38.
32. B. Einhorn & M. Kripalani, 2003, Move over India: China is rising fast as a services outsourcing hub, *Business Week,* August 11: 42–43.
33. M. J. Leiblein, J. J. Reuer, & F. Dalsace, 2002, Do make or buy decisions matter? The influence of organizational governance and technological performance. *Strategic Management Journal,* 23: 817–833.
34. J. Greene, J. Carey, M. Arndt, & O. Port, 2003, Reinventing corporate R&D, *Business Week,* September 22: 74–76.
35. G. Ray, J. B. Barney, & W. A. Muhanna, 2004, Capabilities, business processes, and competitive advantage: Choosing the dependent variable in empirical tests of the resource-based view, *Strategic Management Journal,* 25: 23–37.
36. G. Edmondson & K. Kerwin, 2003, Can Ford fix this flat? *Business Week,* December 1: 51–52.
37. K. Kranhold, 2004, China's price for market entry: Give us your technology, too, *Wall Street Journal Online,* http://www.wsj.com, February 26.
38. C. Prystay, 2004, VW makes bet on a new class of Asian buyers, *Wall Street Journal Online,* http://www.wsj.com, March 3; B. Dolven, 2004, China grooms global players, *Wall Street Journal Online,* http://www.wsj.com, February 24.

part 3

Strategic Thinking

CHAPTER 5

Business-Level Thinking

Reading and studying this chapter should enable you to:

*Knowledge Objectives

1_
Define business-level strategy.

2_
Define and explain the differences among five business-level strategies.

3_
Describe how to successfully use each business-level strategy.

4_
Identify the risks of each business-level strategy.

5_
Describe the structures to use to implement each business-level strategy.

Focusing on Strategy

Brown: "How Can We Help You Today?"

"We'd lost track of whole trainloads of cars. It was crazy." (Jerry Reynolds, president, Prestige Ford, Garland, Texas)

This comment from a person running a car dealership highlights what was once a serious problem. The problem was that Ford Motor Company typically wasn't able to tell dealers exactly which cars and trucks were being shipped to them or when they would arrive. Put yourself into Reynolds' shoes: Can you imagine trying to run a business without knowing what you were going to have available to sell to customers and when?

To correct its distribution problem, Ford turned to United Parcel Service (UPS) for help. Based on information and data provided by Jerry Reynolds and other U.S. dealers, UPS engineers redesigned Ford's entire North American delivery network. The redesign involved UPS streamlining the routes taken by cars and trucks from Ford's factories as well as the processing procedures at regional sorting hubs before the vehicles are sent to their final destinations.

Have these changes helped Ford? To date, the answer to this question is a resounding "Yes!" The delivery network UPS designed for Ford has reduced the time it takes for cars and trucks to arrive at dealer locations by 40 percent. This time reduction enables dealers to receive vehicles much more quickly while saving Ford money. Thus, cars and trucks spend less time being transported and more time in front of prospective customers. What UPS accomplished for Ford was no small feat, given that the UPS-designed network is delivering more than four million cars annually from Ford's 19 North American manufacturing facilities. In describing the results of UPS's work, Jerry Reynolds said, "It was the most amazing transformation I had ever seen."

UPS's Supply Chain Solutions group is responsible for the redesign of Ford's distribution network. This fast-growing UPS business unit provides logistics and distribution services, international trade management, and transportation and freight services using multimodal transportation. Analysts believe that this business unit could be the fastest growing of UPS's business operations for some time to come. UPS wants to use this business unit to "serve as the traffic manager for Corporate America's sprawling distribution networks," which would enable UPS to provide a variety of new services to customers, including the scheduling of planes, ships, and trains on which goods are shipped. This has opened a new area of business for UPS—services—in addition to its standard delivery business. UPS is using its decades-long experience in managing its own global delivery network as the foundation for understanding how to help other companies solve their distribution woes. Its proprietary distribution-related skills enable UPS to provide services to customers that its competitors are not able to imitate. UPS is spending large sums of money to upgrade its capabilities so it can continue to provide superior logistics services to its clients.

SOURCES: D. Foust, 2004, Big Brown's new bag, *Business Week,* July 19, 54–56; 2004, United Parcel Service, *Argus Research,* https://argusresearch.com, July 15; United Parcel Service, Inc., *Callard Research,* https://www.callardresearch.com, July 9.

In Chapter 1, we defined *strategy* as an action plan designed to move an organization toward achievement of its vision. The different types of strategies firms use to do this are shown in Figure 1.1 in Chapter 1.

Business-level strategy, the topic of this chapter, is one of the types of strategies firms develop to achieve their vision. A **business-level strategy** is an action plan the firm develops to describe how it will compete in its chosen industry or market segment. A business-level strategy describes how the firm will compete in the marketplace on a day-by-day basis and how it intends to "do things right."[1] UPS's Supply Chain Solutions group has a business-level strategy as does each of UPS's other business units (such as UPS Consulting, UPS Air Cargo, and Mail Boxes Etc.).[2] Additional information about UPS's business units is presented in the next chapter's "Focusing on Strategy."

A firm's main objective in using a business-level strategy is to consistently provide a good or service to customers that they will buy because it creates more value (in the form of performance characteristics or price) for them than does a competitor's good or service. This is illustrated in "Focusing on Strategy" in this chapter which describes Ford's satisfaction with the new delivery system designed by UPS's Supply Chain Solutions group. A business-level strategy is most successful when everybody in the firm fully understands the chosen strategy[3] and when it is used with relentless zeal and efficiency.[4] In other words, firms must be precise in describing what they seek to accomplish with their strategy. The strategy must "connect" with the target customers as well. For example, the goal of BMW North America's business-level strategy is clear: "to be the leader in every premium segment of the international automotive industry."[5] Of course, as is the case with all of the firm's strategies, ethical practices should guide how the business-level strategy is used.[6] Often, a firm's intended ethical practices are made public by recording them in written documents such as a code of ethics, a code of conduct, and a corporate creed. The statements in these documents signal to stakeholders how the firm intends to interact with them. This means that a firm's employees are expected to adhere to the behaviors specified in these documents.

A business-level strategy is intended to help the firm focus its efforts so it can satisfy a group of customers.[7] In the case of BMW North America, the group of customers to be satisfied is the one wanting to purchase a high-quality vehicle that is different from "average" automobiles. Customers are satisfied when a firm's product creates value for them.[8] An effective business-level strategy has a clear statement of the value to be created for customers. This point is illustrated by the founding of Wal-Mart. Through the strategic leadership of Sam Walton, its founder, Wal-Mart initially formed a business-level strategy that was intended to offer a large assortment of many different products, at very low prices, to consumers living in towns with a population no greater than 25,000.[9] Thus, for early Wal-Mart customers, the value this firm provided to them was the opportunity to buy goods at prices that were always lower than the prices of those goods from locally owned stores. Everyone working at Wal-Mart understood the value the firm was creating for its customers, which helped the firm effectively implement its chosen business-level strategy. In addition, by comparison shopping and then buying from Wal-Mart, customers quickly understood the value the firm was providing to them in the form of lower prices on a wide assortment of items.

We fully discuss five business-level strategies in this chapter. These five strategies are sometimes referred to as *generic* because they are used in all industries and by all types of firms. A properly chosen business-level strategy favorably positions the firm relative to the competitive forces we talked about in Chapter 3. Being effectively positioned enables the firm to simultaneously create value for customers and returns for shareholders. We also use the value chain (see Chapter 4) to show the primary and support activities that are required to successfully use each business-level strategy. Not surprisingly, the firm accepts some risks when it decides to use a particular business-level strategy. We also discuss the risks of each type of strategy. Strategic leaders ensure that these risks are carefully monitored so the firm will recognize when it is time to make changes to its business-level strategy. As we discuss in "Understanding Strategy," JCPenney has changed its business-level strategy to improve its performance. In this chapter, we also describe the particular organizational structure (defined later in the chapter) that should be used to effectively implement each generic strategy. Because it affects the behavior of individual employees, the responsibilities assigned to them, and the leadership style they experience, organizational structure is an important aspect of how business-level strategies are implemented.

As the JCPenney example shows, a firm's business-level strategy is never set in stone. As an action plan, a business-level strategy is a living document that is

understanding strategy:

CHANGING FOR THE BETTER AT JCPENNEY

"The turnaround story is in the sixth inning and continues to be fueled by technology, merchandising and marketing initiatives that will drive and sustain margin improvements going forward." This comment from an industry analyst is great news for those interested in JCPenney's success. But this analyst paints a picture that is strikingly different from what was said about the firm's fortunes beginning in roughly the 1990s. Let's see how this firm has emerged from less-than-desirable performances to again become an impressive retailer.

© Neal Hamberg/Bloomberg News/Landov

According to company documents, JCPenney has always aspired to be the customers' first choice when buying the goods and services it offers. Moreover, the firm claims that it always had a single goal—"to serve the public as nearly as we can to its complete satisfaction." The breadth of this goal, though, contributed to JCPenney's loss of customers in the 1990s. Think of it this way. The "general" public is certainly a broad target market with multiple needs. This is why mass merchandisers, which is what JCPenney was from the time of its founding until about five years ago, carry a wide assortment of merchandise. Clothing for all members of a family, tools for the person wanting to handle repairs around the household, lawn mowers, refrigerators, perfumes, lawn equipment, and sporting goods are just some of the items a mass merchandiser stocks to satisfy the "general" public's needs. However, discount retailers such as Wal-Mart and Target had developed core competencies that enabled them to distribute a wide assortment of items at lower prices and with a level of service that was at least comparable to some firms, including JCPenney. In essence, JCPenney's poor financial performance during the 1990s resulted from the firm's inability to compete against competitors who had used their resources and capabilities to form core competencies that enabled them to better serve the needs of the "general" public.

What was JCPenney to do to improve its situation? A first step, newly appointed top-level managers concluded, was for JCPenney to identify a specific target market and thus shed its image as a mass merchandiser. Today, JCPenney is a moderately-priced department store chain serving the needs of middle-class consumers (households with income ranging from $30,000 to $80,000). In particular, the firm is concentrating on serving middle-class women between the ages of 35 and 54. Focusing on middle-class consumers' needs, JCPenney now provides competitive, fashionable assortments of merchandise. For 35–54 year-old women, JCPenney is offering what it calls "dressy causal" clothing items. Thus, JCPenney has changed its target customer from the "general public" to middle-class consumers. This means that JCPenney's market scope is now narrower than it was previously.

To present the firm's new assortments of merchandise to middle-class consumers in the most positive manner, JCPenney stores have been refurbished; the firm's marketing program is also thought to be more vibrant and certainly more oriented to telling its target customers exactly how its products can satisfy their needs. To support this change from being a mass merchandiser to a moderately priced department store chain, JCPenney is emphasizing its human capital. The firm has hired experienced personnel and continuously trains its workforce—a workforce the firm's executives see as the key to providing maximum satisfaction for its customers. The firm has developed a new distribution channel network to make certain that its products are delivered to its stores in a timely manner. Today, JCPenney is able to create value in the distribution part of the value chain while only a few short years ago, its distribution channel was a source of competitive disadvantage. For 2005, JCPenney was expected to reach profit margins of six to eight percent, something that was unthinkable at the end of the 1990s.

SOURCES: E. Byron, 2005, New Penney: Chain goes for "missing middle," *Wall Street Journal Online*, http://www.wjs.com, February 14; M. Halkias, 2004, So far, so good. *Dallas Morning News*, October 19: D1, D12; 2004, JCPenney Home Page, Short history of JCPenney, http://www.jcpenney.com, October 23; 2004, JCPenney Company, Inc., *Standard & Poor's Stock Report*, http://www.standardandpoors.com, October 16.

constantly subject to changes based on opportunities and threats emerging in the firm's external environment as well as changes in the competitive advantages that are a product of the resources, capabilities, and core competencies in the firm's internal environment.

Types of Business-Level Strategies

Firms choose from five business-level strategies: *cost leadership*, *differentiation*, *focused cost leadership*, *focused differentiation*, and *integrated cost leadership/differentiation* (see Figure 5.1). As shown in this figure, the firm's business-level strategy has two key dimensions—competitive advantage and competitive scope. This means that the business-level strategy the firm chooses is a function of its competitive advantage (either cost or uniqueness) and the breadth (either broad or narrow) of the target market it wishes to serve. When using the cost leadership or differentiation strategy, the firm seeks to apply its competitive advantage in many customer segments. When using either focused cost leadership or focused differentiation, the firm uses its cost advantage or its uniqueness advantage in narrower market segments. Specifically, with focus strategies, the firm "selects a segment or group of segments in the industry and tailors its strategy to serving them to the exclusion of others."[10]

Procter & Gamble's Tide soap is an example of a product that has a broad target market, while Porsche's 911 Carrera is designed to serve the needs of a narrow group of customers.[11] Each firm's decision about competitive scope (broad or narrow) is influenced by opportunities and threats in its external environment. Interestingly, though, the fact that markets today are increasingly being segmented into smaller and smaller groups with clearly identifiable needs[12] is affecting firms' decisions about competitive scope. A *market segment*

FIGURE 5.1 Five Business-Level Strategies

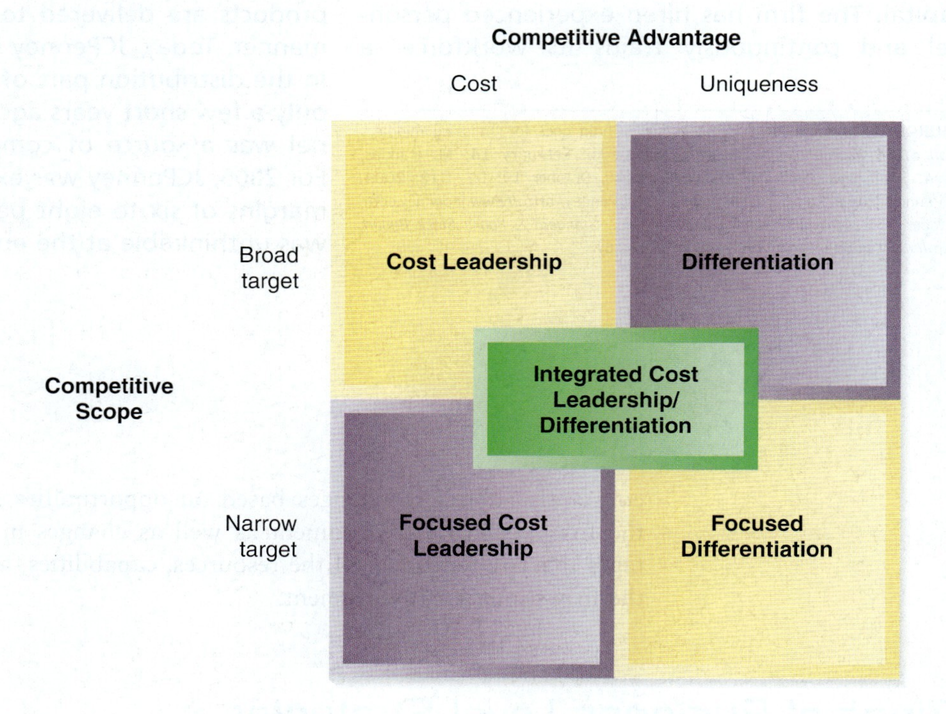

SOURCE: Adapted with the permission of The Free Press, an imprint of Simon & Schuster Adult Publishing Group, from *Competitive Advantage: Creating and Sustaining Superior Performance* by Michael E. Porter, p. 12.

is a group of people with similar needs with respect to certain variables such as price, quality, and product features. Segmenting markets into smaller and smaller groups with similar needs can be a threat to firms with a relatively standardized product serving the needs of multiple customer segments. Tide, for example, in terms of competitive scope, is designed to fit a broad target market. Simultaneously, though, being able to identify people with a specific need that isn't being satisfied by the product aimed at a broad target market creates opportunities for other firms. For instance, a company named SoapWorks produces a laundry detergent as well as other hypoallergenic cleansing products for people who want to avoid the types of chemicals in products such as Tide that are targeted to broader customer segments.[13]

In general, a firm's competitive advantages enable it either to produce standardized products at lower costs than those of their competitors or to produce unique products that differ from competitors' products in ways that create value for customers. In the first instance, the firm has a *cost competitive advantage* while in the second it has a *uniqueness competitive advantage* (see Figure 5.1).

By *standardized* products, we mean products that are widely available and have a large customer demand. Think of automobile tires as an example. We all need tires for our vehicles, such as cars, trucks, and motorcycles. Cooper Tire & Rubber is known for producing relatively inexpensive (yet reliable) tires for cars and trucks. Cooper can do this because its production, distribution, and service costs are lower than those of its rivals (such as Michelin, Goodyear, and Pirelli). Cooper remains committed to being lean in all of its operations as a way of continuously holding its costs down relative to competitors' costs.[14]

Unique products have features different from or in addition to the standardized product's features. SoapWorks' products, for example, are made without certain chemicals that some customers believe may harm users' health. As another example, although more expensive than beers designed for the broad target market, Guinness believes that its beers "awaken the taste buds in the consumer's mouth."[15] Guinness beers are more expensive because Guinness targets customers who may be willing to pay more for what some perceive to be a distinctive taste—a taste that is more expensive to produce. Let's turn our attention to learning about each of the five generic business-level strategies.

Cost Leadership Strategy

A **cost leadership strategy** is an action plan the firm develops to produce goods or services at the lowest cost.[16] Producing at the lowest cost enables the firm to price its product lower than competitors can, and therefore gain a larger share of its target market. Firms using the cost leadership strategy sell standardized products to the industry's typical or "average" customer because this is usually the largest target segment. Thus, Cooper Tire & Rubber intends to sell its tires to the customer with "average" or "typical" needs. Successful use of the cost leadership strategy across time results when the firm continuously finds ways to lower its costs relative to competitors' costs by constantly thinking about how the costs of its primary activities and support activities could be lowered without damaging the functionality of its products. Firms implementing the cost leadership strategy have strong process engineering skills, emphasize manufacturing processes permitting efficient production of products, have performance evaluation systems that reward employees on the quantity of their output, and know how to buy raw materials needed to produce their products at low costs.

In Chapter 4, we described how firms use value-chain analysis to identify the primary activities and support activities in which they are able to create value. In Figure 5.2, we show how the cost leader could create value in each primary activity and in each support activity. A firm does not need to outperform competitors in every one of these activities to successfully use the cost leadership strategy; however, the more primary and support activities in which the firm can outperform its competitors, the more likely that its costs will be lower than its competitors' costs.

Effective use of the cost leadership strategy positions the firm in the marketplace in a way that enables it to create value for customers, especially through lower prices. Also, as we describe in the next five subsections, effectively implementing the cost leadership strategy enables a firm to establish a strong market position relative to the five competitive forces we introduced in Chapter 3.

FIGURE 5.2 Examples of Value-Creating Activities Associated with the Cost Leadership Strategy

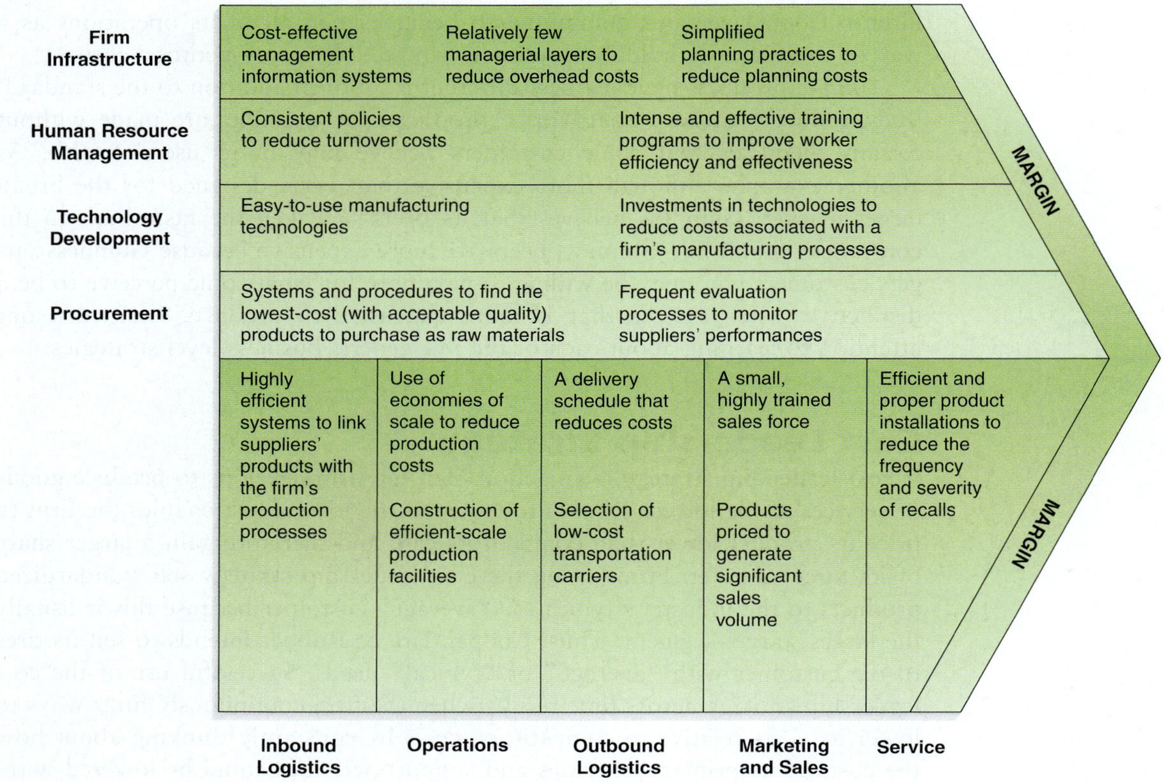

Support Activities			
Firm Infrastructure	Cost-effective management information systems	Relatively few managerial layers to reduce overhead costs	Simplified planning practices to reduce planning costs
Human Resource Management	Consistent policies to reduce turnover costs	Intense and effective training programs to improve worker efficiency and effectiveness	
Technology Development	Easy-to-use manufacturing technologies	Investments in technologies to reduce costs associated with a firm's manufacturing processes	
Procurement	Systems and procedures to find the lowest-cost (with acceptable quality) products to purchase as raw materials	Frequent evaluation processes to monitor suppliers' performances	

Inbound Logistics	**Operations**	**Outbound Logistics**	**Marketing and Sales**	**Service**
Highly efficient systems to link suppliers' products with the firm's production processes	Use of economies of scale to reduce production costs	A delivery schedule that reduces costs	A small, highly trained sales force	Efficient and proper product installations to reduce the frequency and severity of recalls
	Construction of efficient-scale production facilities	Selection of low-cost transportation carriers	Products priced to generate significant sales volume	

MARGIN

MARGIN

SOURCE: Adapted with the permission of The Free Press, an imprint of Simon & Schuster Adult Publishing Group, from *Competitive Advantage: Creating and Sustaining Superior Performance* by Michael E. Porter, p. 47. Copyright © 1985, 1988 by Michael E. Porter. All rights reserved.

Rivalry with Existing Competitors

Competitors find it extremely difficult to compete on the basis of price against the cost leader. To meet the cost leader's sales price, a competing firm must reduce its profit margins when selling its products. In turn, lower margins leave that firm with less capital to invest to improve its operational efficiency. Therefore, competing on the basis of price against the cost leader places a competitor in a cycle of falling farther and farther behind in terms of efficiency and cost reductions. Kmart encountered this competitive circumstance when trying to compete against cost leader Wal-Mart on the basis of price. Kmart's cost structure, compared to Wal-Mart's, was higher. The higher cost structure prevented

Kmart from being able to offer products at prices as low as Wal-Mart's. Having emerged from bankruptcy, Kmart no longer attempts to compete against Wal-Mart on the basis of costs and product prices. Instead, the firm is changing its product mix to reduce the degree to which it competes directly with cost leader Wal-Mart.[17] Moreover, the proposed merger between Kmart and Sears (announced in late 2004) makes it even less likely that Kmart will directly compete against Wal-Mart.

Bargaining Power of Buyers (Customers)

As buyers, customers can exercise power against the cost leader under several conditions, but especially if they purchase a large quantity of the cost leader's output. The cost leader successfully positions itself against buyers' potential power by selling to a large number of buyers to avoid becoming dependent on any one customer for a significant portion of its sales.

Bargaining Power of Suppliers

A supplier can exercise power over the cost leader if it provides a significant amount of a key input to the cost leader's production process. Firms dependent on key natural resources to produce their products when sources of supply are limited may have to pay higher prices. Airline companies, for example, are highly dependent on aviation fuel, a product that is sold by a relatively small number of firms. Successfully positioned cost leaders try to develop long-term contracts with a number of suppliers at favorable rates to reduce the potential of suppliers raising their prices, which would affect the cost leader's position in terms of costs. Cost leader Southwest Airlines is quite savvy about forming long-term contracts with fuel suppliers. These contracts often keep Southwest's fuel costs lower than those of its competitors.

Potential Entrants

The favorably positioned cost leader operates at a level of efficiency that can't be matched by firms thinking of entering the industry in which the cost leader is well established. The cost leader's ability to continuously drive its costs lower and lower while still satisfying customers' needs makes it very difficult for potential entrants to the market to compete against the cost leader.

Product Substitutes

A *product substitute* is a product that can replace the focal product because it has essentially the same functionality. For example, NutraSweet is a replacement or substitute for sugar. To compete against a cost leader, though, a substitute must offer something in addition to the same functionality. This "something different" could be a lower purchase price (which is unlikely when competing against the cost leader) or a feature that customers value that isn't a part of the cost leader's product. (As you know, NutraSweet's "something different" is a taste similar to that of sugar but without sugar's calories.) The successfully positioned cost leader thwarts product substitutes by lowering the purchase price of its product, which makes it difficult for a substitute to attract the attention of the cost leader's customers.

Competitive Risks of the Cost Leadership Strategy

The cost leadership strategy has two major risks. First, competitors' innovations may enable them to produce their good or service at a cost that is lower than that of the cost leader. For the price-conscious, "typical" consumer, the lower cost is attractive. Second, concentrating too much on reducing costs may eventually find the cost leader offering a product at very low prices to customers who are less inclined to purchase it. While the cost leader must keep its costs down, it can't lose contact with its customers to the point that it fails to fully understand changes in customers' expectations relative to the product in terms of price and features. At some point, for example, customers wanting to buy low-cost products may become willing to pay more for additional features such as increased product safety and extended product warranties. The cost leader must stay in close touch with its customers so it will be able to detect changes in their needs.

Differentiation Strategy

A **differentiation strategy** is an action plan the firm develops to produce goods or services that customers perceive as being unique in ways that are important to them. UPS's Supply Chain Solutions business unit, discussed in this chapter's "Focusing on Strategy," uses a differentiation strategy.

The "uniqueness" a firm provides when using the differentiation strategy may be physical or psychological. It can be created by the way in which the firm uses one or more of either the primary activities or the support activities. Product durability, ease of repair, and superior installation services are examples of physical sources of differentiation. Perceptions of the quality of service after the sale and of the courtesy of salespeople are examples of sources of psychological differentiation. Think of differentiated products you buy. Are the sources of these products' differentiation physical or psychological? Does the source of differentiation make a difference to you as long as the product you buy creates the unique value you want?

The cost leader serves an industry's typical or average customer. In contrast, the firm using the differentiation strategy serves customers who want to buy a good or service that is different from the good or service purchased by an industry's typical or average customer. Think of goods offered by Ralph Lauren as an example of differentiated items. The logo appearing on many of the firm's clothing products is one way these goods differ from those made for the clothing industry's typical customer. In addition to the logo, the firm's dress shirts for men, for example, are made of high-quality raw materials and lack a pocket. The logo, the materials, and the absence of a pocket are differentiated features that create value for customers desiring to wear something other than a "typical" dress shirt.

Think about goods and services (cars and clothes, for example) that you believe are different from those serving the typical customers in an industry. In all likelihood, you'll conclude that the ways goods and services can differ from one another are virtually endless. Different tastes, responsive customer service, product design, alternative distribution methods, and customer loyalty programs are but a few examples of how goods or services can offer unique value to customers.

© TANNEN MAURY/Bloomberg News/Landov

Pottery Barn started in 1949 as a single store in lower Manhattan and now has stores in more than 40 states. Are its loyal customers buying more than furniture?

Pottery Barn is another example of a firm using the differentiation strategy. The firm is known for the eclectic mix of its products, clever merchandising, and first-rate customer service as ways that its goods and services differ from those offered to the furniture industry's typical customer. The combination of these differentiated features has created a loyal group of customers who want to be a part of the Pottery Barn lifestyle, as suggested by an analyst who believes that Pottery Barn "has built a furniture brand into a lifestyle brand in a way that nobody else has done."[18]

The value chain can be used to highlight the primary and support activities where value should be created to use the differentiation strategy. The focus here is for the firm to emphasize the primary and support activities shown in Figure 5.3 to create more value than competitors can create for customers. This means, of course, that the firm using the differentiation strategy wants to develop core competencies in one or more of the primary and support activities. The more unique value the firm can create for customers, the more likely that the firm will be able to successfully use the differentiation strategy.

Next, we explain how the firm effectively using the differentiation strategy is able to position itself in the marketplace. In the next five subsections, we explain how an effective differentiation strategy results in a strong market position for the firm by countering each of the five competitive forces discussed in Chapter 3.

Rivalry with Existing Competitors

Customers tend to be loyal buyers of products that create unique value for them. Because of this, firms using the differentiation strategy do everything they can to increase the loyalty of their customers. With increasing loyalty, customer sensitivity to the price of the product they are buying is reduced. This is important, because the firm using the differentiation strategy needs to establish large profit margins on its products to earn the resources required to continuously reinvest in its products so that the valued sources of difference can be maintained. Think of it this way: providing differentiated goods and services can be expensive. The firm needs to earn high returns on what it sells to be able to pay for the costs of creating differentiated features while producing its products.

Bargaining Power of Buyers (Customers)

The uniqueness of a differentiated good or service reduces customers' sensitivity to the product's price. Firms using the differentiation strategy continuously stress the uniqueness of their products to customers (often through advertising campaigns) to reduce their sensitivity to price. Think of the Lexus slogan of "The Relentless Pursuit of Perfection" as an example. Toyota, the manufacturer of Lexus products,[19] is signaling to the customer that while the product's price is higher than that of cars aimed at the typical customer, the Lexus is a superior product because it is made by people seeking perfection in their work. When a

FIGURE 5.3 Examples of Value-Creating Activities Associated with the Differentiation Strategy

Firm Infrastructure
Highly developed information systems to better understand customers' purchasing preferences
A company-wide emphasis on the importance of producing high-quality products

Human Resource Management
Compensation programs intended to encourage worker creativity and productivity
Somewhat extensive use of subjective rather than objective performance measures
Superior personnel training

Technology Development
Strong capability in basic research
Investments in technologies that enable the firm to produce highly differentiated products

Procurement
Systems and procedures used to find the highest-quality raw materials
Purchase of highest-quality replacement parts

Inbound Logistics	Operations	Outbound Logistics	Marketing and Sales	Service
Superior handling of incoming raw materials to minimize damage and to improve the quality of the final product	Consistent manufacturing of attractive products Rapid responses to customers' unique manufacturing specifications	Accurate and responsive order-processing procedures Rapid and timely product deliveries to customers	Extensive granting of credit buying arrangements for customers Extensive personal relationships with buyers and suppliers	Extensive buyer training to ensure high-quality product installations Complete field stocking of replacement parts

MARGIN

MARGIN

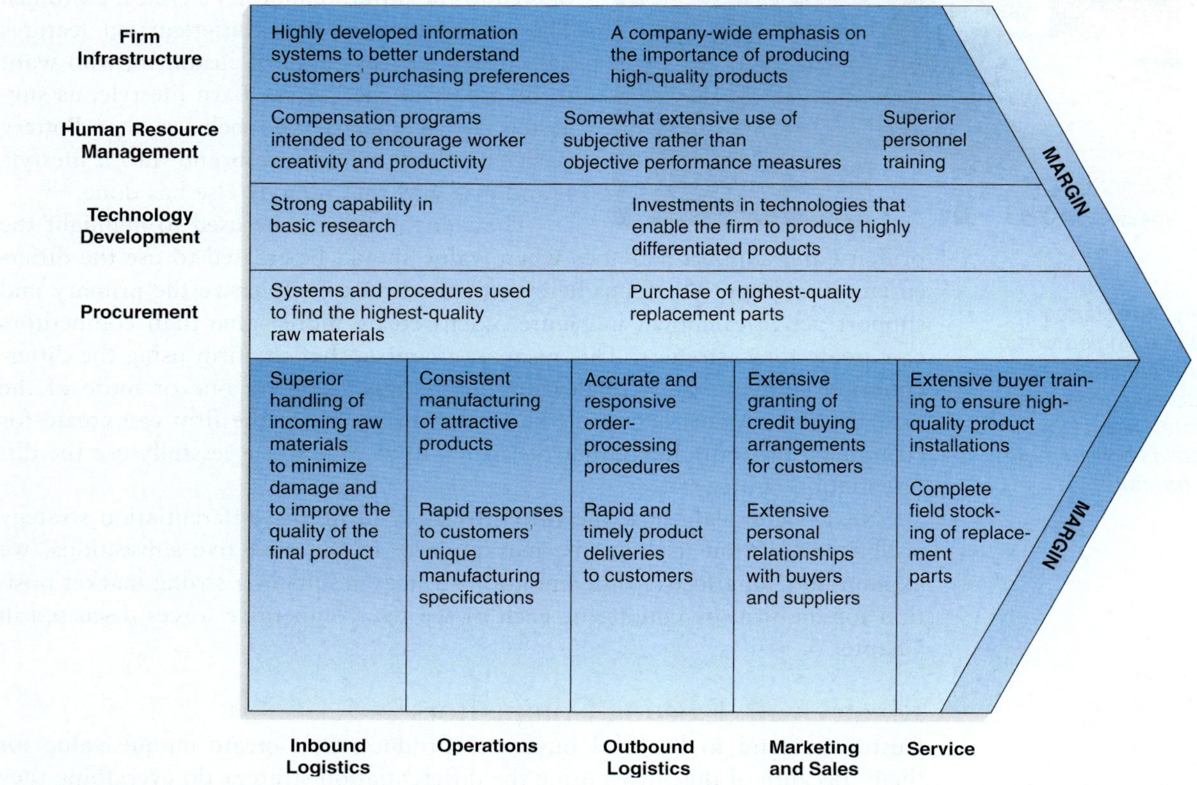

SOURCE: Adapted with the permission of The Free Press, an imprint of Simon & Schuster Adult Publishing Group, from *Competitive Advantage: Creating and Sustaining Superior Performance* by Michael E. Porter, p. 47.

firm's effort to emphasize product uniqueness is successful, customers' sensitivity to price will be reduced, thus enabling the firm to continue selling its products at a price that permits constant reinvestment in the products' differentiated features.

Bargaining Power of Suppliers

The firm using the differentiation strategy typically pays a premium price for the raw materials used to make its product. For a good, this means that some of the raw materials will be expensive (think of high-quality cotton used to make expensive, yet differentiated clothing items). Alternatively, for a service, the firm may pay a premium price to hire highly talented employees (think of the consultants McKinsey & Company must hire to provide differentiated service to its clients). However, the returns earned from a premium sales price of a differentiated good or service yields the funds the firm would need to pay its suppliers' higher prices. In addition to this, a firm providing goods or services that create differentiated value to customers may be able to pass supplier price increases on to its satisfied and loyal customers in the form of higher prices.

Potential Entrants

Customer loyalty and the need to provide customers with more value than an existing firm's product provides to them are strong challenges for those thinking about competing against a firm successfully using the differentiation strategy. Customer loyalty is hard to earn (doesn't a firm have to consistently meet your needs for quite a while before you'll become loyal to it?), meaning that a new entrant typically faces a long battle. In addition, the established firm has the margins necessary to reinvest in ways that will further enhance the differentiated value it creates for customers, making it even more difficult for a new competitor to compete against it.

Product Substitutes

It is difficult for competitors to create substitute products that will satisfy loyal customers of a firm that provides them differentiated value in the form of a good or service. Perceived unique value is hard to replace, even when a product substitute has a better performance-to-price ratio that favors substitution. Think of a good or service to which you have a great loyalty. What would it take for you to switch to a product substitute? For most of us, it would take a lot to get us to switch to a substitute when we are satisfied with the product we've been buying for perhaps a long time. Thus, firms with loyal customers tend to be insulated from competitors' substitute products that are intended to provide different value to the focal firm's customers.

Competitive Risks of the Differentiation Strategy

The differentiation strategy is not risk free. The first risk is that customers may decide that the price they are paying for a product's differentiated features is too high. This can happen especially when a cost leader learns how to add some differentiated features to its product without significantly raising the product's price. When this occurs, the customers buying the differentiated product may decide that the value being received is simply too expensive relative to the combination of some differentiation and low cost of the cost leader's good or service. A second risk is that the source of differentiation being provided by the firm may cease to create value for the target customers. For example, men buying Ralph Lauren dress shirts might conclude that the logo, lack of a pocket, and high-quality cotton no longer provide value for which they are willing to pay. Customer experiences are the third risk; by using a differentiated product and comparing its performance with lower-cost alternatives, the customer may conclude that the cost of the differentiation isn't acceptable. When first introduced, the IBM brand name enabled the firm to charge premium prices for its personal computers (PCs). However, through experience, many customers learned that the performance of competitors' lower-priced products was virtually equivalent to that of the IBM PC. Finally, differentiated products run the risk of being somewhat effectively counterfeited. Haven't many of us seen counterfeit purses, wallets, watches, and jewelry offered by street vendors?

Some of us may have even purchased one of these products! Although of much lower quality, the counterfeit product that looks like "the real thing" can be appealing, even for the customer capable of buying the true differentiated product. Here, the customer thinks about why he or she should pay the higher price for "the real thing" when the counterfeit product looks about as good.

Focus Strategies

A **focus strategy** is an action plan the firm develops to produce goods or services to serve the needs of a specific market segment. Therefore, focus strategies serve a narrower segment within a broader market. Firms using the focus strategy intend to serve the needs of a narrow customer segment better than their needs can be met by the firm targeting its products to the broad market (see Figure 5.1). A particular buyer group (such as teenagers, senior citizens, or working women), a specific segment of a product line (such as professional painters rather than "do-it-yourself" painters), and particular geographic markets (such as the West Coast or the East Coast of the United States) are examples of different target market segments on which a firm might focus. Recall that SoapWorks serves the segment of the household cleaning products' market that wants to buy hypoallergenic products. The firm uses either the focused cost leadership strategy or the focused differentiation strategy to successfully serve the needs of a narrow market segment.

Focused Cost Leadership Strategy

The **focused cost leadership strategy** is an action plan the firm develops to produce goods or services for a narrow market segment at the lowest cost. Based in Sweden, Ikea uses the focused cost leadership strategy.

Ikea is a global furniture retailer with locations in more than 30 countries. Some of you reading this book may be customers Ikea is targeting, in that the firm focuses on young buyers desiring style at a low cost.[20] Ikea offers home furnishings with good design and function and acceptable quality at low prices to young buyers who, according to Ikea's research, aren't wealthy, work for a living, and want to shop at hours beyond those typically available from firms serving the broad furniture market.

To successfully use its focused cost leadership strategy, Ikea concentrates on lowering its costs and understanding its customers' needs. According to the firm, "low cost is always in focus. This applies to every phase of our activities."[21] To keep the firm's costs low, Ikea's engineers design low-cost modular furniture that customers can easily assemble. To appeal to young buyers, who often are short of time and are inexperienced when it comes to buying furniture, Ikea arranges its products by rooms instead of by products. These configurations enable customers to see different living combinations (complete with sofas, chairs, tables, and so forth) in a single setting.

Focused Differentiation Strategy

The **focused differentiation strategy** is an action plan the firm develops to produce goods or services that a narrow group of customers perceive as being unique in ways that are important to them. Thomas Pink is a business unit of LVMH Moet Hennessy Louis Vuitton, which produces clothing and apparel.

All of LVMH's business units, including Thomas Pink, use the focused differentiation strategy. Recently, Thomas Pink introduced men's shirts made of 170-count cotton. This count of cotton is quite high and is the main way the product is differentiated in the marketplace (in comparison, a T-shirt from Old Navy is made of 18-count cotton). When introduced, these shirts were priced at $195 each. What unique value does a 170-count cotton shirt provide to a customer? According to a company official, one of these shirts helps a man "feel comfortable and confident in himself. This could be the one shirt he wears to board meetings."[22] Thus, this shirt is targeted to a very narrow target market—men who have achieved a great deal of success in corporate settings and who want to feel comfortable about the shirt they are wearing.

To successfully use either focus strategy, the firm must perform many of the value chain's primary and support activities in ways that enable it to create more value than competitors can create for a narrow group of target customers. The specific activities required to successfully use the focused cost leadership strategy are identical to those shown in Figure 5.2, while the activities needed to be successful with the focused differentiation strategy parallel those shown in Figure 5.3. The difference in the value chains shown in these two figures is that each activity is performed with a narrow market instead of a broad market segment in mind. Therefore, Figures 5.2 and 5.3 and the text regarding the five competitive forces describe how a firm successfully using one of the focus strategies is favorably positioned against the five competitive forces. However, to maintain its favorable position, the firm must continually drive its costs lower compared to competitors when using the focused cost leadership strategy and continue to find ways to differentiate its product in ways that are meaningful to the target customers when using the focused differentiation strategy.

Designers reevaluate their focus strategies each season in order to compete. These models are showing the Polo Ralph Lauren fall collection.

© AP Photo/Richard Drew

Competitive Risks of Focus Strategies

Using a focus strategy carries several risks. First, a competitor may learn how to "outfocus" the focusing firm. For example, Charles Tyrwhitt Shirts is using its skills to try to outfocus Thomas Pink in men's high-quality dress shirts. Tyrwhitt introduced a 180-count cotton shirt priced at $160, creating significant competition for Thomas Pink.[23] Second, a company serving the broad target market may decide that the target market being served by the focusing firm is attractive. Ralph Lauren, for instance, could introduce a dress shirt with a cotton count lower than that used by Thomas Pink and Charles Tyrwhitt and a slightly lower price. Ralph Lauren could rely on its brand image to entice its competitors' customers to try its dress shirt. Finally, the needs of the narrow target customer may change and become very similar to those of the broad market. Increases in their disposable income and experience with buying furniture might change some of Ikea's young buyers' needs to those that can be satisfied by a firm serving the broad market.

Integrated Cost Leadership/Differentiation Strategy

The **integrated cost leadership/differentiation strategy** is an action plan the firm develops to produce goods or services with strong emphasis on both differentiation and low cost. With this strategy, firms produce products that have some differentiated features (but not as many as offered by firms using the differentiation strategy) and that are produced at a low cost (but not at a cost as low as those of the firm using the cost leadership strategy). This strategy can be used to serve the needs of a broad target market or a narrow target market. McDonald's uses this strategy to serve the needs of a broad market, while Anon uses it to focus on the needs of a narrow target market. (Anon makes semicustomized rooftop air-conditioning systems for large customers such as The Home Depot, Wal-Mart, and Target.) Because the integrated cost leadership/differentiation strategy requires firms to be somewhat differentiated while producing at relatively low costs, firms must develop the flexibility needed to serve both of these objectives.

The possibility of being "neither fish nor fowl" is the main risk of using the integrated cost leadership/differentiation strategy. This means that when a firm fails to produce somewhat differentiated products at relatively low costs, it becomes "stuck in the middle."[24] The risk of this strategy and the problem of being stuck in the middle is highlighted in the following quote from the CEO of BMW North America: "The car market seems to be bifurcating between more expensive, prestige products and very inexpensive, high-volume products. The middle ground is the killing fields—the worst business to be in."[25]

Implementing Business-Level Strategies

To be successful, business-level strategies must not only match the needs of the marketplace, they also need to be implemented effectively. Organizational structure is an important dimension of implementing strategies. An **organizational structure** specifies the firm's formal reporting relationships, procedures, controls, and authority and decision-making processes.[26] Matching the right structure with the chosen strategy enhances firm performance.

Three major types of organizational structure are used to implement strategies: a simple structure, a functional structure, and a multidivisional structure.[27] Only the simple structure and the functional structure can be used to implement business-level strategies. A **simple structure** is an organizational structure in which the owner/manager makes all of the major decisions and oversees all of the staff's activities. This structure calls for very few rules, a dependence on informal relationships, and limited task specialization. The work is coordinated through frequent informal communications between the owner/manager and staff. This type of structure is best suited for use in a small business. The **functional structure** is an organizational structure consisting of a CEO and a small corporate staff. Here, the managers of major functional areas usually report to the CEO or a member of the corporate staff. This structure emphasizes functional specialization and facilitates active information sharing within each function. However, the functional orientation sometimes makes it difficult to communicate and coordinate across functions.

Implementing the Cost Leadership Strategy

so people "closest to the customer" can decide how to appropriately differentiate the firm's products. Jobs in this structure aren't very specialized and characteristics of this form of the functional structure enable employees to frequently communicate and to coordinate their work. Communication and coordination are vital parts of being able to understand customers' unique needs in order to produce unique products to satisfy those needs.

highly centralized authority in the corporate staff (see Figure 5.4). Recall that the cost leadership strategy finds the firm producing a relatively standardized

Implementing the Focus Strategies

When firms following a focus strategy have only a single product line and operate in a single geographic market, a simple structure is effective for implementing the strategy. These firms are often small and the focus is direct. However, in firms that are larger and more complex (such as those that have several product lines or operate in multiple geographic markets), a functional structure usually is more effective. The type of functional structure used is matched to the type

The functional structure used by firms implementing the differentiation strategy

this version of the functional organizational structure, the R&D and marketing

differentiate its products in ways that create value for customers, and marketing

ized functional structure that emphasizes efficiency. However, firms using a focused differentiation strategy should use a functional structure that is decen-

the firm relies on to continuously differentiate its products.

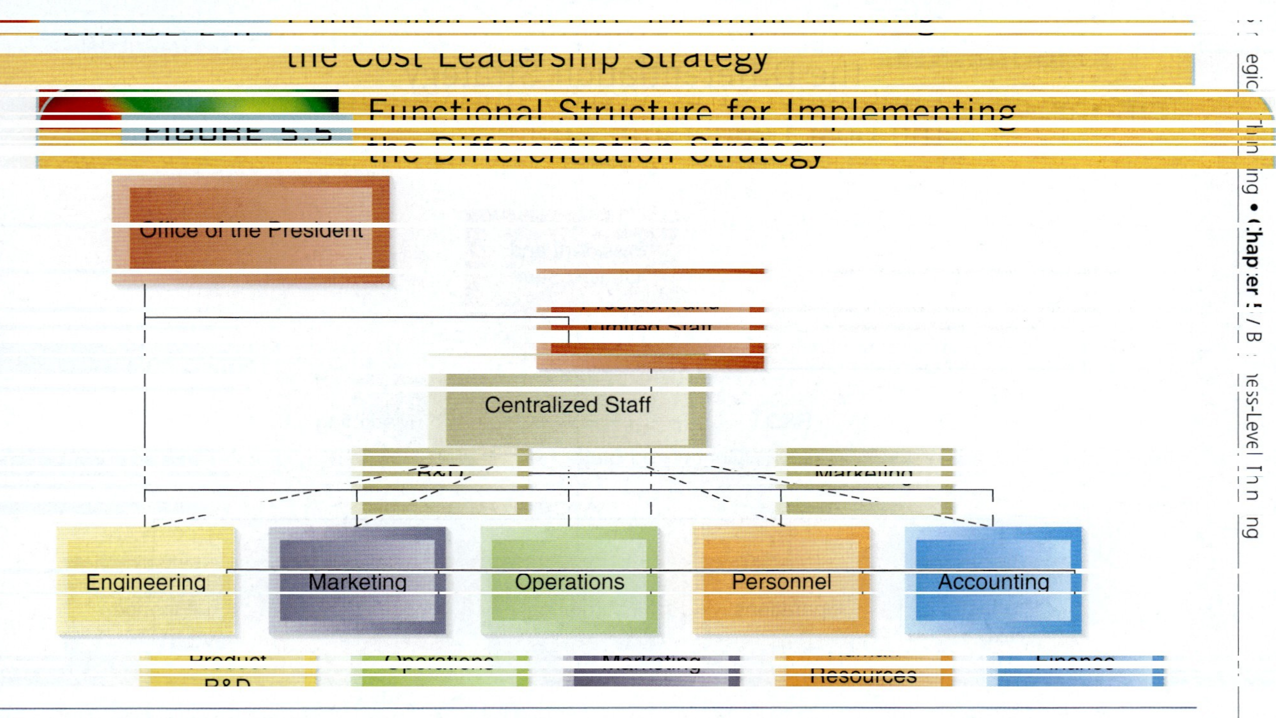

NOTES: • Operations is the main function
• Process engineering is emphasized rather than new product R&D

NOTES: • Marketing is the main function (to track new product ideas)

Implementing the Integrated Cost Leadership/Differentiation Strategy

Because of the competing demands of the cost leadership strategy's concern with efficiency and the differentiation strategy's concern with innovation, an integrated cost leadership/differentiation strategy is difficult to implement. To satisfy these competing demands, a firm using this strategy needs a structure in which decisions are partly centralized and partly decentralized. Jobs are semispecialized and some formal rules and procedures are needed, as well as some informal behavior. In short, flexibility is required. This strategy requires efficient processes to maintain lower costs. Yet the ability to change is also important in order to develop and maintain differentiated goods or services. Flexible manufacturing systems, quality-control systems, and sophisticated information systems can all contribute to simultaneous efficiency and flexibility. For example, ABB Ltd., a Swiss company manufacturing power and automated technologies that other firms buy to help them improve their performance, was well known for decentralizing decision-making authority to individual profit centers (the company once had 5,000 profit centers). But it also had effective information systems that gave top managers real-time information about each profit center's revenues and costs.[28]

Business-Level Strategy Success across Time

As we've described in this chapter, a business-level strategy is based on the firm's competitive advantages and is used to position the firm favorably in the marketplace relative to its rivals. Once formed, though, the firm must continuously evaluate its business-level strategy and change it as needed to create more value for customers or bring the firm back on course. Being "on course" means that the strategy is helping the firm reach its vision as well as the mission that is a core part of the vision, as explained in Chapters 1 and 2. Recently, brokerage house Charles Schwab concluded that the business-level strategy it was using to broaden its target market and product offerings wasn't working well. An important reason for this was the fact that the new strategy was taking Schwab too far from its original mission. According to a business writer, "Schwab executives [are saying] that salvation lies in returning to the firm's original mission of serving mom-and-pop, buy-and-hold investors who generate recurring advisory fees."[29] Schwab is changing its business-level strategy so the firm will again be "on course."

One way the firm can learn how to create more value for customers by using its business-level strategy is to ask them how it can do so. Sam Walton was known for recommending that firms trust their customers and frequently talk to them to find out what they want. In "Understanding Strategy," we describe how two firms talk to their customers to learn how to create more value for them.

Diversified firms, ones with multiple businesses competing in many industries and market segments, develop business-level strategies for each of their business units. For example, GE has more than a dozen business units, each of which develops a business-level strategy to describe how it intends to compete in its industry or market segments. In addition, UPS, the company described in this chapter's "Focusing on Strategy," has seven business units, each of which has a separate business-level strategy. We describe the multiproduct strategies that firms like UPS and GE use in the next chapter.

learning from success

understanding strategy:

MINING GOLD BY TALKING TO CUSTOMERS

"Companies very often employ bright people but only use them to do the task at hand," says Mark Turrell, CEO of Imaginatik, a firm that helps companies interpret information from customers in ways that will enable them to create new, innovative products. The CEO's comments reflect his belief that companies too often fail to use all of their employees' skills. One of their unused skills, he believes, is identifying customers' unmet needs.

In a recent assignment, Imaginatik worked with Grace Performance Chemicals, a division of W. R. Grace, to make sense of customers' innovative applications of the division's products. Grace sales representatives observed customers using the products they had sold to them in unexpected, creative ways. The uses from these observations are being integrated and catalogued to see if the chemicals unit can find ways to sell its current products to different customers or to tap latent demand (suggested by how current customers are using the unit's current products) as the foundation for developing new products.

Dow Chemical recently launched a new stretch fiber, XLA. This product was created after asking customers to describe the functionality they wanted in fibers. Dow gathered insights from firms competing in 26 industries to understand the characteristics of fiber that these firms thought would best serve their needs. What Dow learned is that apparel makers (one of the 26 industry groups Dow surveyed) wanted a "soft stretch" fiber with a natural feel and an ability to resist heat and chemicals. Armed with this insight, Dow's scientists developed XLA. To date, three apparel makers have introduced shirts using XLA as the core fiber. This was important customer input for Dow. Prior to learning about customers' preferences, Dow believed that it should concentrate its efforts to develop a spandex-type fiber that could be sold at a price lower than competitors' prices for this type of fiber. According to business writers, "That critical insight—that the market wanted an alternative to spandex, not a low-cost imitator—helped Dow avoid a huge error."

Customers may not always know what they want. Grace Performance Chemicals is trying to develop new products based on latent customer needs as inferred by observing their innovative uses of current products. Dow, on the other hand, directly asked customers what functionality they wanted in a product and then used its scientific skills to develop a product that could deliver what customers wanted. Both of these companies are working with customers to learn how to better serve those customers' needs.

SOURCES: 2004, About Imaginatik, Imaginatik Home Page, http://www.imaginatik.com, September 22; J. Esty, 2004, Those wacky customers! *Fast Company,* January: 40; L. Lavelle, 2004, Inventing to order, *Business Week,* July 5: 84–85.

Unlike UPS and GE, nondiversified firms that compete in a single product market develop only one business-level strategy. Your neighborhood dry-cleaning store and favorite locally owned restaurant are examples of firms with a single business-level strategy. Every firm needs a business-level strategy, and diversified firms need multiple business-level strategies plus a multiproduct strategy (see Chapter 6) as well as an international strategy (see Chapter 7) if they compete in more than a single country's markets.

Summary

The primary purpose of this chapter is to discuss the different business-level strategies firms can use to compete in the marketplace. In doing so, we examined the following topics:

- **Business-level strategy** is an action plan the firm develops to describe how it will compete in its chosen industry or market segment. A business-level strategy details how the firm intends to compete in the marketplace on a day-to-day basis to satisfy customers' needs.
- There are five generic business-level strategies. These strategies are called generic because they can be used by any firm regardless of the industry. Opportunities and threats in the external environment and the firm's core competencies and competitive advantages suggest the business-level strategy the firm should choose to implement.
- Each business-level strategy has two dimensions—competitive advantage (either a cost advantage or a uniqueness advantage) and competitive scope (either broad or narrow). The cost leadership and differentiation strategies are used to serve a broad market, while the focused cost leadership and focused differentiation strategies serve the specialized needs of a narrow market. The integrated cost leadership/differentiation strategy strikes a balance between the competitive advantage and competitive scope dimensions.
- When using the **cost leadership strategy**, a firm produces standardized products that are intended to satisfy the needs of the typical or "average" customer, which is usually the largest market segment. These products are produced at costs lower than those of competitors. To use this strategy successfully across time, the firm must continuously drive its costs lower than competitors' costs so it can sell its products at lower prices.
- Firms use the **differentiation strategy** to produce products that customers consider unique in ways that are important to them. Target customers for this strategy are willing to pay for product uniqueness. Uniqueness can be physical (such as superior reliability) or psychological (such as perceived status). Earning margins that are sufficient to support continuous reinvestment in sources of differentiation that customers value is the key to long-term success with this strategy.
- **Focus strategies** (cost leadership and differentiation) rely on either the cost or uniqueness advantage to better serve the specialized needs of a narrow target market, as compared to serving a broad target market.
- Firms use the **integrated cost leadership/differentiation strategy** to produce products that have some differentiation at a relatively low price. With this strategy, a firm's products have some differentiated features (but not as many as products coming from the firm using the differentiation strategy) and are produced at a low cost (but not as low as are the cost leader's costs). Because both low cost and differentiation are sought simultaneously, the firm must be very flexible to successfully use this strategy so it won't become "stuck in the middle." The main risk of the integrated cost leadership/differentiation strategy is being outperformed by firms successfully using the cost leadership or differentiation strategy.
- Two versions of the **functional structure** are best suited to implement the cost leadership strategy and the differentiation strategy. These two versions differ in their degree of centralization, specialization, and formalization. To promote efficiency, the functional structure for the cost leadership strategy holds decision-making authority in centralized staff functions, is highly specialized, and uses formal rules and procedures. In contrast, the functional structure used to implement the differentiation strategy is decentralized to different organizational functions. The emphasis here is on R&D and marketing to promote innovation. There is less specialization, with the use of cross-functional teams and fewer formal rules and procedures. Structures for the focus strategies largely match the emphasis of structures used to implement the cost leadership or differentiation strategy. However, if a firm using a focus strategy is small, a **simple structure** is used. The structure for the integrated cost leadership/differentiation strategy is more complex. It must be flexible with some centralization and some decentralization. The structure must be flexible in order to promote efficiency and innovation. Use of flexible manufacturing systems, quality-control systems and sophisticated information systems aid the flexibility.

Key Terms

business-level strategy 94
cost leadership strategy 99
differentiation strategy 102
focus strategy 106
focused cost leadership strategy 106
focused differentiation strategy 106
functional structure 108
integrated cost leadership/differentiation strategy 108
organizational structure 108
simple structure 108

Discussion Questions

1. What is a business-level strategy? Why is a business-level strategy important to a firm's success?
2. What are the definitions of the five business-level strategies discussed in this chapter? What are the differences among the five business-level strategies?
3. What specific and unique set of actions should a firm take to effectively use each business-level strategy?
4. What risks are associated with using each business-level strategy?
5. What organizational structures should be used to implement the business-level strategies?

Endnotes

1. M. E. Porter & E. Olmstead-Teisberg, 2004, Redefining competition in health care, *Harvard Business Review,* 82(6): 64–76.
2. 2004, UPS Home Page, About UPS, http://www.ups.com, September 21.
3. M. Beer & R. A. Eisenstat, 2004, How to have an honest conversation about your business strategy, *Harvard Business Review,* 82(2): 82–89.
4. G. Stalk Jr. & R. Lachenauer, 2004, Hardball: Five killer strategies for trouncing the competition, *Harvard Business Review,* 82(4): 62–71.
5. B. Breen, 2002, BMW: Driven by design, *Fast Company,* September: 123–127.
6. L. K. Trevino & M. E. Brown, 2004, Managing to be ethical: Debunking five business ethics myths, *Academy of Management Executive,* 18(2): 69–81.
7. B. C. Skaggs & M. Youndt, 2004, Strategic positioning, human capital, and performance in service organizations: A customer interaction approach, *Strategic Management Journal,* 25: 85–99.
8. E. Waaser, M. Dahneke, M. Pekkarinen, & M. Weissel, 2004, How you slice it: Smarter segmentation for your sales team, *Harvard Business Review,* 82(3): 105–111.
9. 2004, Becoming the best: What you can learn from the 25 most influential leaders of our times, Knowledge @ Wharton, http://www.knowledge.wharton.upenn.edu, February 11.
10. M. E. Porter, 1985, *Competitive Advantage,* New York: Free Press, 15.
11. G. Edmondson, 2004, Porsche's latest entry hits a crowded track, *Business Week,* July 5: 55.
12. A. Bianco, 2004, The vanishing mass market, *Business Week,* July 12: 61–67.
13. D. M. Osborne, 2000, Bootstrap marketing: Taking on Procter & Gamble, *Inc.,* http://www.inc.com, October.
14. 2004, About Cooper, Cooper Tire & Rubber Home Page, http://www.coopertire.com, September 18.
15. D. Sacks, 2004, Guinness: Brew a connection, *Fast Company,* August: 39–44.
16. M. E. Porter, 1980, *Competitive Strategy,* New York: Free Press, 35–40.
17. A. Bary, 2004, Barron's insight: Attention, Kmart holders: Game plan has pitfalls, *Wall Street Journal,* July 25: 2.
18. J. Samuelson, 2003, How Pottery Barn wins with style, *Fast Company,* June: 106–110.
19. S. J. Spear, 2004, Learning to lead at Toyota, *Harvard Business Review,* 82(5): 78–86.
20. K. Kling & I. Goteman, 2003, Ikea CEO Andres Dahlvig on international growth and Ikea's unique corporate culture and brand identity, *Academy of Management Executive,* 17(1): 31–37.
21. 2004, About Ikea, Ikea Home Page, http://www.ikea.com, September 22.
22. K. H. Hammonds, 2004, Thread-count wars, *Fast Company,* January: 31.
23. Ibid.
24. Porter, *Competitive Advantage,* 16.
25. Breen, BMW: Driven by Design.
26. B. Keats & H. O'Neill, 2001, Organizational structure: Looking through a strategy lens, in M. A. Hitt, R. E. Freeman & J. S. Harrison (Eds.), *Handbook of Strategic Management,* Oxford, UK: Blackwell, 520–542.
27. R. E. Hoskisson, M. A. Hitt, & R. D. Ireland, 2004, *Competing for Advantage,* Mason, Ohio: South-Western, 44.
28. Ibid.
29. 2004, Schwab is renovating to be more competitive, *Dallas Morning News,* September 14: D3.

CHAPTER 6

Product Strategies

Reading and studying this chapter should enable you to:

*Knowledge Objectives

1_
Define a multiproduct strategy.

2_
Understand the differences between the levels of diversification.

3_
Discuss the related-diversification multiproduct strategy.

4_
Explain the unrelated-diversification multiproduct strategy.

5_
Understand two motives that top-level managers have to diversify the firms they lead.

6_
Describe the organizational structures used to implement the different multiproduct strategies.

Focusing on Strategy

Brown: How Many Services Does It Offer?

"We see every aspect of our business working cohesively to synchronize commerce—helping companies simultaneously manage goods, information, and funds with speed, precision, security, and efficiency." (Michael L. Eskew, chairman and CEO of UPS)

In Chapter 5's "Focusing on Strategy," we described how UPS's Supply Chain Solutions group worked with Ford Motor Company to solve Ford's distribution problem. Do you recall that the president of a Ford dealership said that UPS's work brought about the most amazing transformation he had seen over his career as a dealer? Not surprisingly, being able to solve customers' logistics or supply-chain management problems is the goal of people working in UPS's Supply Chain Solutions group.

But logistics or supply-chain management isn't the main product (we use the word *product* to refer to either a good or a service) that comes to mind for most of us when we think about UPS and what it does. In fact, many of us likely picture a large brown truck delivering packages to individuals or businesses when we think of UPS. And such an image is quite understandable, in that UPS is the world's largest express and package delivery company. However, UPS has diversified its product lines, meaning that it sells multiple products. For example, the firm has formed what it calls its "non-package businesses" group as well as its "international package delivery service." The Supply Chain Solutions group is at the core of UPS's non-package businesses, although UPS Capital (which provides asset-based lending to businesses) and UPS Consulting (which provides supply-chain design and re-engineering advice to clients) are also part of the group. In essence, the Supply Chain Solutions group helps firms increase the efficiency of their supply chains, viewed as a network of actors or companies that convert raw materials into products for distribution. Currently, UPS's international package delivery service is growing faster than its domestic service.

The decisions to move into non-package businesses and to deliver packages in more than 200 countries means that UPS is using a multiproduct strategy along with an international strategy. Collectively, this means that UPS is diversified in terms of the services it offers and is diversified in terms of the countries it serves.

Why would UPS choose to diversify? For example, why would the firm decide to make a major commitment to delivering packages in China? The president of UPS International answers this question by noting, "The most exciting and fastest growing market is China." The growth in package delivery in China and other countries outside the United States exceeds the growth in UPS's domestic package delivery business. Therefore, building its operations in China and other emerging economies outside the United States is understandable. UPS diversified into non-package services as a result of building a sophisticated technological infrastructure to support its international transportation network, as follows: The decision to expand internationally resulted in the firm's developing technological and information processing capabilities that could be used to complete tasks in addition to servicing the firm's sprawling international delivery service. With its technological and information processing capabilities, UPS decided to diversify its service offerings by adding logistics or supply-chain management services as well as other related services to its portfolio of services. Given all of UPS's actions to diversify, we can understand CEO Eskew's comment indicating that UPS is working to "synchronize commerce."

SOURCES: 2004, Today's UPS, UPS Home Page, http://www.ups.com, December 2; D. Foust, 2004, Big Brown's New Bag, *Business Week,* July 19: 54; N. Harris, 2004, UPS expands direct control of China business, *Wall Street Journal Online,* http://www.wsj.com, December 3; B. Stanley, 2004, Delivery services expand role, *Wall Street Journal Online,* http://www.wsj.com, November 26.

As described in "Focusing on Strategy," UPS has diversified its service offerings and is using a multiproduct strategy. A **multiproduct strategy** is an action plan the firm develops to compete in different product markets. The focus of this chapter is on diversification in the form of multiproduct strategies, while the next chapter focuses on diversification in the form of international strategies. Think about Figure 1.1 and consider that UPS is using a multiproduct strategy and an international strategy to compete against its rivals such as FedEx and DHL. Of course, UPS is using business-level strategies in each of its three product groups (U.S. domestic package, international package, and non-package).

As with business-level strategies, a firm's multiproduct strategy is used to improve its performance.[1] A firm improves its performance by using a multiproduct strategy when it learns how to use its core competencies to pursue opportunities in the external environment in more than one product market.[2] Successful multiproduct strategies enable a firm to smooth out its revenue and earnings flows and earn additional profits by using its core competencies in additional ways.[3] We present additional reasons why firms use multiproduct strategies to diversify their operations in Table 6.1.

Firms such as UPS deal with two issues when developing a multiproduct strategy: What products will be offered and how will those products be man-

TABLE 6.1 Reasons Why Firms Use Multiproduct Strategies to Diversify

- Achieve profitable growth
- Reduce the risk of being involved with a single product line
- Learn how to apply core competencies in other value creating ways
- Gain exposure to different technologies
- Develop economies of scope
- Extend the firm's brand into additional product areas

aged?[4] As noted earlier, the groups of services that UPS offers are U.S. domestic package (74 percent), international package (17 percent), and non-package (nine percent). The percentages shown indicate the percentage of total sales revenue generated by each group during UPS's 2003 fiscal year.[5] The manner in which UPS generates sales revenue across its product divisions means that the firm is using a dominant-business multiproduct strategy. We define this and the other multiproduct strategies in the next section. Later in the chapter, we discuss the type of organizational structure UPS uses to implement its multiproduct strategy.

To explain multiproduct strategies, we first describe how diversified a firm becomes (from low to high) when it selects a particular multiproduct strategy. We then examine two levels of diversification (related and unrelated) in some detail. We do this because of how frequently firms use these multiproduct strategies. Following these discussions, we describe two motives that top-level managers have to diversify the firm in ways that may or may not create value for stakeholders. The chapter closes with presentations of the different organizational structures firms use to implement the different multiproduct strategies.

Levels of Diversification

We show five levels of diversification (from low to high) in Figure 6.1. Firms using the single-business multiproduct strategy are the least diversified, while companies using the unrelated-diversification multiproduct strategy are the most diversified. A firm with low levels of diversification has a smaller total number of different products and generates a larger percentage of its sales from its major product group; a firm with high levels of diversification has a larger number of different products and generates a smaller percentage of its sales revenue from one product group.

Low Levels of Diversification

As shown in Figure 6.1, the sources of a firm's sales revenue are used to determine its level of product diversification. This technique of determining a firm's degree of diversification is based on a classic work completed by Richard Rumelt.[6]

FIGURE 6.1 Levels of Diversification

Low Levels of Diversification

Single business: More than 95 percent of revenue comes from a single business.

Dominant business: Between 70 and 95 percent of revenue comes from a single business.

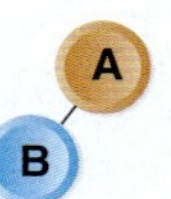

Moderate to High Levels of Diversification

Related constrained: Less than 70 percent of revenue comes from the dominant business, and all businesses share product, technological, and distribution linkages.

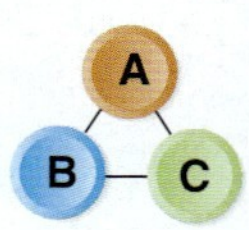

Related linked (mixed related and unrelated): Less than 70 percent of revenue comes from the dominant business, and only limited links exist between businesses.

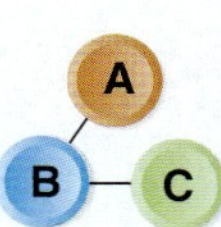

Very High Levels of Diversification

Unrelated: Less than 70 percent of revenue comes from the dominant business, and no common links exist between businesses.

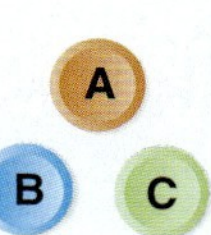

SOURCE: Adapted from R. P. Rumelt, 1974, *Strategy, Structure, and Economic Performance,* Boston: Harvard Business School.

Single-Business Diversification Multiproduct Strategy

A firm pursuing low levels of diversification uses either the single- or dominant-business multiproduct strategy. With the single-business multiproduct strategy, the firm generates at least 95 percent of its sales revenue from a single business. A *single business* is one in which the firm makes and sells a single product or a variety of a single product. Let's consider a famous chewing-gum manufacturer to understand the single-business diversification multiproduct strategy.

Historically, Wrigley has used the single-business multiproduct strategy. Chewing and bubble gums, of course, are the firm's core product. Wrigley produces and sells multiple types of gums, including Juicy Fruit, Spearmint, Doublemint, and Hubba Bubba. The few other products Wrigley produced for many years (which accounted for less than five percent of total sales revenue) were all related to derivatives of chewing gum. Therefore, for many decades, Wrigley produced and sold a number of versions of a single type of product—chewing gum and bubble gum.

Recently, though, Wrigley decided to diversify its product offerings so it could become a global confectionery business. Chewy and hard candies are a primary new product area for Wrigley.

© Getty Images

Wrigley has traditionally produced one product, gum, in a variety of flavors, such as Big Red, advertised here by Carmen Electra.

Dominant-Business Diversification Multiproduct Strategy

A firm using the dominant-business multiproduct strategy generates between 70 and 95 percent of its sales revenue from a single business. As mentioned earlier, UPS, the focal firm in "Focusing on Strategy," recently earned 74 percent of its revenue from its U.S. package delivery business, 17 percent of revenue from its international package business, and nine percent of revenue from its non-package business. This means that UPS has three businesses, with each business delivering some unique services. Therefore, compared to firms using a single-business multiproduct strategy, companies similar to UPS produce and sell a larger number of products and so are more diversified.

Given current trends, the nature of UPS's diversification is likely to change. There are two reasons for this. First, its international package delivery business is growing faster than its domestic package delivery business. Second, UPS's non-package business is also growing rapidly and is the product area that company leaders believe holds the most promise for UPS's future growth. Indeed, if the "world of synchronized commerce" evolves as UPS's leaders anticipate, the percentage of the firm's total revenue generated by its non-package products and its international package delivery businesses may continue to increase and eventually eclipse the amount of revenue generated by its U.S. package delivery business. If this trend continues, UPS is likely to pursue either a moderate or a high level of diversification.

Moderate to High Levels of Diversification

Related-Diversification Multiproduct Strategy

A firm generating less than 70 percent of its sales revenue from its dominant business is using either the related-diversification or the unrelated-diversification multiproduct strategy (see Figure 6.1). Let's see what the differences are between these strategies.

Firms using a related-diversification multiproduct strategy try to create economies of scope. **Economies of scope** are cost savings the firm accrues when it successfully shares some of its resources and activities or some of its core competencies between its businesses.

The related-diversification strategy actually has two forms, with a subtle but important difference between the two. With the *related constrained* multiproduct strategy, most (but not necessarily all) of the firms' businesses are related to each other.[7] The relatedness between the businesses occurs as they share some products, markets, and/or technologies.[8] As shown in Figure 6.1, the hypothetical firm using the related constrained multiproduct strategy has three businesses (A, B, and C). The lines connecting all three businesses show hypothetically that the three businesses are somewhat constrained in the activities used to produce their goods or services because they share some products (such as raw materials as inputs to the manufacturing processes used to make the business's final product), markets (that is, they serve the same customers), and/or technologies (that is, the same or very similar technologies are used to produce the three business's products). Consumer product giant Procter & Gamble (P&G) uses the related constrained strategy. A few paragraphs below, we describe an example of how P&G's businesses are related to one another.

In the *related linked* diversification strategy, only limited links or relationships exist between the firm's businesses. As shown in Figure 6.1, the hypothetical firm using the related linked strategy has three businesses (A, B, and C). The line connecting business A and business B reflects a hypothetical relationship, as does the line between business B and business C. Notice however, that business A and business C do not share products, markets, and technologies. In addition to some sharing of resources and activities between businesses, a firm using the related linked strategy concentrates on transferring core competencies between businesses. Firms using this strategy organize strategic business units (SBU). A **strategic business unit (SBU)** is a semiautonomous unit of a diversified firm with a collection of related businesses. An important point about strategic business units is that resources and activities are shared and core competencies are transferred among the product divisions within each SBU. However, resources, activities, and core competencies are not shared or transferred respectively between product divisions *across* SBUs. We'll talk more about this at the end of the chapter when we describe relationships between multiproduct strategies and organizational structures. Also, firms using the related linked strategy share fewer resources and activities between divisions within individual SBUs, concentrating on transferring core competencies (such as knowledge) between the businesses instead.

Unrelated-Diversification Multiproduct Strategy

A firm that does *not* try to transfer resources, activities, and/or core competencies between its businesses or divisions is using an unrelated-diversification multiproduct strategy. Commonly, firms using this strategy are called *conglomerates*. The unrelated-diversification multiproduct strategy is frequently used in both developed markets (for example, the United Kingdom and the United States) and emerging markets. In fact, firms using this strategy dominate the private sector in Latin American countries and in China, Korea, and India.[9] Conglomerates account for the greatest percentage of private firms in India.[10] Similarly, the largest business firms in Brazil, Mexico, Argentina, and Colombia are family-owned, highly diversified enterprises.[11]

We now turn our attention to discussing the related- and unrelated-diversification multiproduct strategies in detail and how firms use them to generate economies of scope by achieving either operational relatedness or corporate relatedness. **Operational relatedness** is achieved when the firm's businesses successfully share resources and activities to produce and sell their products. **Corporate relatedness** is achieved when core competencies are successfully transferred between some of the firm's businesses. Most commonly, these transfers involve intangible core competencies such as marketing knowledge, design skills, and brand name.

Notice by looking at Figure 6.2 that firms using the related constrained multiproduct strategy create economies of scope by achieving operational relatedness (see cell 1 in Figure 6.2), while firms using the related linked multiproduct strategy create economies of scope by achieving corporate relatedness (see cell 2 in Figure 6.2). As noted earlier, we concentrate on the related- and unrelated-diversification multiproduct strategies instead of on the single-business and dominant-business multiproduct strategies because they are more frequently used by larger firms.

FIGURE 6.2 Value-Creating Strategies of Diversification: Operational and Corporate Relatedness

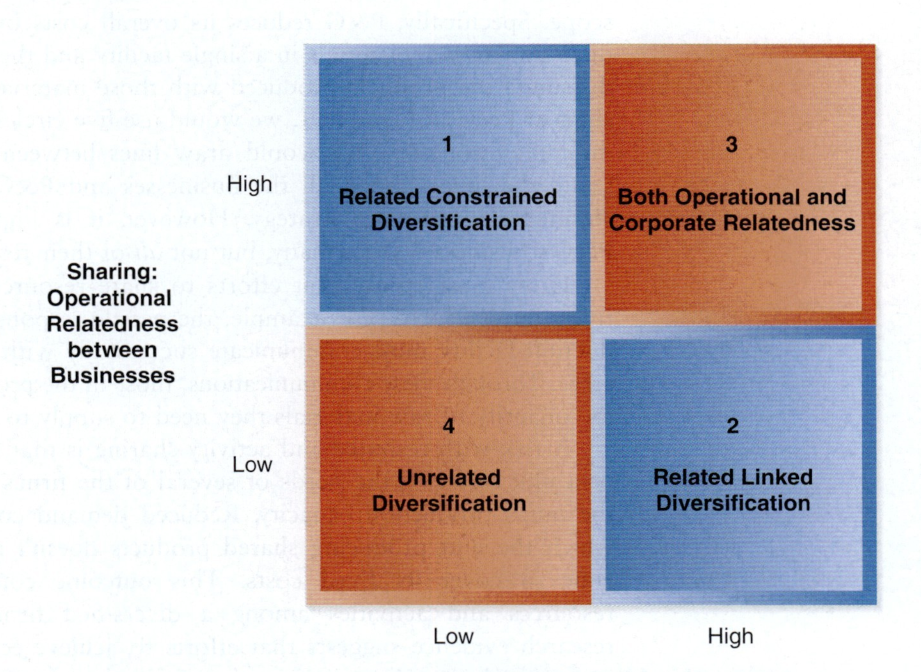

Operational Relatedness and the Related Constrained Multiproduct Strategy

Economies of scope are created through operational relatedness when the firm successfully shares primarily tangible resources (such as plant and equipment) and/or when a primary activity (such as inventory delivery systems) or a support activity (such as purchasing procedures) is successfully used in more than one of the firm's businesses. We'll use Procter & Gamble (P&G) to describe how economies of scope are created in firms using the related constrained multiproduct strategy.

Currently, P&G has five businesses (Personal and Beauty, House and Home, Health and Wellness, Pet Nutrition and Care, and Baby and Family) that share some resources and activities. (P&G calls its businesses product divisions.) The total number of P&G's businesses may change as it integrates its recent acquisition, Gillette, into its operations. All five businesses produce one or more products that use materials based on paper. P&G operates a paper production facility that provides raw materials to all five businesses. Of course, there are some differences in what the paper production facility makes for each business. However, the paper-based raw material inputs needed by the five businesses are similar enough that one facility can produce many if not most of those items. Because many of the businesses' products are sold in some of the same outlets (grocery stores, for example), these products also share distribution channels and networks of sales representatives.[12] The sharing of these resources (raw materials) and activities (distribution) enables P&G to generate economies of scope. Specifically, P&G reduces its overall costs by combining assets to produce similar raw materials in a single facility and then using similar channels to distribute the products produced with those materials. To show these relationships at P&G in Figure 6.1, we would use five circles (A–E) to represent P&G's different businesses. We would draw lines between the businesses to demonstrate the links among all the businesses and P&G's use of the related constrained multiproduct strategy. However, it is important to emphasize that P&G's businesses share many, but not *all* of their resources and activities.

Firms must ensure that efforts to share resources and activities are effectively implemented. For example, the people responsible for P&G's paper production facility must communicate successfully with all businesses its products serve. Through these communications, those in the production facility learn about the quantity of raw materials they need to supply to P&G's five businesses.

A risk with resource and activity sharing is that the demand for the output of a unit servicing the needs of several of the firm's businesses may fall below the unit's production capacity. Reduced demand could lead to a situation in which the unit producing shared products doesn't generate enough sales revenue to cover its fixed costs. This outcome complicates efforts to share resources and activities among a diversified firm's businesses.[13] However, research evidence suggests that efforts to achieve economies of scope through operational relatedness are worthwhile in that they help create value for stakeholders.[14] Creating value through operational relatedness is what Hyatt intends to do as a result of acquiring the AmeriSuites chain. We discuss how Hyatt will attempt to do this in "Understanding Strategy."

learning from success

understanding strategy:

HYATT CORPORATION: CREATING VALUE BY SHARING ACTIVITIES

The privately held Hyatt Corporation uses the related constrained multiproduct strategy. Hyatt Regency hotels are the core brand of accommodations offered by this firm.

As with other multiunit hoteliers such as Hilton Hotels, Hyatt offers a number of different hotel concepts as parts of its core brand. For example, Hyatt introduced the Grand Hyatt and Park Hyatt concepts in 1980 "to further identify and market the diverse types of Hyatt properties worldwide." Grand Hyatt units serve leisure and business travelers as well as conventioneers wanting a "grand scale" of refinement during their stays. Park Hyatt is the firm's smaller, luxury hotel that caters to "the discriminating individual traveler seeking the privacy, personalized service, and elegance of a small European hotel." But Hyatt has diversified beyond hotel accommodations, offering other products and services. The firm owns and operates time-share properties, freestanding golf courses, and gaming operations. Hyatt opened its first freestanding golf course in 1995 in Tierra del Sol on the island of Aruba. Hyatt also provides management services to golf courses owned by other companies. Hyatt entered the riverboat gaming industry in 1994 when it opened the Grand Victoria Casino in Elgin, Illinois. As you see, Hyatt is much more than a collection of hotels.

© EMILE WAMSTEKER/ Bloomberg News/Landov

© TANNEN MAURY/ Bloomberg News/Landov

Hyatt continues to diversify its hotel accommodation concepts or products, as shown by its recent purchase of AmeriSuites for more than $600 million. When it was purchased, AmeriSuites was an upscale limited-service hotel chain with 143 hotels in 32 states. Hyatt acquired AmeriSuites partly to diversify away from its core high-end lodging accommodations. By buying AmeriSuites, Hyatt entered the fastest-growing segment of the lodging industry—limited service, all-suites hotels targeting frequent travelers.

Hyatt intends to generate economies of scope through its acquisition of AmeriSuites by sharing resources and activities. In particular, Hyatt uses its purchasing power (a support activity) to buy upgraded furnishings for AmeriSuites rooms at a lower cost than AmeriSuites could have obtained as an independent company. Additionally, AmeriSuites facilities will use Hyatt's reservations systems and will participate in Hyatt's frequent-stayer program. Thus, by sharing activities (such as its reservations systems) and resources (such as its frequent-stayer program) with its new AmeriSuites unit, Hyatt intends to gain economies of scope based on operational relatedness while using its related constrained multiproduct strategy.

SOURCES: 2004, Company overview, Hyatt Corporation Home Page, http://www.hyatt.com, December 15; 2004, Hyatt to buy AmeriSuites hotel chain, *Reuters*, http://www.reuters.com, December 9; C. Binkley, 2004, Hotels are lifting rates, profits a deals disappear, study finds, *Wall Street Journal Online*, http://www.wsj.com, December 9; J. Kimelman, 2004, Real estate pro likes hotels, retail, *Barron's Online*, http://www.barrons.com, December 7; M. Maremont, 2004, Hyatt to buy AmeriSuites hotel chain, *Wall Street Journal Online*, http://www.wsj.com, December 9.

Corporate Relatedness and the Related Linked Multiproduct Strategy

Economies of scope are generated through corporate relatedness when the firm successfully transfers core competencies between one or more of the businesses within individual SBUs. Remember that with the related linked multiproduct strategy, only limited relationships exist between the firm's businesses in each SBU and that core competencies are transferred only between the businesses *within* each SBU. A firm using the related linked multiproduct strategy does not seek to transfer core competencies between businesses housed in its different SBUs. Next, we examine how GE (a firm using the related linked strategy) transfers core competencies between the businesses within individual SBUs.

GE has 11 "primary business units, each with its own number of divisions."[15] As an SBU, GE Commercial Finance has eight divisions (such as Aviation Services, Fleet Services, and Healthcare Financial Services). Fleet Services is another division in this SBU. This division received the 2004 CRM (Customer Relationship Management) award from Gartner,[16] a firm that provides research and analysis on the global information technology industry. CRM is a technique firms use to establish and maintain long-term, positive relationships with their customers. Because the division's CRM system received an award for its excellence, this system may be a core competence that could be transferred from Fleet Services to one or more of the remaining seven divisions in the GE Commercial Finance SBU.

One way that intangible core competencies can be transferred from one business to another within a particular SBU is to reassign personnel. In these cases, the people in charge of an activity in a core competence within one business are assigned to another business to teach those employees how to develop the value-creating core competence. Personnel can sometimes be reluctant to transfer from one business to another; in these instances, the firm may have to pay them a premium to gain their cooperation.

Another way that core competencies are transferred is through knowledge acquired by participating in managerial and leadership training programs. One of the objectives of GE's executive education programs, for example, is for participating managers to develop knowledge (an important source of core competencies) that can be shared between some of the firm's businesses within one of its strategic business units. Here's an example of how this works in one of GE's SBUs. GE's NBC Universal SBU was formed in May 2004 "through the merger of NBC and Vivendi Universal Entertainment."[17] Managers from Universal are participating in executive education programs to work on the "integration" of its businesses with other parts of the SBU that GE has created, while "GE is shipping company-trained CFOs west to scope out the Hollywood units."[18]

Simultaneously Seeking Operational Relatedness and Corporate Relatedness

As shown in cell 3 in Figure 6.2, firms can develop economies of scope by simultaneously seeking high levels of operational relatedness and corporate relatedness.[19] Essentially, this means that the firm's multiproduct strategy is a hybrid with characteristics of both the related constrained and related linked multiproduct strategies.

Experience shows that it is very difficult for firms to simultaneously achieve operational and corporate relatedness.[20] Although sharing is difficult with tangible resources, in which primary and support activities are combined to achieve operational relatedness, transferring intangible resources can be even more challenging. Transferring intangible resources (such as knowledge about how to interpret market trends) between businesses within a SBU to generate economies of scope by achieving corporate relatedness is more difficult because the potential outcome is less visible (that is, it is difficult to know that an intangible resource is being transferred unless that resource is an individual manager). So you can imagine how difficult it is for a firm to simultaneously focus on *sharing* tangible resources and activities among businesses within each SBU while simultaneously concentrating on *transferring* intangible core competencies among those businesses. Although it is challenging to simultaneously attain operational relatedness and corporate relatedness, evidence suggests that firms able to do so have developed a competitive advantage that is difficult for competitors to imitate.[21] Walt Disney Studios, one of Disney's divisions, can share resources and activities as it creates, produces, and promotes movies in its different studios (such as Walt Disney Pictures and Miramax). However, within the same division, knowledge about how to promote movies as a source of entertainment could be transferred to other parts of the division such as television programs and live theater productions, which are also attempting to promote activities as a source of entertainment.[22]

Unrelated-Diversification Multiproduct Strategy

As indicated by cell 4 in Figure 6.2, firms using the unrelated-diversification multiproduct strategy do not attempt to develop economies of scope by achieving either operational relatedness or corporate relatedness. When using the unrelated-diversification multiproduct strategy, firms try to generate financial economies instead of trying to develop economies of scope through operational relatedness and/or corporate relatedness.

Financial economies are cost savings or higher returns generated when the firm effectively allocates its financial resources based on investments either inside or outside the firm.[23] With respect to internal investments, the firm creates financial economies when it allocates its resources efficiently through the efforts of corporate headquarters personnel who represent a capital market for the entire organization. In terms of investments outside the firm, the company using the unrelated-diversification strategy creates financial economies when it is able to buy another firm, restructure that firm's assets in value-creating ways, and then sell that company at a price exceeding its investment (price paid plus amount invested to increase the quality of the purchased company's assets). We consider each type of financial economy in greater detail in the next two sections.

Efficient Internal Capital Market Allocation

As you'll recall from your study of economics and finance in particular, capital markets are assumed to be efficient in the allocation of capital. Efficiency results as investors take an equity position in firms by purchasing shares of stock in companies they believe have high future cash flow value. Efficient markets also allocate capital in the form of debt as shareholders and debtholders seek to improve the value of their investments by taking stakes in firms that they believe have high growth and profitability prospects.

In companies using the unrelated-diversification multiproduct strategy, corporate headquarters personnel allocate the firm's capital across its portfolio of product divisions. At Textron, which uses the unrelated-diversification strategy, corporate headquarters personnel allocate capital across the firm's five strategic business units—Bell, Cessna, Fastening Systems, Industrial, and Finance (Bell accounts for the largest amount of Textron's revenues—24 percent).[24]

At Textron and other firms using the unrelated-diversification strategy, capital is allocated on the basis of what headquarters personnel believe will generate the greatest amount of financial economies for the organization as a whole. At Japan Tobacco, for example, additional capital is currently being allocated to the firm's cigarette manufacturing SBU so it can acquire other firms. The purpose of the acquisitions is for Japan Tobacco's cigarette manufacturing SBU to increase the breadth and depth of its cigarette product lines. Financial capital is allocated to the firm's cigarette SBU because headquarters personnel believe that its growth and profitability prospects are greater than those of the firm's other SBUs (foods, pharmaceuticals, agribusiness, engineering, and real estate).[25] In Japan Tobacco and Textron, as well as in other firms using the unrelated-diversification multiproduct strategy, financial capital is allocated only after extensive, in-depth analyses of each SBU's prospects for revenue and profitability growth.

Internal capital market allocations in firms using the unrelated-diversification strategy may be the basis for superior returns to shareholders compared to returns shareholders would receive as a result of allocations by the external capital market.[26] Access to information is the main reason for this possibility. Indeed, while managing the firm's portfolio of SBUs, headquarters personnel may gain access to detailed information that isn't available to the external capital market about the ability of one or more of the firm's SBUs to create value by growing its revenue and profitability streams. In addition, those evaluating the performance of all of a firm's SBUs can internally discipline poorly performing units by allocating fewer or different types of resources to them.[27] Disciplined SBUs' managers are likely to respond favorably by working hard to improve their units' performance as the first step to receiving a larger percentage of the entire firm's financial capital.

The external capital market relies on information produced by the firm to estimate the organization's ability to generate attractive future revenue and earnings streams. Annual reports, press conferences, and filings mandated by various regulatory bodies are the most common sources of information available to the external capital market. In these communication media, firms may overemphasize positive news while either ignoring or de-emphasizing negative news about one or more of their SBUs. Beyond this, firms may not want to divulge information when using these media because it might help competitors better understand and imitate the competitive advantages of product divisions within SBUs. Therefore, in-depth knowledge about the positive and negative performance prospects and competitive advantages for all of the firm's SBUs creates a potential informational advantage for the firm relative to the external capital market.

As we've described, the firm's internal capital market can create value in the form of financial economies when it efficiently allocates the organization's total set of financial capital. However, firms sometimes fail in their efforts to do this effectively. When this happens, the conglomerate must either improve its internal capital market allocation skills or divest either SBUs or product divisions within SBUs until it reaches the point where once again, the SBUs the firm owns are creating more value through financial economies than they would generate while operating as independent entities.

We describe a failed unrelated-diversification multiproduct strategy in "Understanding Strategy." As noted earlier, firms may decide to become less diversified (often referred to as refocusing or downscoping[28]) when they are unable to achieve financial economies through allocations of their financial capital. This is what happened at Campbell Soup.

Restructuring

A firm using the unrelated-diversification multiproduct strategy can also produce financial economies by learning how to create value by buying and selling other companies' assets in the external market.[29] As in the real estate business, buying assets at low prices, restructuring them in value-creating ways, and then selling them at a price exceeding their purchase cost plus the restructuring cost generates a positive return on the firm's invested capital.

United Technologies Corporation (UTC) uses the unrelated-diversification strategy and restructures purchased firms' assets to create financial economies. In May 1999, for example, UTC sold its long-held automotive division (a composite of several previous acquisitions) to Lear for $2.3 billion because UTC's top-level managers concluded that the firm could not create additional value by further restructuring the unit's assets. UTC takes a deliberate approach in buying and selling restructured assets, often requiring several years to realize full value from restructuring its assets.[30]

In general, it is easier to create financial economies by restructuring the assets of firms competing in relatively low-technology businesses because of the uncertain future demand for high-technology products. All businesses that UTC purchases, for example, are involved in manufacturing industrial and commercial products, many of which are relatively low-technology (such as elevators and air conditioners). Of course, firms seeking financial economies by buying and selling restructured assets must be able to restructure those assets at a cost below their expected future market value when they are sold to another company.

Managerial Motives to Diversify

In addition to the reasons for diversification that are shown in Table 6.1, top-level managers may have two additional motives to diversify their organization. These motives may or may not be in the best interests of the firm's stakeholders.

Reducing the risk of losing their job is the first motive for top-level executives.[31] If a firm has multiple businesses and one business fails, the firm is unlikely to experience total failure if the other businesses are doing well. Therefore, additional diversification reduces the chance that top-level executives of a diversified firm will lose their jobs.

learning from failure

understanding strategy:

CAMPBELL SOUP RETURNS TO LOWER LEVELS OF DIVERSIFICATION TO IMPROVE ITS PERFORMANCE

Founded in 1869, Campbell Soup is a global manufacturer of high-quality convenience foods. Today, Campbell operates with four product divisions: North American Soup and Away from Home (39 percent), North America Sauces and Beverages (19 percent), Biscuits and Confectionery (26 percent), and International Soups and Sauces (16 percent). The percentages indicate the total of the firm's sales revenues earned by each product division during Campbell's 2003 fiscal year. Obviously, Campbell is using a related diversificaton multiproduct strategy. Because some resources and activities are shared among the firm's divisions, we know that Campbell is using the related constrained multiproduct strategy. Only a few years ago, though, the firm was using the unrelated diversification multiproduct strategy. Let's talk about why the firm first became more diversified and then why it decided to reduce its level of diversification to again use the related constrained strategy.

© David Young-Wolff/ Photo Edit

R. Gordon McGovern was CEO of Campbell Soup from 1980 to 1989. McGovern decided early in his tenure to rapidly expand Campbell's product lines to increase its revenues and profits. McGovern felt that it was difficult to rapidly expand a packaged-goods company's product lines by developing new products internally. Therefore, McGovern concluded that Campbell should acquire other firms to quickly gain access to new products and new product markets. Instead of acquiring only food products, though, Campbell began to use the unrelated diversification strategy to acquire firms that it felt were positioned to capitalize on consumer trends, whatever they might happen to be. So McGovern and his top-level managers intended to create financial economies through their efficient allocation of financial capital across Campbell's increasingly diverse product divisions. During the course of McGovern's tenure, Campbell bought firms involved in all types of businesses. Triangle Manufacturing Company, a fitness products maker, is an example of a firm Campbell acquired that is clearly unrelated to what were historically the firm's core products. At one time during McGovern's tenure as Campbell's CEO, the firm had 50 product divisions.

A major reason for Campbell's failure to generate financial economies while using the unrelated diversification strategy is that the firm's approach to managing its core product divisions never changed. This means that instead of managing the core product divisions to control costs and use financial capital as efficiently as possible (which is necessary to achieve financial economies), managers in the firm's historical core product divisions continued to focus on creating economies of scope by sharing resources and activities. At the same time, corporate headquarters personnel didn't implement the strong financial controls necessary to efficiently manage an internal capital market.

David Johnson succeeded McGovern as CEO in 1990. He quickly decided that Campbell should no longer use the unrelated diversification strategy and that it should divest businesses that weren't related to its historical core products and product markets. As a result of divestitures that continued throughout much of the 1990s, Campbell is again using the related constrained multiproduct strategy to create value through operational relatedness.

SOURCES: 2004, Campbell Soup Co., *Reuters*, http://www.reuters.com, December 1; 2004, Campbell Soup, *Standard and Poor's Stock Report*, http://www.standardandpoors.com, November 27; 2004, Campbell Soup Company, About us, Campbell Soup Company Home Page, http://www.campbellsoup.com, December 2.

However, the managerial/leadership challenge increases greatly when a firm diversifies beyond the level of the single-business multiproduct strategy. The risk here is that managers who believe that keeping their top-level positions depends on greater levels of diversification may overdiversify the firm. Similar to business-level strategies, the multiproduct strategy used by the firm should be a function of opportunities in the firm's external environment and the degree to which the firm has core competencies that can create value in product markets beyond its core product market. A firm's board of directors must ensure that the level of diversification top-level managers pursue is based on a match between opportunities in the external environment and the company's core competencies.

The relationship between firm size and executive compensation is the second managerial diversification motive. Research shows that as a firm's size increases, so does the compensation for top-level managers.[32] Of course, increasing a firm's level of diversification increases the firm's overall size. The relationship between firm size and managerial compensation is perhaps not surprising, in that larger, more diversified organizations are more difficult to manage than smaller, less diversified firms.[33] Common sense suggests that more complex and difficult work should be more highly compensated. However, the board of directors desires to use compensation incentives that encourage managers to diversify the firm in value-creating ways rather than compensating them simply on the basis of the firm's size.

In Chapter 5, we noted that after choosing a business-level strategy, the firm must effectively implement it to fully benefit from its use. Organizational structure plays a major role in implementing a strategy. Because of their importance, we next discuss the appropriate organizational structures for implementing the different multiproduct strategies.

Implementing Multiproduct Strategies

We mentioned the multidivisional structure in Chapter 5 and indicated that it is not used to implement business-level strategies. Indeed, the multidivisional structure is used only to implement multiproduct strategies with moderate and high levels of diversification. Firms using the single-business and dominant-business multiproduct strategies still rely on the different forms of the functional structure used to implement the cost leadership strategy or product differentiation strategy. UPS uses a functional structure to implement its business-level strategies in its three product groups. Because UPS is rapidly becoming more diversified, a new structure will be required to implement the related constrained multiproduct strategy. When this happens, UPS will likely discard its functional structure in favor of a form of the multidivisional structure. Indeed, firms often change their multiproduct strategy from dominant-business to a related-diversification strategy (typically related constrained first) as they grow. With the change in strategy, the firm must also change its structure from the functional form to the appropriate form of the multidivisional structure.

The **multidivisional (M-form) structure** is an organizational structure in which the firm is organized to generate either economies of scope or financial economies. The M-form has three versions (see Figure 6.3). As we describe next, the different versions of the M-form are designed to implement multiproduct strategies in firms with moderate to high levels of diversification.

FIGURE 6.3 Three Variations of the Multidivisional Structure

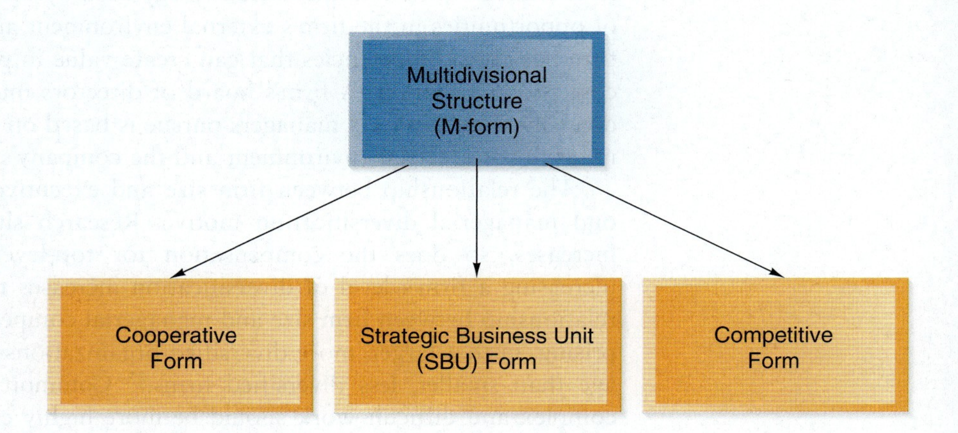

The Cooperative M-Form and the Related Constrained Multiproduct Strategy

The **cooperative M-form** is an organizational structure in which horizontal integration is used so that resources and activities can be shared between product divisions. As you can see in Figure 6.4, firms using the related constrained multiproduct strategy (such as P&G) adopt the cooperative M-form. The product divisions in a firm's M-form structure must cooperate with one another to share resources and activities and generate economies of scope by achieving operational relatedness.[34] Thus, as we noted earlier, P&G's five product divisions share some resources and some activities.

Success with the cooperative M-form is significantly affected by how well product divisions process information about the resources and activities they intend to share and how they intend to share them. *Horizontal linkages* are the mechanisms used to facilitate information sharing between product divisions. One obvious horizontal linkage is holding frequent meetings among product division managers in which they discuss each division's products. In addition, each division head describes his or her division's available resources (especially new ones) and how they are used to complete different activities in the value chain. A key objective of division heads during these meetings is to determine whether two or more divisions' resources could be combined to create an intangible capability that could become a core competence.

Temporary teams or task forces are a second horizontal integrating mechanism. These groups are typically formed for a project that requires sharing the resources and activities of two or more divisions. Developing a new product or finding a way to create more value by completing one or more activities in the value chain are the objectives sought by temporary teams and task forces.

As shown in Figure 6.4, division managers in the cooperative M-form are held accountable for their divisions' performance. Because of this, headquarters personnel should also use compensation systems that reward sharing. As a

FIGURE 6.4 Cooperative Form of the Multidivisional Structure for Implementing the Related Constrained Strategy

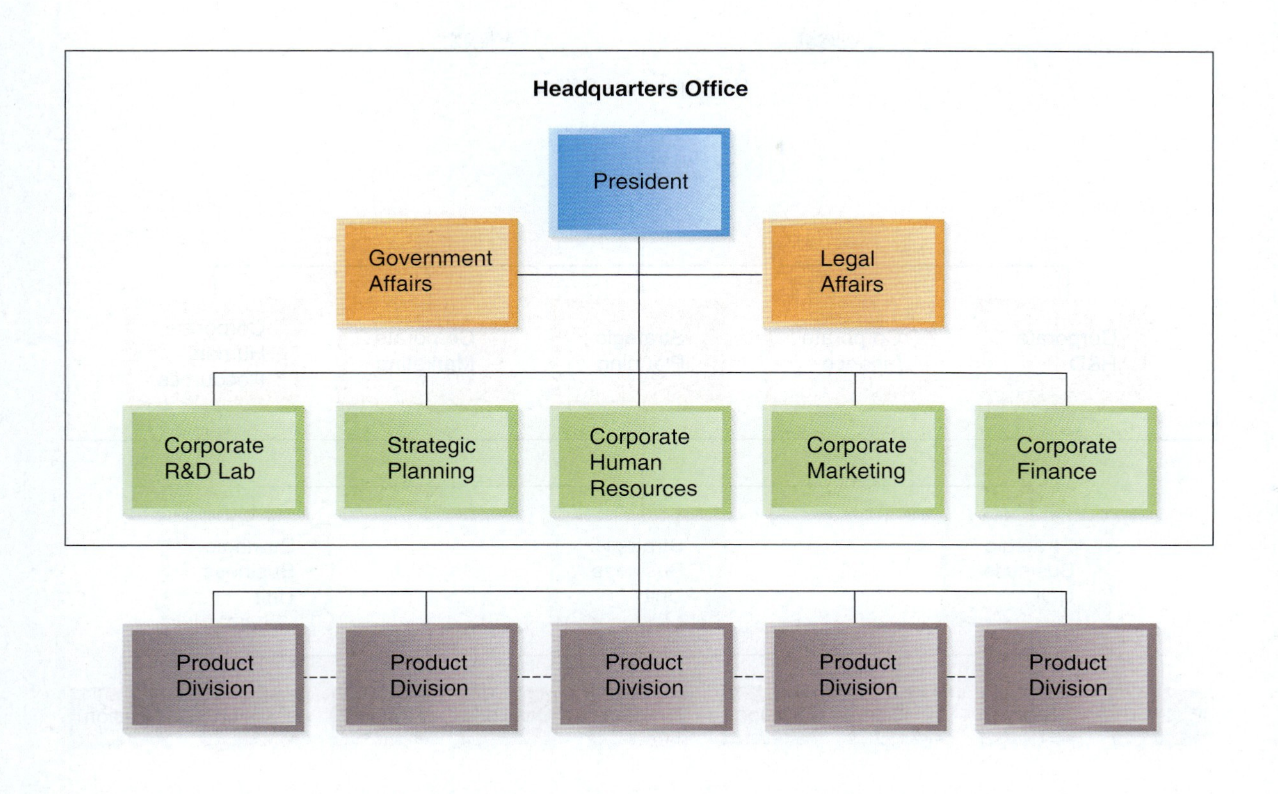

NOTES:
- Structural integration devices create tight links among all divisions
- Corporate office emphasizes centralized strategic planning, human resources, and marketing to foster cooperation between divisions
- R&D is likely to be centralized
- Rewards are subjective and tend to emphasize overall corporate performance in additon to divisional performance
- Culture emphasizes cooperative sharing

result, for example, each division head's compensation might be based on a composite of her division's performance as well as that of the firm's other divisions, especially those that are cooperating on joint product development and management. This type of compensation signals to division heads that each person's success is at least partly a function of the success of cooperation.

The SBU M-Form and the Related Linked Multiproduct Strategy

The **strategic business unit** (SBU) **M-form** is an organizational structure in which the divisions within each SBU concentrate on transferring core competencies rather than on sharing resources and activities. As you can see in Figure 6.5, firms using the related linked multiproduct strategy (such as GE) adopt the SBU M-form.

In the SBU M-form, each SBU is a profit center that is evaluated and controlled by corporate headquarters. Although both strategic controls and financial controls are used (recall our discussion of these two types of controls in

FIGURE 6.5 SBU Form of the Multidivisional Structure for Implementing the Related Linked Strategy

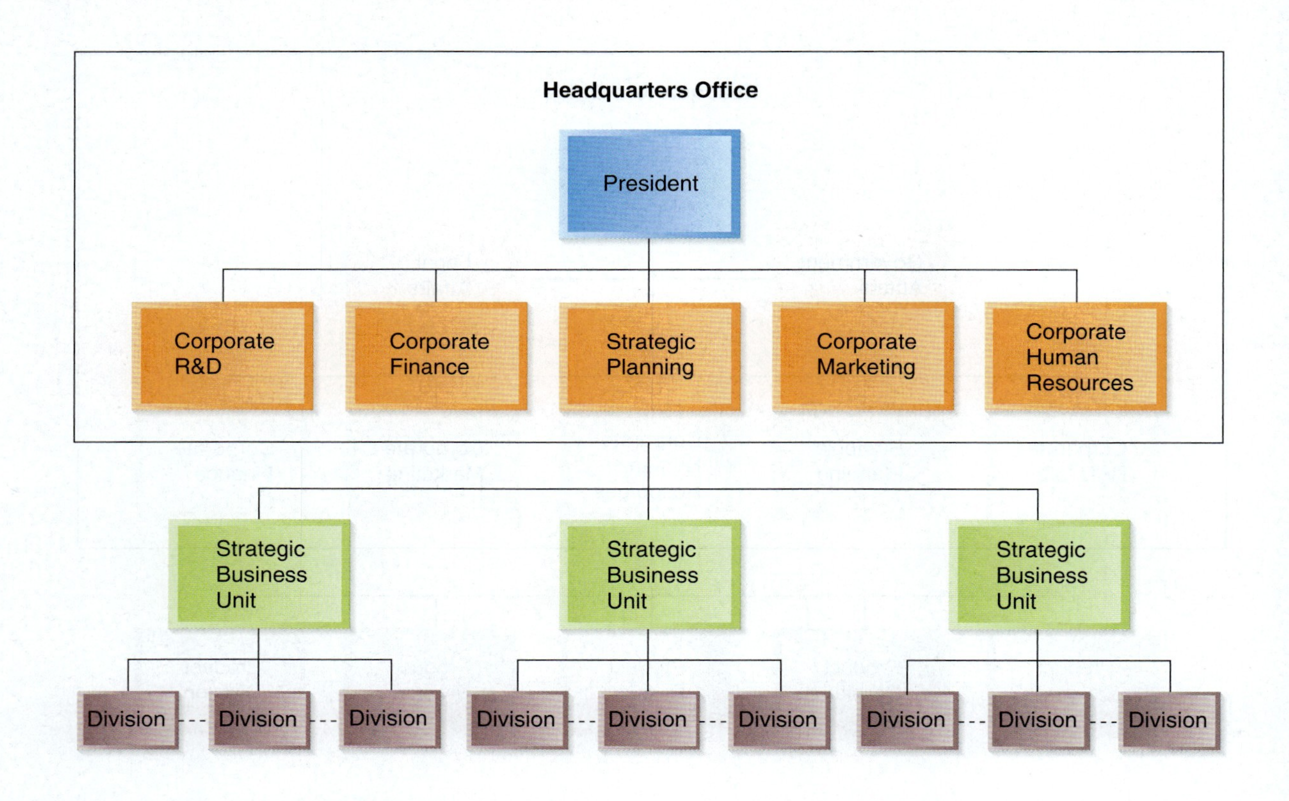

NOTES:
- Structural integration among divisions within SBUs, but independence across SBUs
- Strategic planning may be the most prominent function in headquarters for managing the strategic planning approval process of SBUs for the president
- Each SBU may have its own budget for staff to foster integration
- Corporate headquarters staff serve as consultants to SBUs and divisions, rather than having direct input to product strategy, as in the cooperative form

Chapter 2), financial controls are vital to headquarters' evaluation of each SBU. Strategic controls, on the other hand, are critical when those leading each SBU evaluate the performance of the divisions in their SBU. Strategic controls are also valuable to headquarters personnel as they try to determine whether the businesses the organization has chosen to enter (as shown by its collection of SBUs) are the right ones. As you can imagine, the SBU M-form can be a complex structure. Think of GE's size (11 SBUs with multiple divisions in each SBU). It doesn't take much imagination to conclude that GE's organizational structure is immensely complicated.

The Competitive M-Form and the Unrelated-Diversification Multiproduct Strategy

The **competitive M-form** is an organizational structure in which there is complete independence between the firm's divisions. As shown in Figure 6.6, firms using the unrelated-diversification multiproduct strategy adopt the competitive M-form structure. Recall that with the unrelated-diversification strategy, the

FIGURE 6.6 Competitive Form of the Multidivisional Structure for Implementing the Unrelated-Diversification Strategy

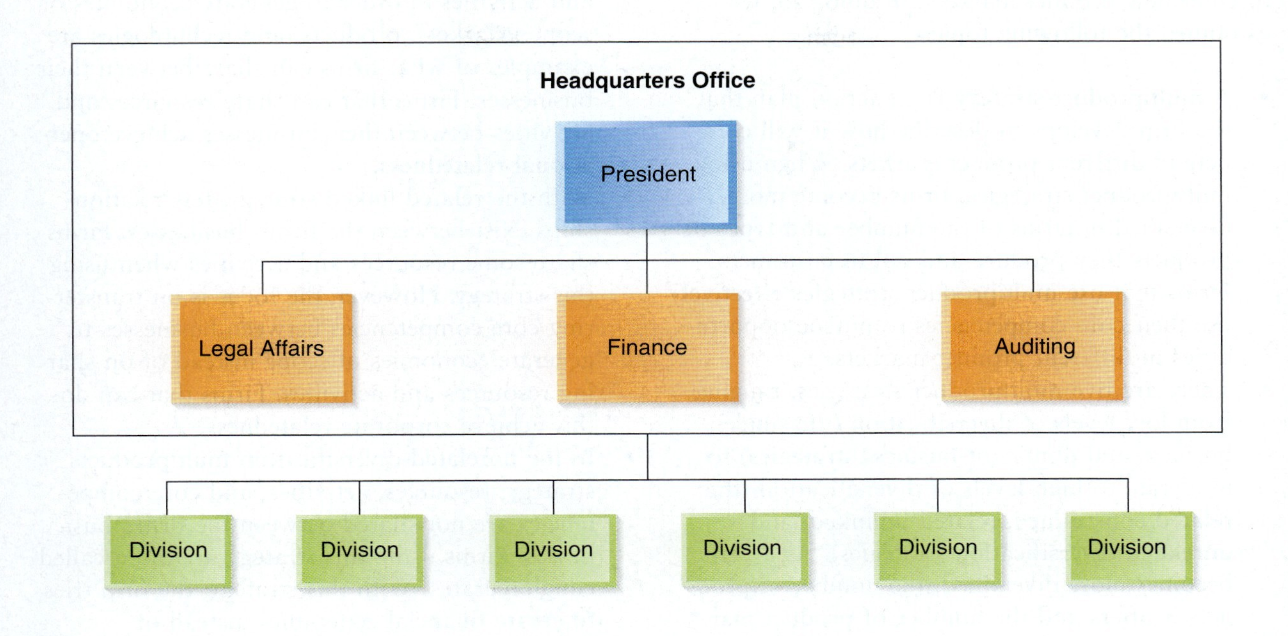

NOTES:
- Corporate headquarters has a small staff
- Finance and auditing are the most prominent functions in the headquarters office to manage cash flow and ensure the accuracy of performance data
- The legal affairs function becomes important when the firm acquires or divests assets
- Divisions are independent and separate for financial evaluation purposes
- Divisions retain strategic control, but cash is managed by the corporate office
- Divisions compete for corporate resources

firm seeks to generate financial economies rather than develop economies of scope through either operational relatedness or corporate relatedness.

Divisions operating in a competitive M-form structure actually compete against one another for the firm's resources. Indeed, an efficient internal capital market allocates resources to the divisions with the greatest probability of generating excess returns on the firm's financial capital. Because of this focus, corporate headquarters personnel make no effort to find ways for sharing to occur between the firm's divisions. Instead, the focus of the headquarters office is on specifying performance criteria that will be used to evaluate the performance of all divisions. At Textron, for example, return on invested capital is the primary criterion used by corporate headquarters to judge the performance of the firm's divisions. According to Textron, "return on invested capital serves as both a compass to guide every investment decision and a measurement of Textron's success."[35]

With the competitive M-form, headquarters personnel rely on strategic controls to establish financial performance criteria; financial controls are then used to monitor divisional performance relative to those criteria. So the focus of headquarters is on performance appraisal, resource allocations, and long-range planning to ensure that the firm's financial capital is being used to maximize financial success.[36]

Summary

The primary purpose of this chapter is to discuss the different multiproduct strategies firms can use to enter new product markets. In doing so, we examined the following topics:

- A **multiproduct strategy** is an action plan that the firm develops to describe how it will compete in different product markets. When using multiproduct strategies, firms become more diversified in terms of the number and types of products they produce and sell to customers. Firms that use multiproduct strategies effectively use their core competencies to pursue opportunities in different product markets.
- There are five multiproduct strategies, ranging from low levels of diversification (the single-business and dominant-business strategies) to moderate to high levels of diversification (the related constrained, related unlinked, and unrelated-diversification strategies). As a firm becomes more diversified, the number of products it offers and the number of product markets in which it competes increase.
- A firm using the single-business multiproduct strategy makes and sells a single product or a variety of a single product and generates at least 95 percent of its sales revenue from its dominant business or product line. As firms continue to develop the ways in which their core competencies can be used to create additional products or to compete in different product markets, they may begin to pursue the dominant-business strategy—a multiproduct strategy through which the firm generates between 70 and 95 percent of its sales revenue from a single business.
- Firms using a related-diversification multiproduct strategy try to create **economies of scope,** which are cost savings that result from successfully sharing some of their resources and activities or core competencies between their different businesses. There are two types of related-diversification multiproduct strategies, both of which suggest that the firm is experiencing a moderate level of diversification. With both strategies, the firm earns less than 70 percent of its sales revenue from its dominant business.
- In the related constrained strategy, most or all of the firm's businesses share some resources and activities in order to generate economies of scope. Markets, products, and technologies are examples of what firms can share between their businesses. Firms that can share resources and activities between their businesses achieve **operational relatedness.**
- With the related linked strategy, few relationships exist between the firm's businesses. Firms share some resources and activities when using this strategy. However, the focus is on transferring core competencies between businesses to generate economies of scope instead of on sharing resources and activities. Firms that can do this achieve **corporate relatedness.**
- In the unrelated-diversification multiproduct strategy, resources, activities, and core competencies are not shared between the firm's businesses. Firms using this strategy are often called conglomerates. With this strategy, the firm tries to create financial economies instead of economies of scope. **Financial economies** are cost savings or higher returns generated when the firm effectively allocates its financial resources based on investments inside or outside the firm. The firm's divisions compete against one another to gain access to a larger share of the entire organization's financial capital. Firms generate financial economies when they successfully allocate their own financial capital across their businesses or by buying other companies, restructuring those firms' assets, and then selling the acquisitions in the marketplace at a profit.
- Managers often have personal motives for increasing the diversification of their firm. For example, increasing the number of product markets in which the firm competes reduces the managers' risk of losing their job (balances firm performance across markets). Additionally, compensation of executives is often related to the size of the firm. Thus, growing the size of the firm through diversification may increase executives' pay. Engaging in a multiproduct strategy for these reasons may or may not create value for the firm's shareholders.

- It is important to match each multiproduct strategy with the proper organizational structure. Firms using the single-business and dominant-business strategies continue to use the functional structure that we discussed in Chapter 5. However, the related- and unrelated-diversification strategies are effectively used only when supported by a version of the **multidivisional structure** (in which the firm is organized to generate either economies of scope or financial economies). The **cooperative M-form** supports the related constrained strategy, the **SBU M-form** supports the related linked strategy and the **competitive M-form** supports the unrelated-diversification multiproduct strategy.

Key Terms

competitive M-form 134
cooperative M-form 132
corporate relatedness 123
economies of scope 121
financial economies 127
multidivisional (M-form) structure 131
multiproduct strategy 118
operational relatedness 123
strategic business unit (SBU) 122
strategic business unit (SBU) M-form 133

Discussion Questions

1. What is a multiproduct strategy? Why do some firms use this strategy?
2. What are the different levels of diversification (from low to high) that firms experience when using a multiproduct strategy?
3. What are the related-diversification multiproduct strategies? How can the firm create value by using these strategies?
4. What is the unrelated-diversification multiproduct strategy? What are the ways that a firm can create value by using this strategy?
5. What are the two additional motives that top-level managers have to diversify their firms?
6. What organizational structure is used to implement each of the different multiproduct strategies?

Endnotes

1. H. Kim, R. E. Hoskisson, & W. P. Wan, 2004, Power dependence, diversification strategy, and performance in Keiretsu member firms, *Strategic Management Journal,* 25: 613–636.
2. W. P. Wan & R. E. Hoskisson, 2003, Home country environments, corporate diversification strategies and firm performance, *Academy of Management Journal,* 46: 27–45.
3. G. T. M. Hult, D. J. Ketchen Jr., & S. F. Slater, 2004, Information processing, knowledge development, and strategic supply chain performance, *Academy of Management Journal,* 47: 241–253.
4. M. E. Porter, 1987, From competitive advantage to corporate strategy, *Harvard Business Review,* 65(3): 43–59.
5. 2003 UPS Annual Report, UPS Home Page, http://www.ups.com, 8.
6. R. Rumelt, 1974, *Strategy, Structure, and Economic Performance,* Boston: Harvard Business School.
7. R. A. Bettis, 1986, The dominant logic: A new linkage between diversity and performance, *Strategic Management Journal,* 7: 485–501.
8. Rumelt, *Strategy, Structure, and Economic Performance.*
9. L. Fauver, J. Houston, & A. Naranjo, 2003, Capital market development, international integration, legal systems, and the value of corporate diversification: A cross-country analysis, *Journal of Financial and Quantitative Analysis,* 38: 135–157.
10. S. Manikutty, 2000, Family business groups in India: A resource-based view of the emerging trends, *Family Business Review,* 3: 279–292.
11. 1997, Inside story, *The Economist,* December 6: 7–9.
12. 2004, P&G products, Procter & Gamble Home Page, http://www.procterandgamble.com, December 15.
13. M. A. Hitt, J. S. Harrison, & R. D. Ireland, 2001, *Mergers and Acquisitions: A Guide to Creating Value for Stakeholders,* New York: Oxford University Press.

14. A. Van Oijen, 2001, Product diversification, corporate management instruments, resource sharing, and performance, *Academy of Management Best Paper Proceedings* (on CD-ROM, Business Policy and Strategy Division).
15. 2005, Our company, GE Home Page, http://www.ge.com, January 11.
16. 2004, GE Commercial Finance and Pitt Ohio Express win Gartner CRM excellence awards, Yahoo Finance, http://www.yahoo.com, October 28.
17. 2005, NBC Universal, GE Home Page, http://www.ge.com, January 11.
18. R. Grover, D. Brady, & T. Lowry, 2004, Lights! Camera! Bean Counters! NBC is set to get its Hollywood studio. Can the GE unit handle the culture clash? *Business Week,* May 17: 82.
19. K. M. Eisenhardt & D. C. Galunic, 2000, Coevolving: At last, a way to make synergies work, *Harvard Business Review,* 78(1): 91–111.
20. R. Schoenberg, 2001, Knowledge transfer and resource sharing as value creation mechanisms in inbound continental European acquisitions, *Journal of Euro-Marketing,* 10: 99–114.
21. Eisenhardt & Galunic, Coevolving, 94.
22. 2005, The Walt Disney Studios, Walt Disney Home Page, http://www.waltdisney.com, January 11.
23. D. D. Bergh, 1997, Predicting divestiture of unrelated acquisitions: An integrative model of ex ante conditions, *Strategic Management Journal,* 18: 715–731.
24. 2004, Textron Inc., *Standard and Poor's Stock Report,* http://www.standardandpoors.com, December 27; M. Maremont, 2004, More can be more, *Wall Street Journal,* October 25: R4.
25. J. Singer & R. G. Matthews, 2004, Investors bid up tobacco, *Wall Street Journal Online,* http://www.wsj.com, October 28.
26. O. E. Williamson, 1975, *Markets and Hierarchies: Analysis and Antitrust Implications,* New York: Macmillan.
27. D. Miller, R. Eisenstat, & N. Foote, 2002, Strategy from the inside out: Building capability-creating organizations, *California Management Review,* 44(3): 37–54.
28. R. E. Hoskisson & M. A. Hitt, 1994, *Downscoping: How to tame the diversified firm.* New York: Oxford University Press.
29. R. E. Hoskisson, R. A. Johnson, D. Yiu, & W. P. Wan, 2001, Restructuring strategies and diversified business groups: Differences associated with country institutional environments, in M. A. Hitt, R. E. Freeman, & J. S. Harrison (eds.), *Handbook of Strategic Management,* Oxford, U.K.: Blackwell, 433–463.
30. D. Brady, 2004, The unsung CEO, *Business Week,* October 25: 76–84.
31. W. Shen & A. A. Cannella Jr., 2002, Power dynamics within top management and their impacts on CEO dismissal followed by inside succession, *Academy of Management Journal,* 45: 717–733.
32. J. J. Cordeiro & R. Veliyath, 2003, Beyond pay for performance: A panel study of the determinants of CEO compensation, *American Business Review,* 21(1): 56–66.
33. J. G. Combs & M. S. Skill, 2003, Managerialist and human capital explanation for key executive pay premiums: A contingency perspective, *Academy of Management Journal,* 46: 63–73.
34. C. C. Markides & P. J. Williamson, 1996, Corporate diversification and organizational structure: A resource-based view, *Academy of Management Journal,* 39: 340–367.
35. 2002, Textron profile, Textron Home Page, http://www.textron.com, February 4.
36. T. R. Eisenmann & J. L. Bower, 2000, The entrepreneurial M-form: Strategic integration in global media firms, *Organization Science,* 11: 348–355.

CHAPTER 7

Mergers and Acquisitions

Reading and studying this chapter should enable you to:

*Knowledge Objectives

1_
Define acquisitions, takeovers, mergers, and acquisition strategy.

2_
Discuss the five basic reasons why firms complete acquisitions.

3_
Describe target screening, target selection, target negotiating, and due diligence.

4_
Understand the importance and process of successful postacquisition business integration.

5_
Discuss the four major pitfalls of acquisitions and remedies for their prevention.

6_
Describe the major restructuring strategies for failed acquisitions.

© Getty Images

Focusing on Strategy

What Makes an Acquisition Successful?

"European banks have been quaking in their boots since last October, when Bank of America swallowed FleetBoston Financial for $47 billion. J. P. Morgan Chase offered even more for Bank One three months later. The Europeans have been slow to merge among themselves—across national borders, at any rate—and fear that big American banks might look across the Atlantic for their next purchases. Some Americans have indeed taken a close look at European targets." (*The Economist*)

Acquisitions are a popular growth strategy for firms competing in many industries. In the banking industry, for example, less restrictive regulations and the sanctioning of branch banking, which permits consumer banking across state lines in the United States as well as across country borders, are contributing to the greater use of the acquisition strategy. As noted in the quote above, two large acquisitions—Bank of America's acquisition of FleetBoston in late 2003 and J. P. Morgan Chase's acquisition of Bank One in 2004—illustrate the use of an acquisition strategy. Transactions such as these between large banks may create economies of scale that often are achieved by combining firms' technology and information systems. After integrating different systems, the larger combined banks can employ powerful systemwide software applications that significantly reduce costs. For example, at the time of its announcement, Wachovia's acquisition of SouthTrust was projected to save $250 million after taxes by cutting 4,300 overlapping jobs (four percent of the combined labor force) and closing 130 to 150 redundant branches.

Firms use an acquisition strategy to compete successfully against their competitors. In the spirits industry, for example, Bacardi, a U.S. producer famous for its rum brands, recently tried to acquire Grey Goose, a dominant vodka producer, to expand its product line. Grey Goose has been growing at a rate of 80 percent annually and has about 50 percent of the market in high-end vodka. If completed, this acquisition would increase Bacardi's strength with distributors relative to Diageo. In 2000, Diageo, a large food and spirits company in the United Kingdom, bought Seagram's liquor business. After this acquisition, Diageo had 25 percent of the U.S. spirits market, compared to Bacardi's eight percent. With larger efficiencies in distribution and power with distributors, Diageo has an advantage relative to Bacardi. Therefore, Bacardi is trying to use an acquisition strategy to gain the product lines, resources, and market power it needs to successfully compete against Diageo.

Acquisitions are also resulting in consolidation in parts of the global retail clothing industry. For example, Philip Green, a billionaire retail entrepreneur, has shaken up the British retail landscape by acquiring nine store chains. As a result of these acquisitions, Green controls about 13 percent of the women's clothing market in the United Kingdom. Green is now targeting Marks & Spencer, a venerable U.K. retailer selling clothing and food. Marks & Spencer also owns King Supermarkets in the United States. If he is able to acquire Marks & Spencer, Green intends to cut costs by using more direct sourcing from overseas factories and more direct purchasing from manufacturers rather than using multiple distributors as Marks & Spencer has traditionally done. Although the Marks & Spencer board has rejected Green's offer, he is determined to buy the admired chain.

SOURCES: 2004, Finance and Economics: Westward, ho!; Retail banking, *The Economist,* May 8, 90; R. D. Atlas, 2004, Wachovia hopes SouthTrust deal repeats success of 2001 merger, *New York Times,* http://www.nytimes.com, June 22; D. K. Berman & C. Mollenkamp, 2004, Wachovia, SouthTrust in talks as hunt for consumers intensifies, *Wall Street Journal,* June 21: A3, A11; A. Dolbeck, 2004, M & A in the U.S., making mergers work, *Weekly Corporate Growth Report,* April 19, 1–3; C. Lawton, 2004, Bacardi aims for vodka shot, *Wall Street Journal,* June 18: B5; C. Mollenkamp, Wachovia to acquire SouthTrust for $13.7 billion, *Wall Street Journal,* June 22: A2; E. White, 2004, Wooing a dowdy retailer, *Wall Street Journal,* June 18: B1, B5.

An **acquisition** is a transaction in which a firm buys a controlling interest in another firm with the intention of either making it a subsidiary business or combining it with its current business or businesses. It is important to understand that for some firms, an acquisition is a "one-time only" event. For example, a firm using a differentiation business-level strategy might decide to acquire only one other company because it has truly specialized skills that the focal firm requires to create unique value for its customers. It is rare, though, for a firm to complete only a single acquisition. Most firms involved with acquisitions form an acquisition strategy. An **acquisition strategy** is an action plan that the firm develops to successfully acquire other companies. An effective acquisition strategy enables significant firm growth.[1] Philip Green (see "Focusing on Strategy") is using an acquisition strategy to establish a prominent competitive position in the United Kingdom's retail clothing industry. Through its acquisition strategy, Green's company has grown to a point where it controls about 13 percent of the women's retail clothing market in the United Kingdom. A **takeover** is a specialized type of acquisition in which the target firm does not solicit the acquiring firm's offer. For instance, in 2004, Comcast made an unsolicited offer to buy (take over) Walt Disney. Disney's board of directors and top-level managers reacted very negatively to the Comcast bid. When a target firm reacts negatively to a proposal, the proposed transaction is called a *hostile takeover.* A **merger** is a transaction in which firms agree to combine their operations on a relatively equal basis. For example, DaimlerChrysler was created by the merger between Daimler-Benz and Chrysler. Mergers are more common than takeovers, while acquisitions are more common than mergers. Because of their frequency of use, our focus in this chapter is on acquisitions and the acquisition strategy. However, we also describe some mergers.

You may not be surprised to learn that the number of acquisitions being completed with firms from different countries (called *cross-border acquisitions*) continues to increase (see Chapter 8). Relaxed regulations and improved trade relations among various countries are contributing to the growth of cross-border acquisitions such as the one between Daimler-Benz and Chrysler. In the European Union, as more countries have been added, the number of regulations and restrictions between firms in these countries has been reduced. As home markets mature, it is expected that governments would facilitate the efforts of firms in their country to seek growth in other countries' markets.

Although the number of opportunities to complete cross-border acquisitions is increasing, it is important to understand that these transactions are challenging. Among the challenges are the difficulties of screening firms, selecting a target firm, and then negotiating with target firm managers. Differences in languages and cultures require understanding and sensitivity from both sides of the transaction.

We think the trend of cross-border acquisitions will continue for years to come. What do you think? Do you think working for a company completing a cross-border acquisition would be exciting as well as challenging?

We use Figure 7.1 as the framework for this chapter's discussion of acquisitions and the acquisition strategy. First, we describe the five major reasons firms complete acquisitions. We then examine target screening and selection, target negotiating, and due diligence. We discuss four questions firms should answer when engaging in due diligence. Our attention then turns to what should be done to successfully integrate the target firm into the acquiring firm. We discuss four major pitfalls to successful integration and what firms can do to avoid them. In spite of good intentions, acquisitions sometimes fail. We close the chapter with a discussion of what firms do when this happens.

FIGURE 7.1 Acquisition Decision-Making and Business Integration Processes

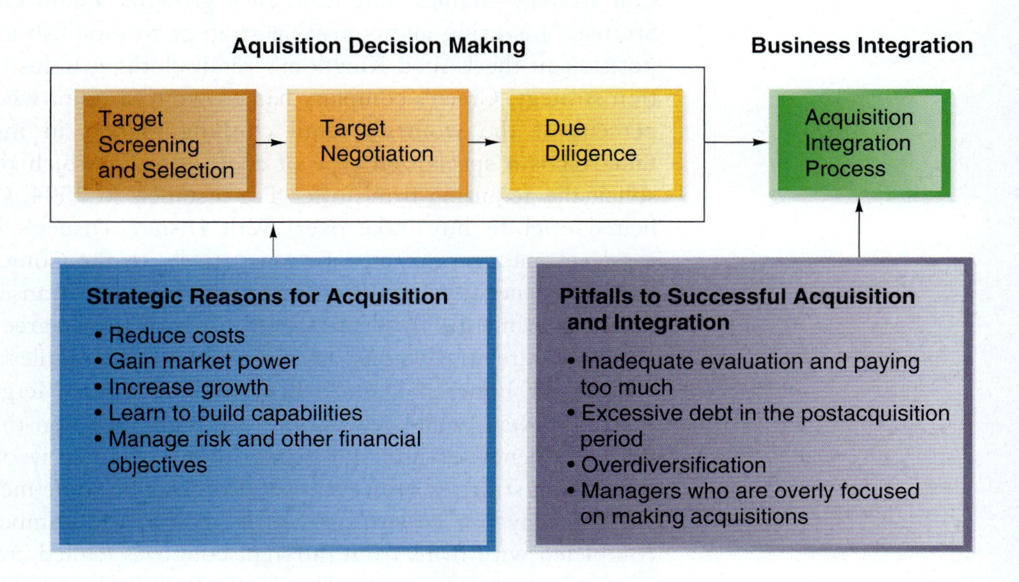

Reasons for Acquisitions

Firms complete acquisitions and use an acquisition strategy for many reasons. We discuss five major reasons in the following sections.

Reduce Costs

Firms often use horizontal acquisitions to reduce costs. A **horizontal acquisition** is the purchase of a competitor competing in the same market or markets as the acquiring firm. A manufacturer of women's shoes buying a competitor that also makes women's shoes is an example of a horizontal acquisition.

Firms gain scale economies through horizontal acquisitions. This is one reason why so many horizontal acquisitions take place in the pharmaceuticals industry. As you might imagine, the ability to combine two firms' R&D skills often drives horizontal acquisitions between pharmaceuticals firms. Let's consider the experiences of Aventis with horizontal acquisitions to demonstrate this point.

Aventis, a large French drug manufacturer, is the largest producer of vaccines in its home country. Swiss drug maker Novartis AG wanted to acquire Aventis, primarily to gain access to its competitor's R&D skills. Stalling this transaction was the French government's hesitancy to allow a Swiss company to buy Aventis and thereby gain control over the production of many vaccines used in France. Ultimately, Sanofi, another French drug maker, agreed to purchase Aventis for more than $65 billion, a price greater than what Novartis offered. At the time, the newly formed firm, Sanofi-Aventis, was the third-largest drug producer in the world, behind Pfizer and GlaxoSmithKline PLC (both of which increased their size through acquisitions as well).[2] Sanofi-Aventis believes that combining its complementary skills through this horizontal acquisition makes it a formidable competitor to the industry's other two giants.

A **vertical acquisition** is the purchase of a supplier or distributor of one or more of a firm's goods or services.[3] Vertical acquisitions can also be used to increase scale and to gain market power, which is discussed in the next section. Rupert Murdoch built News Corporation and continues to manage it today. He began acquiring British newspapers in the 1970s, and then began an acquisition program in the United States in 1976 when he acquired the *New York Post*. Books (HarperCollins), magazines (*TV Guide*), television networks (Fox), and movie studios (Twentieth Century Fox) have been added to create News Corporation. Murdoch acquired a controlling interest in DirecTV by offering $6.6 billion to buy General Motors' 20 percent stake in Hughes Electronics. The acquisition of DirecTV by News Corporation is a vertical acquisition, as DirecTV is a satellite TV company through which News Corporation can distribute more of its media content: news, movies, and television shows.[4]

Gain Market Power

Market power exists when the firm sells its products above competitive prices or when its costs are below those of its primary competitors. Firms commonly use horizontal and vertical acquisitions to gain market power. Horizontal acquisitions have been used in the business software industry. Declines in corporate spending because of the global economic malaise in the early part of the twenty-first century influenced the use of horizontal acquisitions in this industry. Because of declining demand for its products, the business software industry continues to suffer from overcapacity. Acquisitions enable the acquiring firm to reduce overcapacity by eliminating duplicate operations during the integration process.

An opportunity to reduce overcapacity may have influenced Oracle's hostile takeover bid and ultimate acquisition of rival PeopleSoft. After Oracle announced its bid for PeopleSoft, Microsoft and SAP, two other large players in the technology infrastructure and application software area, discussed a possible merger. Antitrust concerns prevented serious pursuit of this proposed merger, however. Nonetheless, the highly visible nature of the announced acquisition (involving Oracle and PeopleSoft) and possible merger (involving Microsoft and SAP) signaled the need for smaller firms in this industry to do something to be able to compete against the market power these transactions would create for the two newly formed firms (if the proposed transactions were completed). Some feel that these proposed transactions sent a message to smaller competitors that they needed to "eat or be eaten."[5]

BMC Software seems to understand this message. Acquiring firms with software applications to run on mainframe computers created

Craig Conway, former Peoplesoft CEO, was opposed to the takeover of the company by Oracle and its CEO, Larry Ellison, which occurred in January 2005. The combined companies will now represent more applications and database customers than any other company in the world.

some market power for BMC in its competitive battles with IBM and Computer Associates. BMC's sales grew to $1.7 billion in 2000. However, the firm then began to lose ground, as shown by a decline in its sales revenue to $1.42 billion in 2003. This sales decline suggests that BMC no longer has adequate market power. To address this competitive disadvantage, the firm acquired five additional companies beginning in 2002. Each horizontal acquisition was completed so that BMC could couple its current software with "tools to predict failures and automate fixes so computers one day might remotely patch errant systems without the need for costly technicians."[6] BMC hopes these acquisitions will help it regain lost market power.

However, pursuing market power can be problematic as well. As "Understanding Strategy" suggests, firms can pay too much for an acquisition as they compete to gain market power and the larger share of a market.

Increase Growth

Some industries have significant fragmentation, with many small competitors of equal size. In these instances, some firms use an acquisition strategy to increase their growth rate relative to competitors.[7] Sports Authority's merger with Gart Sports in 2003 demonstrates how this is happening in the sporting-goods retail market. Similarly, Russell and Reebok have acquired equipment companies to expand their apparel businesses. K2, a sports equipment maker, is responding to this consolidation in segments that surround its sporting goods market. Richard Heckman, CEO of K2, is seeking to grow in the sporting-goods equipment industry as Nike and Germany's Adidas-Salomon AG and Reebok International have grown and come to dominate the athletic footwear and apparel businesses. Since 2002, K2 has completed five acquisitions. Furthermore, K2 has agreements to purchase ski maker Volkl Sports Holding AG and Marker Group (a ski bindings manufacturer) as well as Marrot Mountain (an outdoor apparel company). Although K2 started out as a winter sports gear company, it now has 35 brands, which has resulted in the firm's becoming a year-round sports equipment manufacturer and distributor. As Heckman notes, "you don't drive growth from cutting costs, you do it from revenue synergy."[8]

In another example, MGM Mirage has an agreement to acquire Mandalay Resort Group. The acquisition would create the largest casino company in the industry. This acquisition would enable MGM Mirage to grow by expanding its operations and the opportunity to expand along the Las Vegas strip. Mandalay owns a large percentage of the land still available for development in the strip area and had been planning to use some of its land to build a huge beach-theme resort complex. Potential opposition from antitrust regulators is the major hurdle with this proposed acquisition. If the proposed acquisition is allowed, the combined company could control half of the 72,000-room capacity of the Las Vegas strip hotels. If regulators define competition more broadly than the Las Vegas market, then the acquisition is likely to be approved.[9]

Learn to Build Capabilities

Learning from a target firm and building new capabilities are more reasons firms acquire other companies. Target companies often have unique employee skills, organizational technologies, or superior knowledge that are available to

learning from failure

understanding strategy:

THE LACK OF SUCCESS IN LARGE FOOD COMPANY MERGERS HAS PRODUCED CAUTION AMONG INVESTORS REGARDING FURTHER ACQUISITIONS

Several acquisitions of larger food companies were completed during 2000 and 2001. Kellogg acquired Keebler Foods, Philip Morris (now Altria Group) purchased Nabisco, and Diageo acquired Pillsbury, a part of General Foods. There is speculation that General Mills, Campbell Soup, and Heinz may be acquired next. These midsize firms lack the market power of their larger competitors in dealing with strong distributors and retailers (such as Wal-Mart). To reduce their distributors' and retailers' power, some of these firms may merge or agree to be acquired.

However, complications surround these potential transactions. Nestle, which already has a joint venture with General Mills outside the United States focused on cereals, could make an acquisition a long-term goal by buying a piece of General Mills through Diageo. Nestle's goal of growing in health products does not necessarily fit with the bulk of General Mills' products. Additionally, an acquisition of General Mills would likely increase Nestle's debt by six times and thereby threaten its triple-A credit rating. Kraft may have difficulty acquiring General Mills as well because General Mills' recent purchase of another food company, Keebler, may disturb antitrust authorities. Furthermore, Kraft desires smaller acquisitions in its healthy food categories and in areas where it needs additional scale, such as beverages, snacks, and convenience meals. Similarly, Unilever, the largest food company in Europe, is still paying down its $24 billion in debt due to an acquisition of Best Foods in 2000.

In addition, because the market has been disappointed by previous deals, potential shareholders may be unimpressed by the low returns they are likely to receive from the "value-destroying deals" made earlier by these companies. So firms announcing an acquisition might experience a significant decrease in their stock price.

Although General Mills' stock is priced low, its stock has not gained relative to gains in general stock market averages; this lack of performance may suggest to investors that it is unlikely to provide the growth necessary to increase stock prices in the potential acquiring firms. Accordingly, these deals will probably not be made any time soon even though pressure continues for additional transactions. Usually a premium is required to acquire another firm. Currently, though, those investing in firms in the food industry may not support the idea of their firm paying a premium to buy another firm in this low-margin industry. In slightly different words, shareholders of firms in the food industry may feel that acquisition targets are not worth the price that their firm might have to pay to acquire another firm in this industry. In summary, although there are reasons for continued acquisitions, there are also a number of reasons why such acquisitions are not likely to occur among large food companies.

SOURCES: D. Ball & J. Adamy, 2004, Don't ring up a sale of General Mills Inc. just yet, *Wall Street Journal,* June 7: C1, C2; A. Bary, 2004, Cereal appeal: General Mills and Nestle? *Barron's,* June 7: 14.

© Noah Berger/Bloomberg News/Landov

A leader in networking for the Internet, Cisco Systems, founded by a small group of computer scientists in 1984, now has more than 34,000 employees worldwide. Headquarters are in San Jose, California.

the acquiring firm only through acquisitions. Additionally, pooling the companies' combined resources and capabilities may enable development of new "centers of excellence" for specialized products in new markets. Cisco Systems, Microsoft, and Intel are examples of firms completing technology-driven acquisitions to build their capabilities.[10]

"Building capabilities" through acquisitions is a future-oriented reason to complete acquisitions compared to the reasons of reducing costs, gaining market power, and increasing growth. The first three reasons for acquisitions are about exploiting current advantages, while learning how to build the firm's capabilities is about exploring to create tomorrow's advantages. In general, exploitation was the base for many acquisitions in the 1980s and 1990s, while financial reasons (discussed next) influenced acquisitions in the 1970s. It appears that capability-building acquisitions are a dominant reason for many acquisitions in the first decade of the twenty-first century.[11]

Manage Risk and Other Financial Objectives

Facing stiff competition, some firms choose to use acquisitions to diversify their operations, thereby reducing their dependence on performance in an intensely competitive market. Many years ago, GE diversified away from the consumer electronics market into financial services to reduce its dependence on the consumer electronics area. Furthermore, GE has diversified into other service areas rather than basing its revenue solely on industrial products.[12] At times, firms also make acquisitions to gain access to tax advantages or to reduce business or financial risk. Of course, such acquisitions need to be done in a way that cannot be replicated by shareholders through portfolio diversification.

Screening, Selecting, and Negotiating with Target Firms

Research suggests that financial acquirers (such as Kohlberg Kravis Roberts [KKR]) experience higher valuations in their acquisitions than do corporate acquisitions.[13] Financial acquirers such as leverage buyout (defined later in the chapter) firms often complete two or three acquisitions per year. However, these firms may explore as many as 400 or 500 possibilities and examine closely perhaps 25 targets before selecting the four or five transactions they'll actually complete. Acquisition opportunities can come without warning and usually need to be quickly evaluated. Accordingly, it is important for firms to balance the need to think strategically with the need to react to an acquisition opportunity in a timely way. Cisco Systems, a network gear manufacturer that has completed a large number of acquisitions, may examine three potential markets and decide to enter only one of them, and may evaluate five to ten candidates for each deal that it closes. This extra amount of screening enables the acquiring party to identify the acquisition opportunities that exist while at the same time determining the right price. Although this process takes time, it helps managers develop experience in screening, and over time they can increase the speed *and* effectiveness of the screening process.

To focus too strongly on an "exciting" opportunity and set aside the firm's basic strategy can be a major mistake. It is often problematic when one of the senior executives "falls in love" with a target firm and everyone else falls in line, knowing that "we are going to do this deal." After the screening process is completed in a rational and strategic way, negotiations are initiated.

Key issues requiring careful analysis should be identified early in the negotiating process. For instance, it is important to clarify what role the top executives will play in the newly combined organization. Determining the executive positions needed in the newly created firm and who will fill those positions is an important topic for negotiating.

Because most proposed transactions are greeted with skepticism by those in the target firm, acquirers with experience often try to develop a spirit of cooperation to negotiate a mutually beneficial transaction. A cooperative relationship between personnel in the acquiring and acquired firms is the foundation on which the most serious issues can be successfully negotiated. Table 7.1 provides a list of suggestions that are helpful in the negotiation process. In particular, government officials may also need to be included in order to successfully negotiate a deal, especially in cross-border transactions.

Considerations in Successful Acquisition (Including Cross-Border) Negotiation Processes

1. Be very clear about the strategic logic behind the proposed acquisitions.
2. Be patient, acting decisively when needed but in a way that does not create emotion. Take a long term view, which often runs counter to the strategic objective among participants in the negotiation process.
3. Seek to develop government, industry, and company contacts well before the transaction takes place.
4. Identify the potential players in the proposed deal-making process, including government administrators. Understand who will be for the deal and differentiate between those who will be unconditionally opposed and those whose objectives can be met in the negotiation process.
5. Understand who will defer to which group and sequence the negotiation process in a way that will maximize the chance of success.
6. Think about how you will negotiate with potential deal blockers and how you can give them a vision that meets your needs while enabling them to persuade others among their constituents of the transaction's value for their particular group's interests.
7. Act to ensure the sustainability of the deal. Remember that once the transaction is completed, negotiations are not finished. Integration between deal participants can be facilitated by taking a long-term view of the participants involved.

SOURCES: Adapted from J. K. Sebenius, 2002, The hidden challenge of cross-border negotiations, *Harvard Business Review,* 80(3): 76–85; J. K. Sebenius, 1998, Negotiating cross-border acquisitions, *Sloan Management Review,* 39(2): 27–41.

Due Diligence

Due diligence is the rational process by which acquiring firms evaluate target firms. Due diligence is concerned with verifying that the reason for the proposed transaction is sound strategically and financially. To understand how to improve due diligence, Bane and Company, a strategy consulting firm, studied 20 companies, both private and public, known for the quality of their due diligence processes. We summarize the results of their research into four basic questions around which an acquiring firm's due diligence efforts should be framed.[14]

What Is the Acquiring Firm Really Buying?

Acquiring firms frequently form a team to pursue due diligence. Rather than relying on what might be biased secondary sources for information, the due diligence team should build its own "bottom-up view" of the target firm and its industry. To do this, the team collects information from multiple parties, including customers, suppliers, and competitors. This information helps the team carefully examine each assumption the acquiring firm has made about the target and its value.

Studying customers and suppliers enables the due diligence team to answer important questions about the target firm, such as the following: is the target customer group growing? Has the target firm fully explored the needs of its target customers? What distribution channels is the target firm using to serve customers? Are superior channels available? Has the target firm negotiated favorable deals with its suppliers? If not, why hasn't it done so?

Analyzing competitors is another important source of information when it comes to understanding what the acquiring firm may buy. Important questions to pose in terms of the target firm's competitors include the following: is the target firm more profitable than its competitors? In what part of the value chain are most of the profits made? Is the target underperforming its competitors in the key parts of the value chain? How will the target firm's competitors react to an acquisition, and how might this influence competition between the target and its competitors?

Finally, the due diligence team should assess the target firm's capabilities. This is done by considering a host of questions: Does the target have cost advantages relative to its competitors? How could the target's cost position help the acquiring firm's cost position? Could the target's capabilities be used to create sources of differentiation? If so, how valuable would those be and how long would it take to develop those capabilities?

The due diligence team's answers about what the firm is really buying are studied to ensure that no "deal breakers" exist and to verify that the proposed transaction is logical strategically. On a positive note, answering this question sometimes uncovers more expected value for the proposed acquisition than originally anticipated.

What Is the Target Firm's Value?

Acquisitions can be glamorous, a fact that sometimes biases decision makers to quickly conclude that a proposed acquisition is virtually without potential flaws. To thwart this bias, the due diligence team must assess the target's true financial value. True financial value is determined through an objective, unemotional process.

An objective analysis verifies the absence of accounting anomalies at the target firm. Accounting anomalies may signal problems and possibly unethical decisions as well. The team should consider rapid and significant increases in sales revenue a possible accounting anomaly. As we know, rapid and significant increases in sales revenue may be a function of dramatically lower sales prices rather than true growth. While dramatically reducing prices to sell more products makes revenue look good in the current time period, such sales can't be sustained. Of course, the acquiring firm is very interested in future sales when evaluating a target firm. Another accounting anomaly occurs when the firm treats recurring items as extraordinary costs, thus keeping them off the profit-and-loss statement. These and other accounting anomalies must be stripped away to reveal the historical and projected cash flows. The only way to accomplish this is for the due diligence team to extensively interact with target firm personnel about entries to the target's financial statements. Given your knowledge of accounting and finance, what other anomalies do you think might surface when an acquiring firm works to determine a target firm's true financial value? What should be done to deal with the anomalies you have identified?

Where Are the Synergies between the Combined Firms?

Although evaluating the target firm to determine its actual value is wise, caution must be exercised when doing so. The due diligence team should also evaluate the target in light of the synergies that might be created by integrating the target with the acquiring firm. This evaluation should identify specific synergies that might be created, the probability of developing the synergies, and the time and investment required to do so. Acquisitions often fail because of an inability to obtain expected synergies, an outcome that highlights the importance of carefully studying proposed synergies and their costs.

What Is the Acquiring Firm's Walk-Away Offer Price?

The emotional pressure to make an acquisition can be significant. Think of the pressure executives in the acquiring firm might encounter once a proposed transaction is announced to the press. Extensive coverage highlights a transaction's visibility and can make it harder for the acquiring firm to walk away from the possible deal. However, as we would expect, successful acquisitions result from logical, not emotional decisions. To increase the probability that a rational decision will be made, the acquiring firm should develop a purchase price it will not exceed. To do this, the acquiring firm must determine who makes the top-price decision and the decision criteria he or she will use. These determinations should be made before final negotiations begin. Additionally, creating incentive systems for those negotiating transactions can be fruitful. For example, Clear Channel Communications, an international radio, billboard, and live entertainment company, has an incentive system that is focused on an acquisition's results. Thus, Clear Channel's integration teams' compensation is partly based on the profitability of the completed acquisitions.

Based on the results of its due diligence process, the acquiring firm decides whether it will acquire the target firm. If the acquisition is completed, the focus shifts to what must be done to integrate the acquired firm into the acquiring firm's operations. We discuss this topic next.

Integrating the Newly Acquired Business

The activities leading to an acquisition decision (target screening, target selection, target negotiating, and due diligence) influence the success of individual acquisitions as well as acquisition strategies. However, in the final analysis, a particular acquisition will succeed or fail on the basis of how well the target firm and acquiring firm integrate their operations.[15] Integration success is more likely when an integration team, including employees from the acquiring firm and the acquired firm, is formed and charged with full responsibility to integrate the two companies to create value. In "Understanding Strategy," we describe Hilton Hotels' purchase of Promus Hotel Corporation. As you'll see, these firms successfully integrated their operations.

Although there are many difficulties in implementing acquisitions, as acquiring and target firms begin to integrate their operations, unanticipated opportunities for creating new value may be discovered. This is especially true for firms bent on learning from each other or where complementary assets are brought together in ways that enable such value creation.[16] Other research suggests that creating a culture of a merger of "equals" is likely to reinforce existing organizational identities and create expectations for strict equality.[17] Instead, it is suggested that the organization develop a new identity by asking the question, "Who are we?" instead of framing an acquisition or merger as a combination of equals.[18] If the integration process is carried out thoroughly and appropriately, opportunities are likely for increased growth as learning occurs.[19] In a merger such as that between Sears and Kmart, firms with different retail cultures, it will be important not only to perform integration activities well, but also to establish a joint brand that will enable better differentiation than both firms have currently. They will be in a difficult battle with the likes of Wal-Mart, Target, and Best Buy, who have better-recognized brands for value creation in the consumer's mind.[20]

After filing bankruptcy in January 2002, Kmart closed more than 300 stores. Will its recent merger with Sears be beneficial for both companies?

© Getty Images

Pitfalls in Pursuing Acquisitions and Their Prevention

The importance of successful integration in the postacquisition period cannot be overestimated.[21] Because combined firms often lose target firm managers through turnover, it is important to retain key executives and other valuable human capital, especially if the acquiring firm wants to gain new skills from the acquired firm.[22] In addition, because much of an organization's knowledge is contained in its human capital,[23] turnover of key personnel from the acquired firm should be avoided.[24] Involving these employees in the

learning from success

understanding strategy:

HILTON HOTELS' SUCCESSFUL ACQUISITION OF PROMUS HOTEL CORPORATION

In 1999, Hilton Hotels' CEO and co-chairman, Stephen F. Bollenbach, spearheaded the acquisition of Promus Hotel Corporation, owner of several midpriced hotel chains. At the time, the transaction seemed risky, because the cash and stock acquisition valued at $3.7 billion pushed Hilton's debt significantly higher to a total of $5.5 billion. Concerned about the transaction and its potential effects on earnings, investors pushed Hilton's stock price down seven percent. At the time, a number of analysts were concerned about the "fit" of Promus's midpriced hotel chains (such as Hampton Inn, Doubletree, Homewood Suites, and Embassy Suites) with Hilton's luxury brands (such as Hilton's Waldorf-Astoria in New York and Palmer House in Chicago).

However, six-plus years later, this acquisition is yielding impressive dividends for Hilton shareholders. Hilton now generates one-third of its sales and profits from the brands it purchased from Promus. Hilton now owns 2,185 franchise hotels versus the 269 it owned before the Promus acquisition. On sales of $4.1 billion, Hilton's 2004 earnings were expected to be $214 million, up 30 percent from 2003's earnings.

What is contributing to this successful acquisition? As you have imagined, there are several keys to this acquisition's success. One key is the complex reservation system the newly formed firm was able to create by integrating the capabilities of the formerly independent hotel chains. This system enables the seven Hilton hotel brands to operate in a unified way. A reservation operator who receives a request for a Hilton property that is full can secure a reservation for the customer at another Hilton facility that is close to the location of the customer's first choice. This cross-selling of Hilton brands is generating more than $300 million in revenue each year.

Other actions were taken to integrate the acquired and acquiring firm. The HHonors loyalty program was expanded to include customers using the former Promus brands. Also, franchisees can offer rooms on the central Hilton Web site at the same price as third-party Web sites such as Expedia and Travelocity. The technology improvement program has created kiosks in major locations where guests can do self check-in and get a room key in the lobby. The kiosks also enable guests to book rooms online they'll use in the future. This acquisition is the source of Hilton's ability to grow at an average annual return of 12.5 percent from 2001 to 2003. This growth rate is superior to those of rivals Marriott International and Starwood Hotels and Resorts Worldwide.

SOURCES: 2004, Hilton Hotels Home Page, http://www.hilton.com, October 24; C. Palmeri & C. Yang, 2004, The light is on at Hilton, *Business Week*, June 28: 66–68; J. Barsky & L. Nash, 2003, Improved loyalty programs target a dwindling number of travelers, *Hotel and Motel Management*, July 7: 16; M. Frankel, 1999, Hilton's buy brings only yawns, *Business Week*, September 20: 43.

integration process reduces the likelihood that they will leave the newly combined firm.

History tells us that acquisitions are risky. However, learning how to deal positively with prominent pitfalls increases the chance of acquisition success. Next, we discuss four major pitfalls.

Inadequate Evaluation and Paying Too Much

As we've discussed, effective due diligence is important in ensuring that once negotiations start, a rational approach is used. We also highlighted the importance of the acquiring firm's establishing a price above which it will not go. Notwithstanding due diligence and the use of investment bankers to help with this process, many firms still become too romantic about acquiring the target, with the result being that they pay too much for it. Research suggests that "a combination of cognitive biases and organizational pressures leads managers to make overly optimistic forecasts in analyzing proposals for major investments" such as acquisitions.[25] *Anchoring* (quickly becoming committed to a position and being highly resistant to changing it) and overconfidence in one's opinion are two examples of cognitive biases that may surface during an acquisition process. Regardless of the causes, those evaluating a target firm as an acquisition candidate must ensure that the acquiring firm's evaluation of that target is complete and that the acquiring firm doesn't overpay to acquire the target.

Excessive Debt in the Postacquisition Period

As illustrated in "Understanding Strategy," many companies in the food industry have significantly increased their debt levels. As we discussed, it is unlikely that Nestle will acquire General Mills or another large target anytime soon because additional debt would probably threaten Nestle's credit rating. When credit rating agencies such as Moody's and Standard and Poor's reduce a firm's credit rating, the firm will likely incur higher costs to obtain additional financial capital. This makes sense, because firms with lower credit ratings are thought to be riskier investments. And, as we know, investors expect higher returns from risky investments. An acquiring firm should also remember that if its debt load becomes too high, it will have less cash to invest in R&D, human resources, and marketing.[26] Investments in these organizational functions are important parts of what the firm does to be successful in the long term.

Overdiversification

Frequent acquisitions help meet capital markets' expectations for the firm to grow and have the potential to increase top-level managers' salaries. Top-level managers' salaries tend to increase with increases in the firm's overall size. Therefore, capital markets and the relationship between organizational size and salaries for top-level managers may influence top-level managers to make frequent acquisitions. This can be problematic, though, in that firms can become too diversified. When this happens, a firm is said to be overdiversified. In the late 1990s and early 2000s, a number of media companies such as AOL Time Warner, Vivendi, and Bertelsmann completed several acquisitions that did not turn out well. A number of analysts concluded that these firms had become overdiversified, a condition that makes it very difficult for the firm to effectively manage each successive acquisition. The response to overdiversification is for the firm to divest acquisitions that it can't successfully manage. Vivendi has indeed divested a number of the firms it acquired during the late 1990s and early 2000s.[27]

Managers Who Are Overly Focused on Making Acquisitions

Acquisitions require significant managerial time and energy. Managers have opportunity costs for the time and energy spent searching for viable acquisitions, completing due diligence, preparing for and participating in negotiations, and managing the integration process after an acquisition is completed. Time and energy spent to deal with potential acquisitions obviously can't be spent on managing other aspects of the firm's operations. Furthermore, when acquisition negotiations are initiated, target firm managers often operate in suspended animation until the acquisition and integration processes are completed.[28] Therefore, it is important for managers to encourage dissent when evaluating an acquisition target. If failure occurs, leaders are tempted to blame it on others or on unforeseen circumstances. Rather, it is important that managers recognize when they are overly involved in the acquisition process. "The urge to merge is still like an addiction in many companies: doing deals is much more fun and interesting than fixing fundamental problems. So, as in dealing with any other addictions or temptations maybe it is best to just say no."[29]

In Table 7.2, we summarize the four major pitfalls of acquisitions and present possible preventive actions firms can take to avoid a pitfall or to reduce the negative consequences experienced because of a pitfall. As suggested in the table and as we've discussed, it is important for the firm to establish a rational due diligence process and to make certain that the walk-away offer price is fixed when there is temptation to surpass the rational price to pay for a target firm. Paying too much often happens when there are many bidders; this is called the "winner's curse" in the research literature.[30] Similarly, in regard to the problem of taking on too much debt, it is important to ensure that the firm has enough cash on hand and debt capacity to complete the transaction at or

TABLE 7.2 Major Pitfalls of Acquisitions and Their Prevention

Pitfall	Prevention
Paying too much	Establish rational due diligence processes with a walk-away offer price and make certain that when this price is reached, managers involved do walk away.
Taking on too much debt	Ensure that the firm has adequate cash as well as debt capacity to complete the transaction at or below the walk-away offer price.
Becoming overdiversified	Understand fully the nature of synergy in the acquisition and the integration processes necessary to achieve it. Also, ensure that any unrelated transactions are justified based on strong financial rationales. However, even when such justification is in place, the deal may not be positive for strategic-fit reasons because it may lead to overdiversification. Therefore, make certain that strategic fit does not lead to overdiversification.
Managers who are overly focused on acquisitions	Establish checks and balances so that top managers are challenged by the board and other stakeholders regarding proposed acquisitions. These actions are especially important in firms making frequent acquisitions.

below the established walk-away offer price. Regarding the possibility of becoming overdiversified, it is necessary for managers to fully understand the nature of synergy and the actions necessary to create it in the business integration stage. Even if there are potential synergies and the transaction is justified based on its expected financial outcomes, a deal may not be good to execute due to lack of strategic fit with the acquiring firm's core strengths. Finally, it is important to establish a "checks and balances" system in which managers are challenged to support the acquisition decision. This is especially true when a firm regularly uses an acquisition strategy. If these checks and balances can be established with integrity, they will likely protect managers from becoming overly focused on completing acquisitions to the detriment of other issues warranting managerial attention.[31]

Acquisition Failure and Restructuring

Regardless of the effort invested, acquisitions sometimes fail. When this happens, divestiture may be the best course of action. A **divestiture** is a transaction in which businesses are sold to other firms or spun off as independent enterprises. Some divestitures occur because the firm wants to restructure its set of businesses to take advantage of new opportunities.[32] Commonly, though, divestitures are made to deal with failed acquisitions. Sears, Roebuck is a famous example of a firm that failed with its acquisitions. In 1981, Sears acquired Dean Witter Reynolds to diversify into financial services and Coldwell Banker to diversify into real estate. At first, the results of these acquisitions seemed positive. Quickly, though, it became obvious that the synergies Sears expected among its retail, financial services, and real estate businesses would not materialize. The inability to rapidly create synergies caused Sears executives to focus too much time on trying to develop those synergies. The net result of these efforts was that Sears' core retail business received little managerial attention, causing it to lose market share and perform poorly. Pressured by institutional investors to correct the problems, Sears announced the divestiture of its financial services and real estate businesses so that it could concentrate on its retail business. Research suggests that despite initial gains over the period when Sears was diversified, the firm's shareholders suffered significant opportunity losses when compared to a portfolio of firms that maintained a focus on their core retailing sector.[33]

Leveraged buyouts are commonly used as a restructuring strategy to correct for managerial mistakes. A **leveraged buyout (LBO)** is a restructuring strategy in which a party buys all or part of a firm's assets in order to take the firm or a part of the firm private. Once the transaction is completed, the company's stock is no longer traded publicly. Usually, significant amounts of debt are incurred to finance a buyout; hence the term "leveraged" buyout. To support debt payments, the new owners may immediately sell a number of assets in order to focus on the firm's core businesses.[34] Because leverage buyout associations (such as KKR, mentioned earlier) often control these firms, the intent is to restructure the firm to the point that it can be sold at a profit within five to eight years. However, besides improving efficiencies, such buyouts can also represent a form of firm rebirth to facilitate entrepreneurial efforts and stimulate strategic growth.[35]

Summary

The primary purpose of this chapter is to describe acquisitions as the foundation for an effective acquisition strategy. In doing so, we examined the following topics:

- An **acquisition** occurs when one firm buys controlling interest in another firm with the intention of either making the acquired firm a subsidiary business or combining it with a current business. An **acquisition strategy** is an action plan that the firm develops to successfully complete acquisitions. A **takeover** is a specialized acquisition strategy in which a target firm does not solicit the acquiring firm's offer. Takeovers are often hostile transactions. A **merger** is a transaction in which firms agree to combine their operations on a relatively equal basis.
- There are five basic reasons to complete acquisitions: (1) to reduce costs; (2) to gain market power; (3) to increase growth; (4) to learn and to build new capabilities; and (5) for other managerial, financial, and risk-reduction motives.
- Target screening, target selection, and target negotiating are activities firms complete to make an acquisition. Effective screening enables the acquiring firm to gain an overall sense of the acquisition opportunities that exist and helps establish the right price. Once the screening and selection are completed, negotiating with target firm leaders begins. When negotiating, it is important to clarify what roles top executives of the acquiring and target firms will play in the new firm. Also, government officials may need to be consulted to conclude negotiations, especially in cross-border deals.
- Effective **due diligence** is critical to making the right decision about a possible acquisition. Four basic questions are answered when engaging in due diligence: (1) What is the acquiring firm really buying? (2) What is the target firm's true financial value? (3) Where are the synergies between the acquiring and acquired firms? (4) What is the acquiring firm's walk-away offer price?
- Efforts to integrate the acquired firm with the acquiring firm after the transaction is completed may be the strongest predictor of acquisition success or failure. After a transaction is completed, it is critical to assess and improve, as required, the morale of all employees, but especially target firm employees. Building bridges between personnel in the target firm and personnel in the acquiring firm increases the likelihood that the firms will be effectively integrated.
- Besides integration difficulties, there are other pitfalls for acquisitions: (1) inadequate evaluation of the target firm and paying too much for the target; (2) excessive debt in the postacquisition period; (3) overdiversification; and (4) managers who are overly focused on making acquisitions.
- Acquisitions sometimes fail. When this happens, firms divest businesses that are causing performance problems so that they might again focus on their core operations. **Leveraged buyouts** are also used to restructure firms when particular acquisitions have failed or when a firm's whole acquisition strategy has failed.

Key Terms

Discussion Questions

1. What are the definitions of an acquisition, takeover, merger, and acquisition strategy? Why are acquisitions this chapter's focus?
2. What are the five basic reasons why firms complete acquisitions? Over the next ten years or so, do you think any of these reasons will become more important than the other four? If so, why?
3. What are target screening, target selection, target negotiating, and due diligence? In your

opinion, why do some firms fail to successfully complete these activities?

4. What process should be used to successfully integrate acquisitions and why is the process important?
5. What are the four major pitfalls of acquisitions? How can these pitfalls be prevented?
6. What major restructuring strategies do firms use to deal with a failed acquisition? What are the tradeoffs among the restructuring strategies?

Endnotes

1. J. E. Ashton, F. X. Cook Jr., & P. Schmitz, 2003, Uncovering hidden value in a midsize manufacturing company, *Harvard Business Review,* 81(6): 4–12.
2. A. Raghavan, J. Carreyrou, & G. Naik, 2004, Sanofi to swallow Aventis in a deal set at $65 billion, *Wall Street Journal,* April 26: A1, A8.
3. T. S. Gabrielsen, 2003, Conglomerate mergers: Vertical mergers in disguise? *International Journal of the Economics of Business,* 10(1): 1–16.
4. A. Lashinsky, 2004, Murdoch's air war, *Fortune,* December 13: 131–138.
5. D. Bank & D. Clark, 2004, Microsoft, SAP teach a lesson: Eat or be eaten, *Wall Street Journal,* June 9: C1, C4.
6. 2004, At BMC, bigger is still better, *Wall Street Journal,* June 16: B9.
7. B. Mascarenhas, A. Kumaraswam, D. Day, & A. Baveja, 2002, Five strategies for rapid firm growth and how to implement them, *Managerial and Decision Economics,* 23: 317–330.
8. 2004, K2 to buy three ski-gear makers as it continues acquisition spree, *Wall Street Journal,* June 16: B4.
9. 2004, MGM Mirage's board votes for deal, *Wall Street Journal,* June 16: B4.
10. A. L. Ranft & M. D. Lord, 2002, Acquiring new technologies and capabilities: A grounded model of acquisition implementation, *Organization Science,* 13: 420–441.
11. J. Gammelgaard, 2004, Access to competence: An emerging acquisition motive, *European Business Forum,* Spring: 44–48.
12. M. Warner, 2002, Can GE light up the market again? *Fortune,* November 11: 108–117.
13. R. J. Aiello & M. D. Watkins, 2000, The fine art of friendly acquisition, *Harvard Business Review,* 78(6): 100–107.
14. G. Cullinan, J.-M. Le Roux, & R.-M. Weddigen, 2004, When to walk away from a deal, *Harvard Business Review,* 82(4): 96–104.
15. T. Vestring, T. Rouse, & S. Rovit, 2004, Integrate where it matters, *MIT Sloan Management Review,* 46(1): 15–18.
16. M. Blyler & R. W. Coff, 2003, Dynamic capabilities, social capital and rent appropriation: Ties that split pies, *Strategic Management Journal,* 24: 677–697.
17. R. A. Weber & C. F. Camerer, 2003, Cultural conflict and merger failure: An experimental approach, *Management Science,* 49: 400–415.
18. S. Zaheer, M. Schomaker, & M. Genc, 2003, Identity versus culture in mergers of equals, *European Management Journal,* 21(2): 185–195.
19. T. Saxton & M. Dollinger, 2004, Target reputation and appropriability: Picking and deploying resources in acquisitions, *Journal of Management,* 30: 123–147.
20. T. Dougherty & E. Stein, 2004, Doomed for failure: Sears + Kmart, *Brandweek,* December 6: 20.
21. Y. Weber & E. Menipaz, 2003, Measuring cultural fit in mergers and acquisitions, *International Journal of Business Performance Management,* 5(1): 54–72.
22. A. K. Bucholtz, B. A. Ribbens, & I. T. Houle, 2003, The role of human capital in postacquisition CEO departure, *Academy of Management Journal,* 46: 506–514.
23. M. A. Hitt, L. Bierman, K. Shimizu, & R. Kochhar, 2001, Direct and moderating effects of human capital on strategy and performance in professional service firms, *Academy of Management Journal,* 44: 13–28.
24. J. A. Krug, 2003, Why do they keep leaving? *Harvard Business Review,* 81(2): 14–15; H. A. Krishnan & D. Park, 2002, The impact of workforce reduction on subsequent performance in major mergers and acquisitions: An exploratory study, *Journal of Business Research,* 55(4): 285–292.
25. D. Lovallo & D. Kahneman, 2003, Delusions of success: How optimism undermines executives' decisions, *Harvard Business Review,* 87(5): 56–64.
26. M. A. Hitt & D. L. Smart, 1994, Debt: A disciplining force for managers or a debilitating force for organizations? *Journal of Management Inquiry,* 3: 144–152.
27. S. Clow, 2004, Vivendi's asset mix poses new problem; CEO may have restored balance sheet but remaining businesses share little crossover, *Wall Street Journal,* May 27: B2.
28. M. L. A. Hayward, 2002, When do firms learn from their acquisition experience? Evidence from 1990–1995, *Strategic Management Journal,* 23: 21–39; M. A. Hitt, J. S. Harrison, & R. D. Ireland, 2001, *Mergers and Acquisitions: A Guide to Creating Value for Stakeholders,* New York: Oxford University Press.
29. J. Pfeffer, 2003, The human factor: Curbing the urge to merge, *Business 2.0,* July: 58.
30. N. P. Varaiya, 1988, The "winner's curse" hypothesis and corporate takeovers, *Managerial and Decision Economics,* 9: 209–219.
31. C. Gopinath, 2003, When acquisitions go awry: Pitfalls in executing corporate strategy, *Journal of Business Strategy,* 24(5): 22–27.
32. K. E. Meyer & E. Lieb-Doczy, 2003, Post-acquisition restructuring as evolutionary process, *Journal of Management Studies,* 40: 459–483; L. Capron, W. Mitchell, & A. Waminathan, 2001, Asset divestiture following horizontal acquisitions: A dynamic view, *Strategic Management Journal,* 22: 817–844.
33. S. L. Gillan, J. W. Kensinger, & J. D. Martin, 2000, Value creation and corporate diversification: The case of Sears, Roebuck & Co., *Journal of Financial Economics,* 55: 103–138.
34. M. F. Wiersema & J. P. Liebeskind, 1995, The effects of leveraged buyouts on corporate growth and diversification in large firms, *Strategic Management Journal,* 16: 447–460.
35. M. Wright, R. E. Hoskisson, & L. W. Busenitz, 2001, Firm rebirth: Buyouts as facilitators of strategic growth and entrepreneurship, *Academy of Management Executive,* 15(1): 111–125.

Global Competition

*Knowledge Objectives

Reading and studying this chapter should enable you to:

1_
Explain four reasons why firms pursue international strategies.

2_
Understand the two major pressures leading to three dominant international strategies.

3_
Describe the four basic alternative contractual modes for entering international markets and explain the trade-offs for using each mode.

4_
Discuss how three types of advantages affect the decision about which mode of entering international markets to use.

5_
Explain the three alternative types of foreign direct investment and the strategic basis for each one.

6_
Describe the organizational structures that are used to implement each of the international strategies.

Focusing on Strategy

eBay's International Expansion Strategy

"Today, eBay Inc., as it's now known, has catapulted from its early days as the place to trade Beanie Babies to become the Web's most powerful corporate enterprise in its own right, worth more than $70 billion . . . Were eBay a country, its expected gross sales of $34 billion this year would rank as the 59th largest gross domestic product in the world, just behind Kuwait." (Robert D. Hof, *Business Week,* 2004)

In September 1995, Pierre Omidyar launched eBay, an online person-to-person auction or trading forum. eBay receives a fee for a listing and for sales. It competes in markets similar to newspaper classified ads, flea markets, garage sales, and traditional auction houses. Omidyar hoped that the auction community on eBay would reflect the values of openness, honesty, empowerment, and trust. In Omidyar's words, "eBay was founded with the belief that people are honest and trustworthy. We believe that each of our customers, whether a buyer or seller, is an individual who deserves to be treated with respect."

eBay executives worked hard to improve the community and services in order to develop the trust and loyalty needed for its auction business to flourish. Originally, eBay found that serious collectors and small traders were the most active site users. Accordingly, it developed its PowerSellers program to benefit bulk sellers. To expand its opportunities, eBay formed a strategic alliance with AOL in March 1999. This agreement gave eBay a prominent presence across the domestic and international AOL family of brands. eBay also used AOL's brands prominently in its sites to encourage eBay users to use AOL as an Internet service provider.

In 1999, eBay began to expand into international markets. It did so initially in the United Kingdom and Canada by using a greenfield venture (discussed later in the chapter) in these markets. Some German entrepreneurs copied eBay's source code and set up a mirror image of eBay under the name Alandro.de in Germany. However, by the end of 1999, eBay had acquired Alandro.de and renamed the site eBay.de. The firm also started an eBay site in Australia through a joint venture with a leading Internet media company, PBL Online. In February 2000, eBay Japan was launched through a joint venture with NEC. However, Yahoo initiated an auction site in Japan five months earlier through a joint venture with Softbank, a large Japanese Internet company. In 2002, eBay withdrew from Japan's market because Yahoo had an insurmountable lead.

Meg Whitman, CEO of eBay, learned a lesson from the Japanese experience. When considering China as a market opportunity, she invested early to get ahead of the competition. To launch its operations in China, eBay acquired China's Each Net, which eBay renamed eBay Each Net. Although in many parts of Asia, online payment is a novelty, delivery systems are flawed, and theft can be a difficult problem, eBay's China venture has 4.3 million users. Furthermore, eBay is not developing only in Shanghai and Beijing; 52 percent of its users live in largely rural western China. Thus, eBay has extended its geographic reach in China and elsewhere surprisingly quickly and across a vast array of languages and cultures.

eBay's most recent international actions include the acquisition of Baazee.com, Inc., India's largest online auction site, for $50 million and acquisition of Marktplaats.nl, the top classified-listings Web site in the Netherlands. Despite the potential size of India's market, it lags far behind other markets, including China, in Internet usage. However, eBay considers India a huge growth opportunity as it did China; the market is expected to grow as customers become accustomed to shopping and trading online. Currently, India has an estimated 17 million Internet users, compared with 84 million in China and 188 million in the United States. Internet usage is expected to dramatically grow in all three countries.

eBay bought Marktplaats.nl to strengthen its position in the Netherlands, where 70 percent of the population use the Internet, and to learn more about the Internet classified-listing market. Earlier in 2004, eBay purchased a 25 percent position in Craigslist, which offers Web-based classified listings for users in the San Francisco Bay area, New York, Los Angeles and several dozen other cities. Marktplaats.nl will report to eBay Netherlands while operating as a separate business.

Growing approximately 40 percent a year, eBay earned $2.17 billion on gross sales of $24 billion in 2003. Currently, 40 percent of eBay's revenue comes from its international businesses, but it expects relatively more growth from its international operations in the future. Although eBay has expanded rapidly into a number of distinct geographical and cultural markets, the firm must now organize these disparate operations into an overall international strategy as well as structure its organization. To date, eBay has used a number of entry modes: acquisition, joint venture, and greenfield investment. As we've discussed, most of these entries are successful, but some are not (such as the entry into Japan). Meg Whitman has an important challenge in formulating an overall strategy and developing an organization to manage eBay's dispersed international operations.

SOURCES: R. D. Hof, 2004, The Web for the people, *Business Week,* December 6: 18; M. Mangalindan, 2004, eBay buys Netherlands classified-listing site, *Wall Street Journal,* November 11: B11; L. M. Weiss, M. M. Capozzi, & L. Prusak, 2004, Learning from the Internet giants, *MIT Sloan Management Review,* 45(4): 79–84; N. Wingfield, 2004, eBay sets sights on Indian market with acquisition, *Wall Street Journal,* June 23: A3; L. Wozniak, 2004, An online cash machine, *Far Eastern Economic Review,* April 29: 66; R. D. Hof, 2003, The eBay economy, *Business Week,* August 25: 125–128.

As "Focusing on Strategy" indicates, expanding international operations is increasingly important to eBay's strategic and financial performance as it arranges transactions between sellers and buyers at its various auction sites throughout the world. The increase in globalization mentioned in Chapter 3 is based on several historical changes in the global business environment. In the first half of the twentieth century, firms wishing to enter new markets were frustrated because of barriers against foreign trade and investments imposed by national governments. After World War I, many countries imposed tariffs and quotas on imported goods that favored local firms; as a result, international trade declined throughout the 1930s. These tariffs and quotas contributed to the severity of the U.S. depression.

However, after World War II, these policies were reversed as major trading powers negotiated reductions in tariffs and quotas and eliminated many barriers to foreign direct investment (FDI). **Foreign direct investment** is a process through which a firm directly invests (beyond exporting and licensing) in a market outside its home country. These negotiations were embodied in the General Agreement on Tariffs and Trade (GATT) and its successor organization, the World Trade Organization (WTO). Furthermore, regional trading agreements such as the European Union, the Mercosur Accord, and the North American Free Trade Agreement (NAFTA) have also relaxed trade and investment barriers among member countries.

Additionally, investments in technology, particularly communications and transportation technologies, are making international transactions more feasible and more profitable by reducing the costs of transactions. Similarly, the rapidly growing use of the Internet has affected international transactions in at least three ways. First, the Internet and associated technologies are facilitating trade in services such as banking, consulting, retailing, and even gambling. For instance, many U.S. companies have outsourced customer service and data entry operations to low-cost-labor countries outside North America, such as India. Second, the Internet makes competition between large and smaller firms more reasonable regardless of the good or service being sold.[1] This means that the amount of investment needed to expand into foreign markets has been substantially reduced. Consider that Internet technology makes it possible for a company in Missouri, Indonesia, or Brazil to create a Web site and compete with a larger business with facilities located in one of the world's larger cities of commerce. Third, the Internet creates a more efficient networking capability among businesses. General Motors, for instance, expects to reduce its purchase order costs significantly through online purchasing by integrating its suppliers and by monitoring inventory of parts ordering and shipping.[2] Have you used the Internet for transactions with companies overseas? Do you use it to explore international Web sites? If so, hasn't using the Internet in this manner changed how you conduct business transactions?

Even though significant trends have fostered growth in international business, the costs and risks of doing business outside a firm's domestic market can be significant. The research literature labels these costs the **liability of foreignness.**[3] As Chapter 4 indicates, a firm must have resources that enable it to overcome these additional costs. In this chapter, we discuss firm-specific resources as well as location advantages that help to overcome these costs.

In summary, international strategies are becoming more widespread because of the environmental and technological changes taking place in the twenty-first

FIGURE 8.1 International Strategy: Motives, Strategic Approach, Mode of Entry, and Structural Implementation

century.[4] However, firms must still have the resources necessary to formulate and implement a strategy to overcome the continuing costs of the liability of foreign entry. In this chapter, as illustrated in Figure 8.1, we explore the reasons for and types of international strategies that firms use. We begin this important exploration by outlining the motives for using an international strategy. Next, we explore the basic international strategies employed by firms. While reading this chapter, remember that international strategies are sometimes called cross-border strategies. Once a strategy is chosen, managers must choose a mode of international entry. Finally, the firm must choose an organizational structure and accompanying processes to implement the chosen strategy.

Motives for International Strategies

A number of motives drive the use of international strategies. Next, we describe four of the most prominent motives.

Sourcing of Resources and Supplies

Seeking new sources of supply has long been a common reason to engage in international trade. During the Middle Ages, for example, Italy used its political and military strength in Venice, Genoa, and Florence as the foundation for its ability to be a major center of international commerce and banking. During this time, Italy was the major trading link between Europe and Asia. However, after these trade routes were severed by the Turks in 1453, European governments sought new ocean routes to the Far East. This is one of the reasons why the Spanish government backed Christopher Columbus's expedition to sail west from Europe looking for such routes. Inadvertently, as we know, Columbus found new sources of supply in the Americas, a discovery that ultimately led to the colonization of the Americas by European countries. Similarly today, large firms make foreign direct investments largely to reduce the costs they incur to obtain needed supplies. As we explain in "Understanding Strategy," with China's entrance into the WTO, many firms are investing in that country and the seemingly inexhaustible and inexpensive labor. However, as China's markets continue to provide a source of supply, demand for products such as automobiles is growing. Thus, firms also enter China to expand their markets. The motive to expand a firm's potential market is discussed next.

Seeking to Expand or Develop New Markets

As firms mature in their domestic market, they often expand into international markets to increase revenues and profits. This is the case for consumer products giants Procter & Gamble, Unilever, and Colgate-Palmolive. These three firms are using international strategies to expand into a host of countries, including China and India—countries with huge market potential for the firms' products such as toothpaste and detergents. Firms also seek to lower costs of production by developing economies of scale (defined in Chapter 3). International expansion balances a firm's risk. This balance results from the firm's ability to sell in multiple markets, reducing its dependency on sales in any one market.[5] To show the magnitude of international strategies, think of how many of the products you use are made by a nondomestic company. What about your car? Your furniture and stereo system? The clothes you are wearing? For most of us, answering this question clearly highlights the global nature of the world's economy.

Competitive Rivalry

Some businesses enter foreign markets to enhance their ability to compete with major rivals. For example, Coca-Cola and PepsiCo are both aggressively expanding their international operations. Of course, neither firm can allow its competitor to gain a competitive advantage in terms of global markets.[6] Think about this outcome. If either Pepsi or Coke gained a significant advantage in global markets, the additional profitability earned as a result of using that advantage could be used to damage the competitor in the all-important U.S. market. The relationships between earth-moving equipment firms Caterpillar and Komatsu and between photographic firms Kodak and Fuji are similar to the relationship between Coca-Cola and Pepsi. Each firm actively competes against its rival in global markets. This competitive rivalry exists to prevent a competitor from gaining a significant advantage in any one country or region.

Interestingly, other firms pursue international ventures to avoid domestic competition. In the local Japanese automobile market, competition is very intense because of the number of large firms competing in the local market, including Toyota, Honda, Nissan, Mazda, Mitsubishi, Suzuki, Subaru, Isuzu, and Daihatsu. Part of the reason for moving into the international market was the nature of domestic competition. Japanese automakers have largely been successful

learning from success

understanding strategy:

THE EFFECTS OF CHINA'S DEVELOPING MARKET ECONOMY

The annual increase in gross domestic product (GDP) in China has outpaced all other major economies in the world in recent years. China's GDP averaged over eight percent annual growth for 2000–2003. This phenomenal economic growth, however, has been fueled by "bubble" investments in real estate. One analyst estimated that 80 percent of all Zhejiang province bank loans in 2002 and 2003 were given to real estate ventures. Simultaneously the government is spending huge amounts on building bridges, highways, dams, and power plants to fuel a private economy to make up for underinvestment during prior years.

© REUTERS/Claro Cortes IV/Landov

Manufacturers are suffering chronic electricity shortages, a sign that the economy is growing too quickly. China's growth rate has had an impact beyond its borders as well. One of these effects is the dramatic increase in the global prices of raw materials such as crude oil, cement, and scrap steel. This is a classic case of demand and supply relationships. The supply of a number of raw materials (for example, oil) hasn't increased dramatically, while the demand for oil and its derivative products by China and other nations is definitely increasing.

Chinese regulators recognized that the nation's economy is growing too quickly. This knowledge has motivated regulators to establish policies that reduce the annual growth rate to about seven percent. To reach this goal, the Chinese government increased bank reserve requirements; capped the percentage of debt companies can use to purchase cement, steel and aluminum and fund real estate projects; the government also signaled tighter credit policies for commercial lending. These actions must be implemented carefully because the collapse of China's economy would have severe effects on the world and especially on the regional economies of Japan, South Korea, Taiwan, and Hong Kong that feed China's export growth.

China's entrance into the WTO also facilitated changes in government policies that created entry opportunities in many industries. For instance, China is developing legislation to open the telecommunications market more fully, not only to domestic but also to foreign firms. The law will facilitate the continued breakup of state-run monopolies and induce more healthy competition.

In the auto industry, the problem is just the opposite of the telephone industry. China's highly fragmented auto industry means that none of the Chinese manufacturers have the economies of scale needed to compete on a global basis. Although new policies resulting from China's entrance into the WTO are likely to be burdensome for foreign firms because of the requirement to use a higher percentage of parts made in China, it will foster development of the Chinese automobile industry.

To solidify its changes in policy, China is also developing antitrust laws. However, some of this legislation may be targeted toward large multinationals such as Microsoft, Eastman-Kodak, and Tetra Pack AB, a Swedish packaging company.

The impact of the Chinese economy on firms across the world is strong and visible. As we've described, a large number of firms are using

SOURCES: A. Browne, 2004, China charts a tight course, *Wall Street Journal*, May 18: A17; R. Buckman, 2004, China hurries anti-trust law, *Wall Street Journal*, June 11: A7; K. Chen, 2004, Changes are reshaping China, *Wall Street Journal*, June 8, A13; K. Chen, 2004, Giving credit where credit is due in China, *Wall Street Journal*, June 24: C1, C6; K. Chen, 2004, China crafts telecom law to level playing field, *Wall Street Journal*, May 20: B5; J. Cox, 2004, China pulls reins on its economy, *USA Today*, April 28, B1; D. J. Lynch, 2004, China economy zooms ahead, but growth might be too fast, *USA Today*, April 29: B1, B2; R. McGregor, 2004, China's ruling party to lift role in business, *Financial Times*, June 22: 7.

international strategies to compete in China. Large and small firms and companies from both developed and developing economies (such as India) are interested in competing in China. The effects of the Chinese economy are significant for China's domestic companies as well as for firms across the globe wanting to use international strategies to compete in a huge market with seemingly unlimited opportunities.

in their international ventures. In fact, the "big three" in the United States are now the "big two"—Ford and General Motors, plus DaimlerChrysler, which is owned by Daimler-Benz, a German firm.

Leveraging Core Competencies and Learning

As we discussed in Chapter 4, firms invest heavily to develop core competencies. Once it has developed a core competence that is a competitive advantage in its domestic market, a firm may be able to use that competitive advantage in international markets as well. When the competitive advantage is in R&D, the firm may have the foundation needed to rely on innovation as the source of entry to international markets.

Learning is also an important reason for international expansion. Firms often invest in countries that have centers of excellence in industries such as semiconductors. These firms enter international markets to gain access to product and manufacturing process knowledge. For example, large pharmaceuticals firms have formed alliances with foreign partners in order to learn about new drug research that could lead to developing and introducing new products into their domestic market.[7]

We've discussed motives influencing firms to use strategies to compete in international markets. As you would expect, firms can choose from several different strategies to compete in international markets. We discuss these strategies in the next few sections.

International Strategies

Firms consider two important and potentially competing issues when choosing an international strategy—the need for global efficiencies and the need to customize a good or service for a particular host country market.[8] Generally, efficiency increases when the firm can sell its current good or service in multiple international markets. In contrast, the need for customization to serve local, international markets increases when the firm sells a good or service that is adapted specifically to a particular local market.

Despite the initial mistranslation of their famous slogan, Kentucky Fried Chicken restaurants have proven very successful in China with over 900 outlets and approximately 250 more opening per year, such as this one—the first drive-through restaurant in Beijing.

Firms seeking global efficiency may decide to locate in countries where their production and distribution costs will be low. For example, a firm may locate in a country with low labor costs. It might also obtain economies of scale by building factories that can serve customers in more than a single country. Alternatively, by broadening their product line in countries they enter, firms can achieve economies of scope (see Chapter 6) and thereby lower their production and marketing costs for related products.

In some international settings, firms can be more successful by customizing their products to meet local market tastes and interests. For instance, KFC has adapted its restaurant foods to fit the culture and taste preferences of local markets. KFC offers more fish dishes in Asian countries and less chicken, for example. Language can also present challenges as the following indicates: "Pepsi-Cola went into Taiwan and carefully translated its slogan, 'Come alive with the Pepsi generation.' However, the translation came out as 'Pepsi will bring your ancestors back from the dead.' And, KFC's slogan 'Finger licking good,' in Chinese says, 'Eat your fingers off.'"[9]

As shown in Figure 8.2, the need for global efficiency and the need to satisfy a local host country market's unique needs provide a two-dimensional matrix illustrating the different global strategies. We next describe the three international strategies shown in Figure 8.2.

The Multidomestic Strategy

The **multidomestic strategy** is an action plan that the firm develops to produce and sell unique products in different markets. To use this strategy, a firm establishes a relatively independent set of operating subsidiaries in which each subsidiary develops specific products for a particular domestic market. Each subsidiary is free to customize its products' marketing campaign and operating techniques to best meet the needs of local customers. The multidomestic strategy is particularly effective when clear differences between national markets exist; potential economies of scale for production, distribution, and marketing are low; and the cost of coordination between the parent and foreign subsidiaries is high. Because each subsidiary must be responsive to the local market, the parent usually delegates considerable power and authority to managers of host country subsidiaries. Many multinational corporations used the multidomestic strategy during World War II because it was difficult to communicate and transfer technologies. Many European firms also adopted this strategy because of the cultural and language differences they needed to overcome in order to conduct business in each European country. Let's consider a specific firm to demonstrate these points.

The French defense contractor French Thomson-CSF has transformed into a new global defense and aerospace electronics group called Thales SA. Thales has won contracts worldwide by using a multidomestic strategy. It has become a "local

FIGURE 8.2 International Strategies

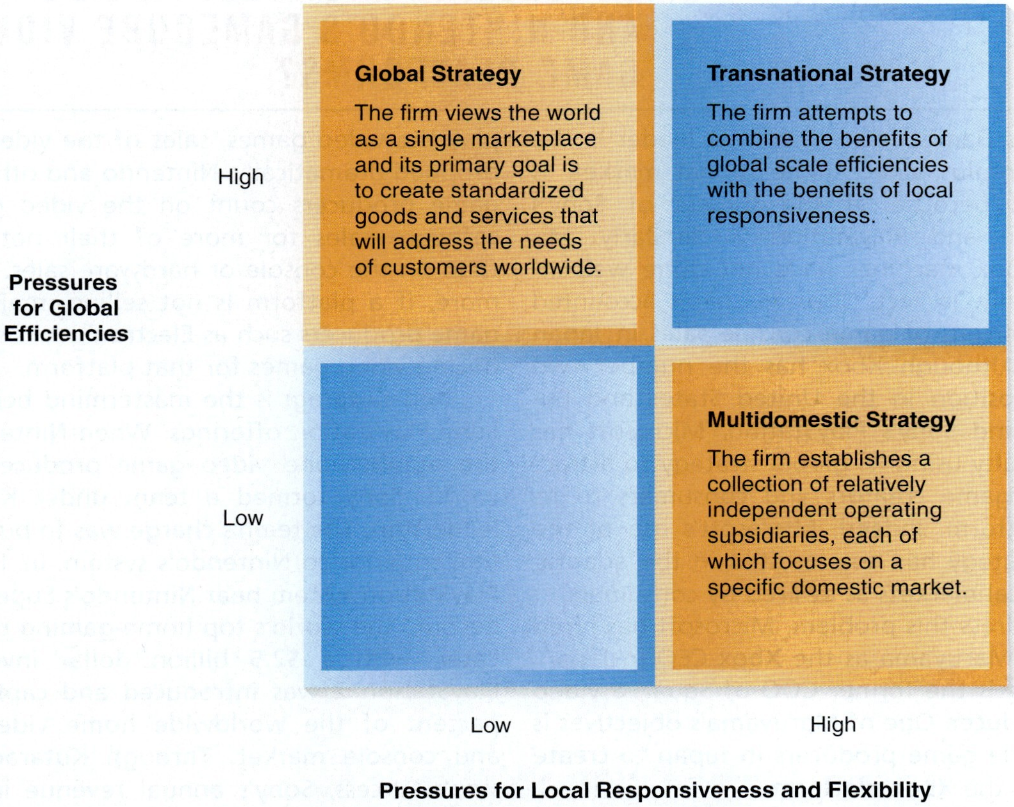

Pressures for Global Efficiencies

High

Global Strategy

The firm views the world as a single marketplace and its primary goal is to create standardized goods and services that will address the needs of customers worldwide.

Transnational Strategy

The firm attempts to combine the benefits of global scale efficiencies with the benefits of local responsiveness.

Low

Multidomestic Strategy

The firm establishes a collection of relatively independent operating subsidiaries, each of which focuses on a specific domestic market.

Low High

Pressures for Local Responsiveness and Flexibility

player in six countries outside France: Britain, the Netherlands, Australia, South Africa, South Korea, and Singapore."[10] It implemented its strategy using a series of joint ventures with and acquisitions of local players in each of these markets.

The Global Strategy

The **global strategy** is an action plan that the firm develops to produce and sell standardized products in different markets. To use this strategy, a firm manages its products from a central divisional office to develop, produce, and sell its standardized products throughout the world. A firm using a global strategy seeks to capture economies of scale in production and marketing as well as economies of scope and location advantage. Because the global strategy requires worldwide coordination, the production and marketing strategies are usually centralized with decisions made at a division headquarters. Mercedes-Benz, a unit of DaimlerChrysler, uses the global strategy to sell its products in many global markets. This strategy is successful for Mercedes-Benz because its products are known for their quality and reliability.[11] However, as discussed in "Understanding Strategy," at times the global strategy leads to difficulties in

understanding strategy:

WHY IS THE SONY PLAYSTATION OUTSELLING MICROSOFT'S XBOX AND NINTENDO'S GAMECUBE VIDEO GAME PLATFORMS?

Nintendo's GameCube, the former leader in the $27 billion-plus video game global market, is struggling because of the success of Sony's PlayStation and PlayStation 2. Similarly, Microsoft Xbox machines have not done well internationally. In fact, Xbox machines accounted for two percent of game console sales in Japan in 2003. Although Xbox has the number two console position in the United States and Europe, behind Sony's PlayStation, Microsoft has had difficulty using its global strategy to attract Japanese game creators and consumers to its game platform. Indeed, Microsoft's use of the global strategy has not resulted in the adaptation to local markets as desired by consumers.

To address this problem, Microsoft has hired Yoshihiro Maruyama as the Xbox CEO in Japan. Maruyama is the former COO of Squar, a video game producer. One of Maruyama's objectives is to persuade game producers in Japan to create games for the Xbox platform.

The lack of sales in the United States in 2003 resulted in Nintendo's reporting a loss for the first time in its history. Apparently, the Japanese firm's game machine and associated games have lost ground in the U.S. market. In other words, Nintendo's international strategy in the United States was not very competitive. In 2002, because it had too many unsold GameCube machines late in the holiday selling cycle, Nintendo had to cut its console price to $99 from $149, which was almost 50 percent less than the price of its rivals, PlayStation 2 and Microsoft Xbox. The lack of console sales harms a firm like Nintendo even more because it tries to make a profit on both its hardware and its software, or video game titles. Without consoles on which to play the video games, sales of the video games dropped dramatically. Nintendo and other video game producers count on the video game or software sales for more of their net income than on the console or hardware sales. Furthermore, if a platform is not selling, major video game producers such as Electronic Arts stop producing video games for that platform.

Ken Kutaragi is the mastermind behind the Sony PlayStation offerings. When Nintendo was the number one video game producer in the world, Sony formed a team under Kutaragi's leadership. The team's charge was to build a system superior to Nintendo's system. In 1994, the PlayStation system beat Nintendo's Super NES to become the world's top home-gaming platform. Later, with a $2.5 billion dollar investment, PlayStation 2 was introduced and captured 75 percent of the worldwide home video game and console market. Through Kutaragi's division's success, Sony's annual revenue increased by $10 billion. The importance of this division is also demonstrated by the fact that in 2002, the division accounted for more than 58 percent of Sony's worldwide operating profits.

Both Microsoft and Nintendo seem to be following global strategies that are centralized and operated mainly from their home countries, the United States and Japan, respectively. Microsoft has not been able to penetrate the Japanese market, which is important because it is Sony and Nintendo's home market. Likewise, Nintendo has not done a good job meeting the competition in pricing and forecasting sales in the U.S. market. These may be symptoms of problems with Nintendo's global strategy because its managers do not understand consumers in markets that are different culturally from their home markets. However, Sony has done well by achieving globally efficient operations and by adapting effectively to demands in foreign markets (such as the United States and Europe). Nobuyuki Idei, Sony's former chairman, was strongly committed to pursuing convergence in music, movies, games, and communications. The Sony PlayStation 2 is an example of this approach; it combines a game platform with the ability to play DVDs and connect to the Internet. Sony's strategy exemplifies the transnational strategy (defined next). Although the transnational strategy is difficult to implement, it is also difficult for competitors to imitate. Having the right strategy is important, but so is implementing it effectively. Sony has demonstrated its ability to effectively formulate and implement its international strategy in the global video game market.

SOURCES: 2004, Business: A serious contest; Video games, *The Economist,* May 8: 73; K. J. Delaney, 2004, Space Invaders: Ads in video games pose a new threat to media industry, *Wall Street Journal,* July 28: A1, A8; P. Dvorak, 2004, Nintendo steers away from the pack, *Wall Street Journal,* May 11: B10; 2004, Nintendo Co.: Weak console sales, firm yen lead to a 51% drop in profit, *Wall Street Journal,* May 28: B6; J. Frederick, 2003, Playing his way to the next level, *Time,* December 1: 84; P. Dvorak, 2003, Nintendo's GameCube sales surge after price cut, *Wall Street Journal,* November 4: B4.

marketing the firm's standardized products to local consumer markets. As we'll see, both Microsoft and Nintendo have had difficulty using the global strategy to sell their video platforms (Xbox for Microsoft; GameCube for Nintendo) outside of their home markets.

The Transnational Strategy

The **transnational strategy** is an action plan that the firm develops to produce and sell somewhat unique and somewhat standardized products in different markets. With this strategy, the firm attempts to combine the benefits of global scale efficiencies with the advantages of being locally responsive in a country or geographic region; it requires both centralization and decentralization simultaneously. Ikea, a worldwide furniture producer, employs the transnational strategy. In using this strategy, Ikea relies on standardization of products with global production and distribution, but it also has a system (called "democratic design") through which new designs for local markets are developed and introduced. Democratic design is helping Ikea produce products that meet the tastes of local customers. Ikea is a world leader in furniture production and distribution and is now one of the top furniture retailers in the United States. In fact, ten percent of American homes have at least one Ikea item.[12]

Although the transnational strategy is more difficult to manage and expensive to implement, it is probably the best international strategy to use to facilitate learning. The balance of centralization and decentralization usually results in a corporate culture that promotes transfer of knowledge among subsidiaries. The multidomestic strategy uses a decentralized authority structure. This structure makes it difficult to transfer knowledge across subsidiaries. The global strategy, on the other hand, centralizes decision making, which also hampers new knowledge development. So when using the global strategy, the firm learns less from different host country markets because of its focus on exploiting the firm's current knowledge in each of the markets rather than learning from each market to adapt the products. As suggested in "Understanding Strategy," Sony has managed the PlayStation video game platform well using the transnational strategy.

Modes of International Market Entry

After a firm decides to pursue an international strategy, it must choose a mode of entry. Factors affecting the choice of an entry mode are presented in Figure 8.3.[13] These factors include firm-specific resource advantages, country-specific or location advantages, internal-coordination or administrative advantages, need for control, and resource availability. We begin with an explanation of each mode of entry followed by a discussion of how each potential advantage affects the choice of entry mode.

Entry Modes

Exporting

Perhaps the simplest and most common form of mode of entry is exporting domestic products to a foreign country. **Exporting** is the process of sending goods and services from one country to another for distribution, sale, and service. The advantage of exporting is that the firm can gradually enter an interna-

FIGURE 8.3 International Modes of Entry and Decision Factors

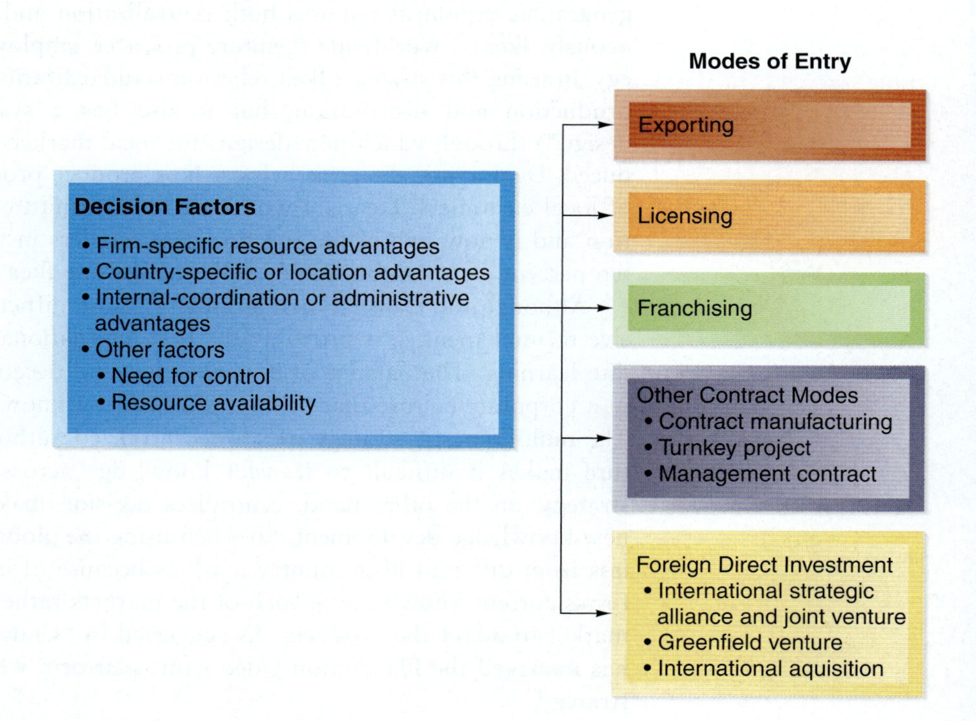

tional market without taking too many risks. Exporting also has the advantage of helping the firm to acquire knowledge about a local market before making large investments. But exporting isn't without problems. Firms exporting their products are vulnerable to tariffs and often encounter logistical challenges in getting products to an international market. Exporting firms also must be aware of possibly being in conflict with local distributors who may want to distribute the firm's products instead.

Licensing

Licensing is the process of entering an international market by leasing the right to use the firm's intellectual property—technology, work methods, patents, copyrights, brand names, or trademarks—to a firm doing business in the desired international market. The firm doing the leasing is the licensor and the firm receiving the license is the licensee. Licensing is popular because it involves little direct cost or risk for the licensor. Electronic Arts successfully uses this strategy as it licenses games worldwide to game platform or hardware producers such as Sony (PlayStation), Nintendo (GameCube), and Microsoft (Xbox). These firms are willing to pay a license fee to Electronic Arts to have rights to the firm's innovative games and titles.[14] Through licensing, Electronic Arts generates revenues and also develops new video games, thereby stimulating further demand for its games and other products. Although licensing has low financial risks, it also provides few opportunities for profit growth. While licensing provides a low-cost means to assess market potential, it also creates dependence on the licensee for exploiting that potential. Another risk is that the licensee can learn the technology and become a competitor of the licensor. Microsoft, for instance, is a software producer and has produced its own video games.

Franchising

Franchising is a special form of licensing and is discussed further in Chapter 9 as a cooperative strategy. **Franchising** is the licensing of a good or service and business model to partners for specified fees (usually a signing fee and a percentage of the franchisee's revenues or profits). The franchisor provides trademarks, operating systems, and well-known products as well as service support such as advertising, specialized training, and quality-assurance programs. McDonald's has developed a successful global franchising system. Pizza Hut, KFC, and Taco Bell have also franchised restaurants worldwide. Benetton uses franchised retail stores to distribute stylish clothing in over 120 countries.

Marriott International has achieved distinction as a franchiser of hotel chains. However, it owns less than three percent of the properties, unlike Hilton and Starwood (St. Regis, Sheraton, and Westin hotel chains), which own more than 30 percent of their properties. One analyst noted that Marriott has "become the industry leader by obsessively whipping its troops into line—not just employees, but hotel owners—while pampering loyal customers and winning bookings away from rivals."[15]

Other Contracting Modes

Contract manufacturing is another popular contractual mode of entry. Large firms in Asia, such as Taiwan Semiconductor Manufacturing Company (TSMC),

© BLOOMBERG NEWS/Landov

A technician checks production of silicon wafers at the Taiwan Semiconductor Manufacturing Company, which works for clients such as Hewlett-Packard.

manufacture chips for large clients such as Hewlett-Packard (HP). Big Asian contract manufacturers like TSMC are expected to do better than smaller U.S. firms because their cost advantage in Asia has attracted large clients such as HP, that can invest significant amounts of capital thereby enabling the manufacturers to keep their competitive edge. The cost of a new chip plant requires more than $2 billion; "The U.S. share of global chip production is expected to fall from 37 percent this year to 34 percent by 2008, while Asia's rises from 20 to 26 percent."[16]

Similarly, turnkey projects, often construction projects to build large infrastructure items such as coal- or gas-fired electrical power plants, are done on a contractual basis. Management agreements to run such facilities are done on a contractual basis as well.

Approaches to Foreign Direct Investment

With FDI entry modes, the firm has greater control of its destiny in the international market it has chosen to enter. But there is greater risk with FDI investments as well. Next, we discuss three approaches to FDI—strategic alliances and joint ventures, greenfield ventures, and acquisitions.

International Strategic Alliances and Joint Ventures

International strategic alliances represent a cooperative agreement in which home and host country firms work closely together. In the case of a joint venture, "working together" results in creating a separate company to promote the partners' mutual interests (joint ventures and strategic alliances are discussed further in Chapter 9). Firms in emerging economies often want to form international alliances and ventures to gain access to sophisticated technologies that are new to them. This type of arrangement can benefit the non-emerging-economy firm as well, in that it gains access to a new market and doesn't have to pay tariffs to do so (because it is partnering with a local company).[17] However, the non-emerging-economy firm needs to be careful to protect its technologies from being copied by its partner.

Greenfield Venture

In a **greenfield venture,** a firm buys or leases land, constructs a new facility and hires or transfers managers and employees, and then independently launches a new operation (usually a wholly owned subsidiary) without involvement of a partner. The firm maintains full control of its operations with a greenfield venture. More control is especially advantageous if the firm has proprietary technology. Research also suggests that "wholly owned subsidiaries and expatriate staff are preferred" in service industries where "close contacts with end customers" and "high levels of professional skills, specialized know-how, and customization" are required.[18] The major disadvantage with a greenfield venture launched in an international market is that it takes time to implement and succeed. A lack of experience with and knowledge about the international local market makes it hard for the greenfield venture to have rapid success. Therefore, firms establishing greenfield ventures in international markets need to be patient in order to achieve success with that venture.

International Acquisition

The final FDI entry mode is one in which a firm acquires an existing host country firm. By acquiring a current business, the purchaser gains control over the acquired firm's assets, employees, technology, brand names, and distribution. Therefore, entry is much quicker than by other modes. In fact, acquisitions are the mode used by many firms to enter Eastern European markets. Wal-Mart has entered Germany and the United Kingdom by acquiring local firms.[19]

Using the acquisition entry mode is not without risk. The main risk centers on the fact that when using this entry mode, the acquiring firm often assumes all of the acquired firm's liabilities. Complicating this matter even more is the fact that the firm acquiring a local company may not be fully aware of the conventional practices used to account for liabilities in the acquired firm's market.[20]

We've explored the entry modes available to firms that want to enter international markets. Next we consider the factors influencing the firm's choice of an entry mode, as illustrated in Figure 8.3.

Factors Affecting the Selection of Entry Mode

Firm-Specific Resource Advantages

Firm-specific resource advantages are the core competencies that provide a competitive advantage over a firm's rivals.[21] As we recall from our discussions in Chapter 4, core competencies are often based largely on intangible resources. When the success of a firm's entry into an international market relies on transferring core competencies, an entry mode should be used that involves an equity stake. Therefore, a joint venture, an acquisition, and a greenfield venture represent the best entry mode choices in these cases, because the firm retains more ownership of its competencies. However, if the firm-specific advantage is a brand name, which is protected by law, a licensing or franchising entry mode may be the best choice. As a precaution, a firm needs to be careful in selecting the right licensee because a brand name's reputation can be easily damaged.

Country-Specific or Location Advantages

Country-specific or location advantages are concerned with the desirability of producing in the home country versus locating production and distribution assets in the host country. If country-specific advantages for production are stronger in the home country, it is likely that exporting is the best choice for entering an international market. Such location advantages can be influenced by costs of production and transportation requirements as well as the needs of the intended customers.[22] Many firms, for instance, have located their assets in Turkey because its geographic, religious, linguistic, and cultural ties provide opportunities to enter Central Asian markets of the former Soviet Union as well as markets in the Middle East.[23]

However, political risks such as the likelihood of terror or war, unstable governments, and government corruption may discourage making direct investments in a host country. Government policies can also influence the mode of entry. For example, high tariffs discourage exporting and encourage local production through direct investments. Similarly, economic risks such as currency fluctuations may create problems for international investment. If a currency is devalued, so are the assets invested through FDI in that country. Currently the dollar has a lower value than other currencies such as the euro which supports U.S. exports. However, it hurts foreign exporters coming into the United States from countries with a higher-valued currency. Cultural influences may also affect location advantages and disadvantages. If there is a strong match between the cultures in which international transactions are carried out, the liability of foreignness is lower than if there is greater cultural distance.[24]

Internal-Coordination or Administrative Advantages

Internal-coordination or administrative advantages make it desirable for a firm to produce the good or service rather than contracting with another firm to produce or distribute it.[25] When a firm outsources the manufacture and distribution of a product, it experiences transaction costs, or the costs of negotiating, monitoring, and enforcing the contract. If these costs are high, a firm may rely on some form of FDI rather than using exporting or contracting (such as licensing or franchising) as an entry mode. Toyota has two advantages that must be maintained internally: efficient manufacturing techniques using a team approach, and a reputation for producing high-quality automobiles.[26] These advantages for Toyota are based on effective management; if Toyota outsourced manufacturing, it would likely lose these advantages. Therefore, Toyota uses some form of FDI (such as greenfield and joint ventures) rather than franchising and licensing for its foreign manufacture of automobiles.

After choosing an appropriate entry mode, the firm must implement its international strategy. Next, we discuss the different organizational structures firms use to implement the multidomestic, global, and transnational international strategies.

Implementing the Multidomestic Strategy

The geographic-area divisional structure is used to implement the multidomestic strategy (see Figure 8.4). The **geographic-area divisional structure** is a decentralized organizational structure that enables each division to focus on a geographic area, region, or country.[27] This structure is particularly useful for firms selling products with characteristics that frequently change (such as clothing). The geographic-area structure facilitates managers' actions that tailor the product mix to meet the cultural or special tastes of local customers. However, cost efficiencies are often sacrificed when using the geographic-area structure. Indeed, economies of scale are difficult to achieve using this structure because each country has unique products. The disadvantage of this structure, then, is duplication of resources across each division; for example, each division has its own

FIGURE 8.4 Using the Geographic-Area Divisional Structure to Implement the Multidomestic Strategy

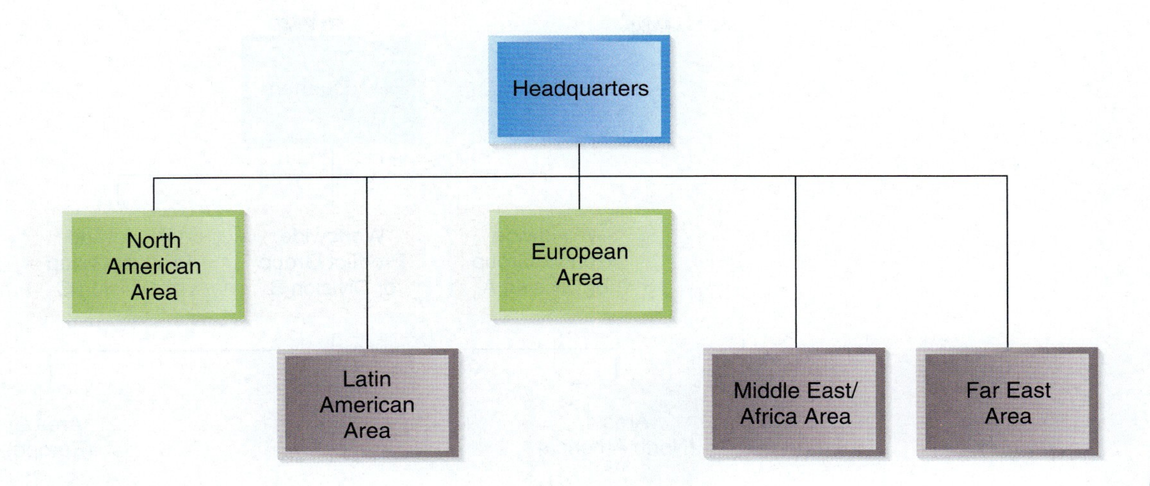

functional marketing specialists and production facilities. Coordination across divisions is also difficult and expensive due to the decentralization.

Implementing the Global Strategy

The worldwide divisional structure is used to implement the global strategy (see Figure 8.5). The **worldwide divisional structure** is a centralized organizational structure in which each product group is housed in a globally focused worldwide division or worldwide profit center.[28] In this structure, the first level of organizational structure below corporate headquarters is that of worldwide product divisions. The global responsibility to develop and manage new products is located in each division. Because a specific division focuses on a single product or product group, division managers are exposed to all aspects of managing products on a global basis. This experience helps managers learn how to integrate the firm's activities to improve manufacturing efficiency and responsiveness—abilities that help the firm adjust production requirements in light of fluctuating global demand. The major disadvantage of the worldwide divisional structure is that it encourages extensive duplication of activities because each division has similar functional skills in marketing, finance, information management, and so forth. Additionally, each product group must develop its own knowledge about the cultural, legal, and political environments of the various regional and national markets in which the various divisions operate. Furthermore, coordination and learning across product groups is difficult. It also results in low responsiveness to specific country needs.

FIGURE 8.5 Using the Worldwide Divisional Structure to Implement the Global Strategy

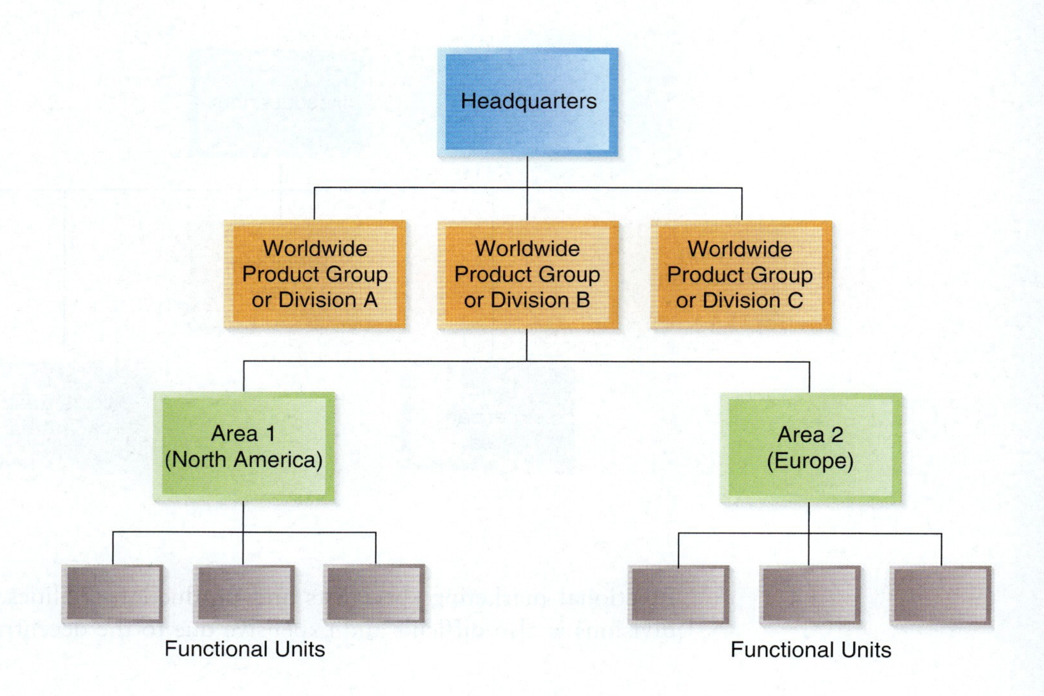

Implementing the Transnational Strategy

The transnational strategy is usually implemented through a global matrix structure[29] (see Figure 8.6). The **global matrix structure** is an organizational structure in which both functional and product expertise are integrated into teams so the teams will be able to quickly respond to requirements in the global marketplace. The global matrix structure promotes flexibility in designing products and responding to customer needs from different geographical areas. However, it places employees in a position of being accountable to more than one manager. In fact, at any given time an employee may be a member of several cross-functional or product or cross-geographical teams and may find it difficult to be loyal to all of them. Although the global matrix structure gives authority to managers who are most able to use it, the corporate reporting relationships are so complex and vague that it often takes longer to approve major decisions.

When you begin your career, you will likely serve on an international project team with people located in several countries. Don't be surprised if this occurs on your first job. Therefore, international strategies and the organizational structures used to implement them are highly relevant to you.

FIGURE 8.6 Using the Global Matrix Structure to Implement the Transnational Strategy

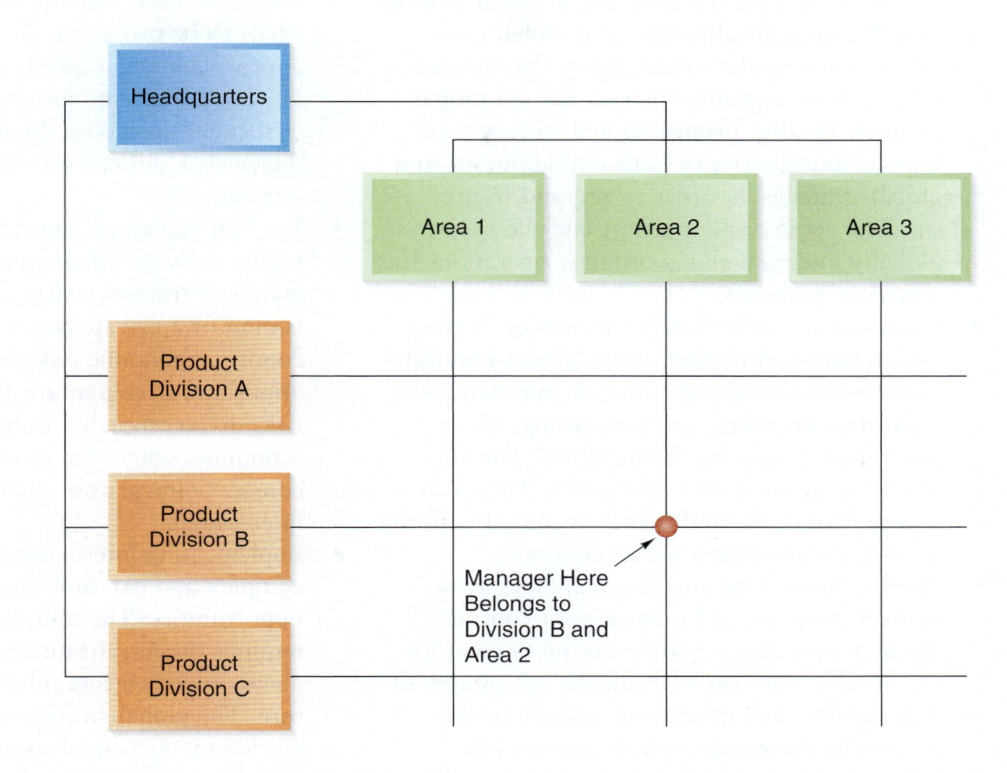

Summary

The primary purpose of this chapter is to examine firm strategies that extend across national borders. In doing so, we examined the following topics:

- The use of international strategies is increasing as firms seek to gain access to new markets and to valuable resources or to reduce their labor costs. The Internet and other technological innovations such as those in logistics are facilitating global business transactions. Reduced regulations and tariffs are also fostering greater opportunities for the use of international strategies.
- International strategies are driven by four major motives: (1) to reduce costs and secure resources; (2) to increase economies of scale and scope and to capitalize on opportunities to secure desirable locations; (3) to respond to pressure by rivals who have moved into regions untapped by others; and (4) to seek learning and other advantages that provide new knowledge from international markets.
- Firms going abroad usually select one of three international strategies. Firms use a **multidomestic strategy** to sell products that are customized to the needs of individual, host country markets. This international strategy works best when decision-making authority is decentralized to each business so it can operate freely in separate

regions or countries. The decentralized authority allows the business to adapt its goods and services to the local geographic market. When global markets demand similar characteristics in a good or service, the firm uses a **global strategy** to sell standardized products to global customers with similar needs. Being able to operate efficiently is critical to the success of a global strategy. Finally, a **transnational strategy** combines characteristics of both multidomestic and global strategies in order to respond to pressures for local responsiveness and the need to globally integrate and coordinate operations for efficiency purposes.

- Firms can use several different modes to enter an international market. Entry modes requiring lower asset commitment include international **exporting, licensing,** and **franchising.** These entry modes have less financial risk but also allow less control over operations. They also reduce profit potential, which is shared with the licensee or franchisee. Other contract approaches include contract manufacturers, turnkey projects, and management contracts. These approaches require more investment by the licensee but also have similar advantages of reduced financial investment relative to the previously discussed contract approaches.
- FDI modes include joint ventures or strategic alliances, **greenfield ventures,** and acquisitions. Each FDI entry mode requires more up-front investment, but allows for more control of the venture. A joint venture includes a separate entity for which control is shared with a local partner. A greenfield venture (new wholly owned subsidiary) allows more control and should be used when proprietary technology needs to be protected. An acquisition is more appropriate when speedy entry is important. However, acquisitions often have significant challenges, including the fact that effective due diligence is difficult to conduct in international settings.
- For FDI strategies, significant political and economic risks are encountered. Political risks include terrorism, wars, and outright nationalization of a private firm's assets by the host country. Economic risks include currency fluctuations and devaluations. Commonly, economic risks are accentuated in transition or emerging economies where the economy is less stable. Of course, political and economic risks are often interrelated.
- Implementing international strategies is often complex and can limit international expansion opportunities. The multidomestic strategy requires decentralization and therefore is implemented with a geographic-area divisional structure. The global strategy is implemented with a worldwide divisional structure. The transnational strategy requires both centralization and decentralization, and is commonly implemented with a **global matrix structure.**

Key Terms

country-specific or location advantages 175
exporting 172
foreign direct investment 163
franchising 173
geographic-area divisional structure 176
global matrix structure 178
global strategy 169
greenfield venture 174
internal-coordination or administrative advantages 176
liability of foreignness 163
licensing 173
multidomestic strategy 168
transnational strategy 171
worldwide divisional structure 177

Discussion Questions

1. What are the basic reasons why firms choose to expand their operations internationally by employing international strategies?
2. What are the two primary pressures leading to three main international strategies?
3. What are the four contract-based international entry modes?
4. What major advantages influence the type of entry mode firms choose to enter international markets?
5. What are the three types of foreign direct investment (FDI) and what rationale supports the use of each one?
6. What structures are used to implement the multidomestic, global, and transnational strategies?

Endnotes

1. J. T. Johnson, 2004, Externalization: Changing the shape of business, *Network World,* June 14: 24.
2. G. Rifkin, 2002, GM's Internet overhaul: How the world's largest manufacturer of cars and trucks is using technology to turn itself into a "small" and profitable company, *Technology Review,* October: 62–67.
3. J. Mezias, 2002, How to identify liabilities of foreignness and assess their effects on multinational corporations, *Journal of International Management,* 8: 265–282.
4. J. E. Ricart, M. J. Enright, P. Ghemawat, S. L. Hart, & T. Khanna, 2004, New frontiers in international strategy, *Journal of International Business Studies,* 35: 175–200.
5. N. Capar & M. Kotabe, 2003, The relationship between international diversification and performance in service firms, *Journal of International Business Studies,* 34: 345–355.
6. D. Luhnow & C. Terhune, 2003, Latin pop: A low-budget cola shakes up markets south of the border; Peru's Kola real takes on Coke and Pepsi by cutting frills, targeting bodegas; how plastic leveled the field, *Wall Street Journal,* October 27: A1.
7. K. T. Yeo, 2003, Factors motivating MNCs to set up local R&D facilities: The case of Singapore, *International Journal of Technology Transfer & Commercialisation,* 2(2): 128–138.
8. P. Ghemawat, 2004, Global standardization vs. localization: A case study and model, in J. A. Quelch & R. Deshpande (eds.), *The Global Market: Developing a Strategy to Manage across Borders,* New York: Jossey-Bass, Chapter 8.
9. G. Hoffman, 1996, On foreign expansion, *Progressive Grocer,* September: 156.
10. D. Michaels, 2003, World business (a special report); Victory at sea: How did a French company capture several British naval contracts? Think "multidomestic," *Wall Street Journal Europe,* September 26: R5.
11. P. Wonacott & L. Hawkins Jr., 2003, A global journal report: Saying 'beamer' in Chinese; Western luxury car makers see sales boom in China as newly rich seek status, *Wall Street Journal,* November 6: B1.
12. C. Daniels, 2004, Create IKEA, make billions, take bus, *Fortune,* May 3: 44; E. Brown, 2002, Putting EAMES within reach, *Fortune,* October 30: 98–100.
13. R. G. Javalgi, D. A. Griffith, & D. S. White, 2003, An empirical examination of factors influencing the internationalization of service firms, *Journal of Services Marketing,* 17: 185–202; J. H. Dunning, 1980, Toward an electric theory of international production: Some empirical tests, *Journal of International Business Studies,* 11: 9–31.
14. C. Edward, 2004, Keeping you glued to the couch; In video games, top developer Electronic Arts zaps the competition, *Business Week,* May 27: 58–59.
15. S. Fitch, 2004, Soft Pillows and Sharp Elbows, *Forbes,* May 10: 66.
16. J. Adams, Chip dip in water? *Newsweek,* October 18: E20.
17. J. Bamford, D. Ernst, & D. G. Fubini, 2004, Launching a world-class joint venture, *Harvard Business Review,* 82(2): 91–100.
18. C. Bouquet, L. Hebert, & A. Delios, 2004, Foreign expansion in service industries: Separability and human capital intensity, *Journal of Business Research,* 57: 35–46.
19. J. Levine, 2004, Europe: Gold mines and quicksand, *Forbes,* April 12: 76.
20. K. Shimizu, M. A. Hitt, D. Vaidyanath, & V. Pisano, 2004, Theoretical foundations of cross-border mergers and acquisitions: A review of current research and recommendations for the future, *Journal of International Management,* 10: 307–353; M. A. Hitt & V. Pisano, 2003, The cross-border merger and acquisition strategy: A research perspective, *Management Research,* 1: 133–144.
21. B. Lev, 2004, Sharpening the intangible edge, *Harvard Business Review,* 82(6): 109–116.
22. R. Tahir & J. Larimo, 2004, Understanding the location strategies of the European firms in Asian countries, *Journal of American Academy of Business,* 5: 102–110.

23. E. Tatoglu, K. W. Glaister, & F. Erdal, 2003, Determinants of foreign ownership in Turkish manufacturing, *Eastern European Economics,* 41(2): 5–41.
24. D. Xu & O. Shenkar, 2004, Institutional distance and the multinational enterprise, *Academy of Management Review,* 27: 608–618.
25. T. W. Malone, 2004, Bringing the market inside, *Harvard Business Review,* 82(4): 107–114.
26. S. J. Spear, 2004, Learning to lead at Toyota, *Harvard Business Review,* 82(5): 78–86.
27. A. Ferner, P. Almond, I. Clark, T. Colling, & T. Edwards, 2004, The dynamics of central control and subsidiary anatomy in the management of human resources: Case study evidence from US MNCs in the UK, *Organization Studies,* 25: 363–392.
28. J. Wolf & W. G. Egelhoff, 2002, A reexamination and extension of international strategy-structure theory, *Strategic Management Journal,* 23: 181–189.
29. G. Ietto-Gillies, 2002, *Transnational Corporations: Fragmentation amidst Integration,* New York: Routledge.

Strategic Alliances

Reading and studying this chapter should enable you to:

*Knowledge Objectives

1_
Define strategic alliances and explain the difference between equity and nonequity alliances.

2_
Explain why firms develop strategic alliances.

3_
Identify business-level strategic alliances and explain vertical and horizontal alliances.

4_
Describe how strategic alliances are used to implement corporate-level strategies.

5_
Explain why strategic alliances represent a common means of entering international markets.

6_
Identify the major risks of strategic alliances.

7_
Explain how strategic alliances can be managed to increase their success.

© AP Photo/Xinhua, Chen Fei

Focusing on Strategy

All Roads Lead to Joint Ventures in China, the Mother of Emerging Markets

"As China's largest steelmaker gathers steam, Western competitors scramble to come up with a game plan." (O. Brown, *Wall Street Journal*)

As the quote from the *Wall Street Journal* writer suggests, the Chinese economy is one of the healthiest and fastest-growing economies in the world. In fact, analysts predict that between 2040 and 2050, the Chinese economy will become the world's largest market. Because of its size and incredible potential, many firms want to enter and build a major presence in Chinese markets. The importance of these markets is shown by General Motors' announcement in 2004 that it and its Chinese venture partners plan to invest $3 billion by 2007 to expand operations in China. GM earned $437 million in net profit from its Chinese operations in 2003. Still, not all firms earn huge profits in China, partly because there is considerable competition in some sectors of the economy. Additionally, as a nation, China is trying to develop larger local automobile manufacturers. Moreover, China limits foreign ownership of joint ventures in most industries to 50 percent. However, exceptions to the ownership rule may be made when a venture is formed with the intention of exporting what it produces.

In spite of some of these potential hurdles, China is a popular destination for investments by foreign firms. Siemens, the German electronics and engineering company, has developed 45 joint ventures in China and its operations there account for about five percent of the firm's total annual revenues. While Siemens wants to be a major player in the Chinese market, it must compete with joint ventures formed by General Electric and Motorola from the United States and Alcatel from France. Likewise, Korean Air has formed an alliance with China Southern Airlines to enter the Chinese high-growth air traffic market. Demand for flights between Korea and China is strong. An executive for Korean Air stated that China was the company's highest priority destination because of predicted increases in annual demand for air travel of 30 percent and air cargo of 20 percent.

Some Chinese firms are the aggressor in forming alliances. For example, several Chinese steel companies, such as Wuhan Iron & Steel, have formed joint ventures with foreign partners to gain access to raw materials to satisfy Chinese demand. Shanghai's Baosteel Group formed a joint venture with Brazil's top iron ore producer, Vale do Rio Doce SA. Through the joint venture, they are building a steel mill in Brazil. Therefore, the alliances provide Chinese companies with access to resources they need to grow.

SOURCES: K. Bradsher, 2004, Made in India vs. made in China, *New York Times,* http://www.nytimes.com, June 12; A. Ward, 2004, Investing in China: Korean Air pushes into Chinese market, *Financial Times,* http://www.ft.com, June 9; L. Yuan & P. Glader, 2004, Looming battle, *Wall Street Journal Online,* http://www.wsj.com, September 27; K. Bradsher, 2004, GM to spend over $3 billion to expand in China, *New York Times,* http://www.nytimes.com, June 8; J. L. Lee, 2004, China seeks formation of large auto groups, *Wall Street Journal Online,* http://www.wsj.com, May 27; M. Karnitschnig, 2004, Siemens to expand business in China and boost sales, *Wall Street Journal Online,* http://www.wsj.com, May 18; O. Brown, 2004, BHP sets China iron-ore deal, *Wall Street Journal Online,* http://www.wsj.com, March 1.

The popularity of Chinese markets is shown in "Focusing on Strategy." Because of its size and subsequent sales potential, firms from many parts of the world want to enter Chinese markets. "Focusing on Strategy" describes companies entering Chinese markets from North America, Europe, and Asia. It also suggests that Chinese firms are accessing needed resources from Latin America. Combined, these actions emphasize the importance of strategic alliances to firms throughout the world. For example, Siemens has set up 45 joint ventures in China as a means of building a strong presence in Chinese markets. GM entered the Chinese markets with a joint venture as well, and the importance of this market to GM is clear from the amount of profit GM earns from it as well as the $3 billion GM plans to invest along with its Chinese partners. Finally, "Focusing on Strategy" shows that strategic alliances provide a means of accessing resources unavailable inside domestic markets. Chinese firms have developed joint ventures with Brazilian companies that have access to iron ore to obtain more of this resource to meet demands of heavy construction projects ongoing in the Chinese market.

A **strategic alliance** is a relationship between firms in which the partners agree to cooperate in ways that provide benefits to each firm. A strategic alliance is a type of cooperative strategy. A **cooperative strategy** is an action plan the firm develops to form cooperative relationships with other firms. Although firms choose to cooperate with one another rather than compete when using a cooperative strategy such as a strategic alliance, the purpose of doing so is the same in both instances: namely, to develop a competitive advantage.[1] Thus, a cooperative strategy adds to the repertoire of strategies firms use to build competitive advantages that can help them successfully compete in one or more markets.

There are at least two types of strategic alliances—equity alliances and non-equity alliances. In an **equity alliance,** each partner owns a percentage of the equity in a venture that the firms have jointly formed. If a separate business is created by this alliance, it is often referred to as a **joint venture.** A **nonequity alliance** is a contractual relationship between two or more firms in which each partner agrees to share some of its resources or capabilities.[2]

In previous chapters, we discussed business-level strategies, corporate (product diversification) strategies, and international strategies, which all concern actions the firm takes to compete in markets against other firms operating in them. In this chapter, we explore the use of strategic alliances, the reasons for them, and their different types. We also examine alliances at the business and corporate levels along with international alliances. Finally, we explore the means of managing alliances, including balancing the risks of using such strategies. We begin with the reasons to develop strategic alliances.

Reasons for Developing Strategic Alliances

As suggested in "Focusing on Strategy," strategic alliances are a highly popular strategy used by firms throughout the world. Strategic alliances represent a major trend in global business primarily because of the potential value they provide to partnering firms. They can help firms grow and often provide 20–35 percent of many firms' revenue.[3] Therefore, alliances can have a major effect on the performance of partner firms.[4] They are an important strategy for many reasons. We present some of these reasons in Table 9.1. Before examining Table 9.1, think of reasons you believe would cause firms to form alliances. You likely identified some of the reasons listed in the table and may have included a few others as well. This shows that alliances can be used to help a firm in many ways.

A major reason for firms to engage in strategic alliances is to allow them to enter restricted markets. China provides a prime example; the Chinese government requires foreign firms to form joint ventures with Chinese partners in

Reasons for Strategic Alliances

- Gain access to a restricted market
- Develop new goods or services
- Facilitate new market entry
- Share significant R&D investments
- Share risks and buffer against uncertainty
- Develop market power
- Gain access to complementary resources
- Build economies of scale
- Meet competitive challenges
- Learn new skills and capabilities
- Outsource for low costs and high quality output

order to enter most Chinese markets. Therefore, GM, Siemens, and Korean Air had to form alliances with Chinese firms to enter and serve Chinese markets. Alliances also can allow a firm to overcome trade barriers to enter a market. In other words, a firm may form a joint venture in a country to produce and market products so it would not have to pay major tariffs on those same products if they were imported.

R&D alliances to facilitate development of new goods and services have become increasingly common. R&D alliances help firms share the costs and risks of developing new products. The success of new products in the marketplace is very low. Therefore, sharing the costs and risks allows individual firms to either invest less in R&D or invest the same amount and increase the number of successes in the market (by introducing more new products, for example). Additionally, partner firms may develop better new-product ideas because by cooperating to integrate resources from each, they can create new and different capabilities.

The value of being able to share costs and risks may be quite significant for firms using international alliances to enter new markets.[5] As we noted previously, risks arise because success with new products is highly uncertain. However, other forms of uncertainty exist as well. For example, entering new international markets presents uncertainty in the form of market demand, government actions, and competitor reactions. Therefore, firms may develop strategic alliances such as R&D alliances to overcome uncertainty and share the risks.[6] Nokia's actions show how this can happen.

Nokia entered the Chinese market in 1996 and by 2001 had seven joint ventures with Chinese companies. In 2004, Nokia announced that it intended to expand its R&D operations in China. Part of the reason is that Nokia experienced a 15 percent revenue decline in the first quarter of the year (see Chapter 3) and felt that it needed to improve the design of its products so they would be more competitive in an intense global market (and, in this market, how a product is designed influences customers' purchases). The CEO stated that China was an important part of Nokia's global R&D network. Nokia also announced that 40 percent of its handsets would be designed at its R&D center in Beijing. So, Nokia is collaborating with Chinese corporations to improve the design of its handsets so they'll be more competitive in global markets, and thereby reduce its risk and uncertainty partly by using the capabilities of its partners.[7]

As suggested by the Nokia example, alliances can provide access to complementary resources. **Complementary resources** are resources that each partner brings to the partnership that, when combined, allow for new resources or capabilities that neither firm could readily create alone. By integrating their complementary resources, partners can take actions that they could not take separately. So, gaining access to complementary resources is a major reason for engaging in strategic alliances.[8] Nokia expects that the complementary resources held by its partners and within its firm can help it create better designs for the products it sells in global markets.

Firms can also use alliances to gain market power. For example, the alliance between Korean Air and China Southern Airlines opened new markets and routes for the Korean airline to serve. In this way, Korean Air increased its market power to compete against its major domestic competitor, Asiana Airlines. It gained market power because of the ability to provide its customers flights into major Chinese markets—an ability already available from its competitor. Market power can be achieved when partners combine their resources to create synergy and when their market share increases as a result of doing so.

At times, firms form alliances to meet competitive challenges. In fact, they may need to gain access to partners' resources to compete effectively. For example, Sematech was formed in Austin, Texas, during the 1980s by a group of U.S. semiconductor firms with the blessing of the U.S. government. It was developed to conduct joint R&D to meet the competitive challenges of foreign semiconductor firms, particularly Japanese businesses at the time. The consortium was so successful that Sematech has a different purpose today, although its general focus remains that of improving knowledge in the semiconductor industry.

Of critical importance is the amount of knowledge a firm holds. In fact, some argue that firms holding greater stocks of knowledge often have a competitive advantage. Because of this, many alliances are formed to gain access to a partner's valuable knowledge. So, a primary reason for developing alliances is to learn from partners, which can contribute to higher performance by the firm.[9] In some cases, firms may attempt to learn from partners in order to explore new areas (such as R&D alliances). In other cases, firms may want to learn from partners in order to know how to better use their current capabilities. For example, large multinational corporations often enter emerging markets to exploit their current technological knowledge. To do so, they must learn the local culture and marketplace. They must also learn how to deal with the foreign government and distributors. This knowledge can be obtained from local partners.[10]

A final reason why firms develop alliances is to outsource an important function or activity of their business. *Outsourcing* (defined in Chapter 4) involves acquiring a capability from an external supplier that contributes to creating value for customers.

As we explained in Chapter 4, outsourcing is a popular trend among U.S. firms. While much outsourcing occurs in manufacturing, outsourcing of information technology, human resources, and other internal staff functions has become increasingly common as well. Outsourcing is commonly used to reduce costs. However, firms also outsource to gain access to special skills for higher-quality output.[11] For example, Ford Motor Company has an alliance with the Pininfarina Group in Italy for the engineering and production of new automobile models, such as the StreetKa. Pininfarina also does design work for Ferrari, product engineering for Jaguar, manufacturing for Mitsubishi, and styling, design, engineering, and production for Peugeot. All of this work resulted in annual revenues for Pininfarina of $826 million in 2003, and revenues are projected to reach $1.2 billion by 2006.[12] Because international outsourcing is believed responsible for exporting jobs to other countries, it is controversial. However, from a strategic management perspective, outsourcing has the potential to help firms successfully implement their strategies and to earn returns for shareholders as a result.

Firms form alliances for use at different levels in their hierarchy of strategies. First, we'll explore business-level alliances.

Business-Level Strategic Alliances

There are two types of business-level strategic alliances—vertical and horizontal. Next we explore how a firm can use either type of business-level alliance to help create or maintain a competitive advantage.

Vertical Strategic Alliances

A **vertical strategic alliance** is an alliance that involves cooperative partnerships across the value chain (the value chain was discussed in Chapter 4). A relationship between buyers and suppliers is a common type of vertical alliance. Some firms use vertical alliances to produce their products. Nike uses quite a few vertical alliances to produce many of its athletic shoes. These alliances are a part of the value chain discussed in Chapter 4.

Although contracts are usually written to form them, vertical alliances are most effective when partners trust each other.[13] Trust enables partners to invest less time and effort to ensure that a contract's terms are fulfilled. Trust also helps partners learn from each other in ways that benefit both firms. In fact, when developed and sustained over long periods of time, trust even facilitates the transfer of technological knowledge from buyers to suppliers. When this happens, the supplier is more likely to provide exactly the materials the buyer needs to be successful.[14]

Both partnerships discussed in "Understanding Strategy" were vertical strategic alliances. Pixar provided Disney with creative animation capabilities and Amazon.com provided market channels and distribution of goods for Toys "R" Us. Vertical alliances can be highly important to a firm's success. For example, an estimated 45 percent of Disney's operating income for its film studio during 2000–2005, more than $1.1 billion, came from Pixar films.[15] Therefore, the disintegration of this partnership appears to have potentially serious implications for Disney's performance.

Horizontal Strategic Alliances

A **horizontal strategic alliance** is an alliance that involves cooperative partnerships in which firms at the same stage of the value chain share resources and capabilities. Horizontal alliances are often intended to enhance the capabilities of the partners to compete in their markets. Firms sometimes develop horizontal alliances to respond to competitors' actions or to reduce the competition they face. DaimlerChrysler created equity-based strategic alliances with Mitsubishi and Hyundai with both purposes in mind. In particular, DaimlerChrysler executives hoped that these alliances would make the firm more competitive in global markets. They expected these alliances to open markets in Asia for DaimlerChrysler products and enable the firm to access technological knowledge with which it could develop and build small autos that are competitive in global markets. However, neither horizontal alliance was successful. Mitsubishi turned out to be a "money pit" into which DaimlerChrysler had to inject much more capital than it originally intended, with no guarantee of earning a return on its investments. The partnership with Hyundai deteriorated, reportedly because of culture clashes and power struggles between the two firms. One DaimlerChrysler manager stated, "The game is over. Strategically, the alliance with Hyundai has fully failed."[16]

learning from failure

understanding strategy:

ENDING FORMERLY GOOD RELATIONSHIPS THAT HAVE GONE BAD

The vertical alliances between Amazon.com and Toys "R" Us and between Disney and Pixar were both highly successful. Toys "R" Us's original effort to reach its market using the Internet failed. However, after creating an alliance with Amazon.com to manage Toys "R" Us Internet sales and distribution, sales blossomed. Likewise, Disney and Pixar formed a vertical alliance to create animated films. Working together, Disney and Pixar developed several highly popular films such as *Monsters, Inc., Toy Story,* and *Finding Nemo.* Yet the partnerships either have been dissolved or are in the process of unraveling. What went wrong?

© Disney/Pixar/The Kobal Collection

In Disney and Pixar's case, negotiations to renew the alliance broke down and the former partners each decided to go their own way. The press reported that the two companies could not agree on the distribution of investments and profits between the partners on future projects. Additionally, Pixar preferred to do one film project per year (to maintain the quality) and Disney wanted to develop two per year. Some felt that the breakdown in negotiations could be attributed largely to the egos of the CEOs for the two firms, Michael Eisner (Disney) and Steven Jobs (Pixar). In recent years, Disney's efforts to produce animated films have been unsuccessful except for films produced with Pixar. The 13-year relationship between the two firms ended in spring 2004.

In the Amazon.com and Toys "R" Us partnership, the problems are less clear and the reasons for the alliance's failure have not been articulated. However, the relationship between the firms seems to have deteriorated even more greatly than between Disney and Pixar. The seriousness of the problems is shown by the fact that Toys "R" Us filed a lawsuit against Amazon.com claiming that Amazon violated the contractual agreement for exclusivity by allowing other companies selling competitive products to sell their goods on the Amazon.com Web site. Returning the favor, Amazon.com filed a countersuit claiming that Toys "R" Us consistently failed to meet the terms of the agreement. Amazon asked that the alliance be terminated and also requested $750 million in damages. It looks as if there is little hope for salvaging this vertical alliance after four seemingly successful years.

SOURCES: N. Wingfield, 2004, Amazon countersues, seeking to end Toys "R" Us partnership, *Wall Street Journal Online,* http://www.wsj.com, June 29; L. Foster, 2004, Amazon sues to cut Toys "R" Us ties, *Financial Times,* http://www.ft.com, June 28; L. Foster, 2004, Toys "R" Us unit files Amazon lawsuit, *Financial Times,* http://www.ft.com, May 24; 2004, Disney-Pixar public row getting down and dirty, *Houston Chronicle,* February 6: C3; 2004, Insiders say clash of egos drove Disney, Pixar apart, *Houston Chronicle,* February 3: B3; 2004, Dream ends for Disney, Pixar, *USA Today,* http://www.usatoday.com, January 29; D. Fonda, 2003, Eisner's wild, wild ride, *Time,* December 15: 46–47.

Because of dynamic and highly competitive markets, firms often face substantial uncertainty. To buffer against this uncertainty, they frequently form alliances to share the risks (as noted earlier in the chapter). High uncertainty has become increasingly common in many markets in addition to high-technology markets—markets that you would expect to be highly uncertain. For example, markets for banks have become highly competitive as they experience significant change. One response has been to acquire other banks to increase market power. However, compared to acquisitions, alliances can accomplish similar objectives, but with a smaller investment of a bank's financial capital. Of course, care must be taken in horizontal alliances to avoid explicit or tacit collusion.

While explicit collusion is illegal, tacit collusion is more difficult to identify.[17] *Tacit collusion* occurs when firms signal intentions to one another through their actions. The market signaling observed when firms tacitly collude is more likely to occur in concentrated industries with only a few large competitors. For example, Kellogg, General Mills, Post, and Quaker have almost 80 percent of the ready-to-eat cereal market.[18] An example of tacit collusion in this industry would be if most or all of these four competitors took no action to reduce the price of their products when the demand for them declined.[19]

Vertical alliances often have the highest probability of producing positive returns, while horizontal alliances usually are the most difficult to manage and sustain. In particular, vertical alliances in which partners have complementary capabilities and the relationship between the partners is strong are likely to be successful. Horizontal alliances are difficult because often the partners are also competitors. Firms in these alliances must guard against opportunistic actions (being unfairly taken advantage of) by their partners because of the potentially serious implications they might have for the firm's ability to remain competitive. Also, because of the differences between competitors, horizontal alliances are ripe for conflict.

While business-level partnerships are important, corporate-level alliances also can have substantial effects on firm performance. We examine these types of alliances next.

Corporate-Level Strategic Alliances

Corporate-level strategic alliances usually focus on the firm's product line and are designed to enhance firm growth. Corporate-level alliances are particularly attractive because they often have the same purpose as acquisitions, but are much less costly.[20] Corporate-level strategic alliances include those for diversification, for synergy, and for franchising.

Diversification by Alliance

R&D strategic alliances may be formed with the intent to develop new products that serve markets distinct from those that the partners currently serve. Partners operating in different industries may be able to integrate unique knowledge stocks to create products that serve new markets and customers. In this way, the new products add to each partner's current product line. In fact, developing new products for markets different from those served may be difficult for firms without help from partners who have the additional knowledge needed. The knowledge held by a firm can be valuable but also create a *path dependence* whereby it is difficult to learn something new that does not fit with the firm's current knowledge base.[21] Diversification alliances can be especially valuable if the new products developed are related to the current products in some way such that synergy can be created.

However, alliances can also be used to refocus the firm and reduce its level of diversification. Using information technology to build partnerships may be useful for reducing the scope of a firm's product offerings and increasing their specialization.[22] Japanese semiconductor manufacturers Fujitsu, Mitsubishi, Hitachi, and NEC formed joint ventures to consolidate and spin off diversified businesses that were earning poor returns. These actions enabled the firms to refocus on their core business and to give the poorly performing business special management attention. These actions have the potential to increase the performance of the spun-off business and the core firm.[23]

Synergy by Alliance

Strategic alliances at the corporate level between firms can be used to create synergy. Synergy is created in this instance when partners share resources or integrate complementary capabilities to build economies of scope. In fact, a synergistic strategic alliance is similar to a complementary business-level alliance in that both types of alliances are intended to synergistically involve partners with new businesses. A relationship between SBC Communications and EchoStar Communications (DISH Network) is an example of such a corporate-level strategic alliance. In 2004, the phone company's customers were able to sign up for EchoStar TV services by calling SBC sales representatives. SBC has similarly improved its broadband offering by partnering with Yahoo. Thus, SBC has been able to "bundle" other services with its telecommunications services to increase its customer base. These relationships rely on partners' complementary capabilities to create value for each partner's diversified service offerings.[24]

Franchising

Franchising is a well-established and successful type of corporate-level strategic alliance. As defined in Chapter 8, *franchising* is the licensing of a good or service and business model to partners for specified fees (usually a signing fee and a percentage of the franchisee's revenues or profits). Franchising allows a firm to expand a successful venture and earn additional returns without taking large financial risks. Franchising has the added advantage of allowing the franchisor to maintain control of its product and business model. Usually, the franchisor establishes tight controls on the actions a franchisee can take with its product and business name.

One successful franchisor is 7-Eleven.

Many well-known firms franchise. McDonald's, Hilton International, and 7-Eleven all have franchisees operating some of the businesses carrying their name and products. 7-Eleven has found franchising to be a particularly successful strategy, with more than 25,000 stores worldwide and in excess of $3 billion in annual revenues.[25]

For franchising to be highly effective, the partners must cooperate closely. The franchisor must develop and transfer successful programs and means of managing the operation to the franchisee. The franchisee must have the knowledge and capabilities necessary to compete in the local market. And franchisees must provide feedback to the franchisor about activities that work and those that do not. Franchisees should

learning from success

understanding strategy:

SONY IS USING STRATEGIC ALLIANCES TO REVITALIZE ITS PERFORMANCE

Sony is taking several actions to renew its performance—cutting costs to increase its efficient use of assets as well as forming strategic alliances to develop attractive new products. In 2001, Sony teamed with Ericsson to create a joint venture to build new products. The joint venture had some rough times in overcoming the cultural differences of the Swedish and Japanese firms. The venture developed the GSM mobile telephone that has been popular in the market. Sales of this product exceeded $8 million at the end of 2003.

Sony also has joint ventures with DoMoCo and Samsung. The venture with DoMoCo is intended to develop smart cards for mobile telephones. As a result, it has the potential to develop synergy with the Sony Ericsson venture. Embedding a smart card in a mobile phone could enable it to work as a security device or as a credit card. The intent is to license the technology to mobile phone manufacturers. Analysts believe that this venture has high potential.

Perhaps Sony's most ambitious alliance is the joint venture it formed with Samsung to develop flat-panel displays. Each company agreed to invest $1 billion in the venture and owns 50 percent equity in it. This venture partners Sony with a competitor and is designed to build a competitive advantage. The joint venture may help Sony leverage Samsung's technology and also take advantage of Samsung's market-leading position in the market for flat panel displays. It also allows each firm to control its capital investment and R&D costs.

While none of these corporate-level alliances is risk-free, they help the partners in each balance their risks. Furthermore, if the capabilities of each firm can be successfully integrated, they should be better able to develop a unique and valuable product. Therefore, this appears to be a potentially successful strategy for Sony's turnaround. In addition, the alliances create synergistic diversification for Sony as well as the partner firms.

SOURCES: A. Lashinsky, 2005, Saving face at Sony, *Fortune,* February 21, 79-86; J. Yang, 2004, A savvy strategy for Sony, *Business Week Online,* http://www.businessweek.com, May 4; B. Einhorn, 2004, DoMoCo's "new business model," *Business Week Online,* http://www.businessweek.com, April 19; P. Dvorak, 2004, Sony, Samsung finalize deal for flat-panel joint venture, *Wall Street Journal Online,* http://www.wsj.com, March 8; A. Edstrom, 2004, Signs of life at Sony Ericsson, *Fortune,* http://www.fortune.com, February 10.

also inform the franchisor about the important characteristics of competitors and market conditions in their local markets. Franchising can also enable a franchisor to gain a first-mover advantage without some of the risks involved in being a first mover.[26]

Sony is trying to develop highly related new products using alliances. Each alliance described in "Understanding Strategy" is intended to create synergy. The most ambitious and probably the most important alliance is the joint venture with Samsung, a competitor. This venture has much potential for Sony, particularly with Samsung's technology and its market-leading position in flat panel displays. Interestingly, Sony's alliances with Ericsson and Samsung are both cross-border alliances, the next topic of discussion.

International Strategic Alliances

Cross-border strategic alliances have become the most prominent means of entering foreign markets. One reason is that some countries require that firms form joint ventures with local firms in order to enter their markets. This is the case for most industries in China, as explained in "Focusing on Strategy." Additionally, foreign firms need knowledge and perhaps other resources to understand and compete effectively in the newly entered markets. As noted earlier, even if the Chinese government did not require joint ventures, foreign firms would do well to form them anyway. They could use the alliances to learn about the different culture and characteristics of the market and to develop relationships with distributors and important government units. Also, the trend toward outsourcing to businesses in foreign countries due to their lower labor costs increases the number of cross-border strategic alliances. Therefore, as noted in Chapter 8, entering foreign markets is an attractive option for many firms.[27]

As we explain shortly, all strategic alliances carry risks. However, the use of international strategic alliances, a popular strategy for entering markets or gaining access to special skills and resources, carries some additional risks and potential costs. In the Sony and Ericsson joint venture, the differing cultures of the two companies' workforces created an early barrier to an effective alliance. Different cultures and a lack of trust can hinder the transfer of knowledge or sharing of other resources necessary to make an alliance successful. Top executives warn against making assumptions when moving into new international markets. A firm's products often must be adapted to the local market. This requires close cooperation of local partners. Firms may have to use different distribution channels as they cross into new international markets. For example, Procter & Gamble sells its goods in the United States largely through drugstores and supermarkets (multi-product retailers), but many of its products are sold through more limited-product pharmacies in Europe.[28]

Managing Risks in Strategic Alliances

Each type of strategic alliance (business-level, corporate-level, and cross-border) has its own risks and there may be some generic ones as well. Many strategic alliances fail, even some that were formerly successful as in the case of Disney and Pixar. Estimates of alliance failure range from 50 percent to 70 percent.[29] Given the substantial conflict in the Amazon.com and Toys "R" Us alliance, the risks related to lack of trust are evident. When partners don't trust each other, they are less likely to share resources, particularly the most valuable ones. Without trust, partners also must invest more time and energy (resulting in extra costs) to guard against possible opportunistic behavior by the other firm. As a result, alliances without trust between partners are unlikely to meet their goals.

Of course, all alliances suffer from the potential differences in corporate and national cultures. These differences reflect emphases on separate values and may also lead to communication problems between partners as well as an inability to understand each other's intentions with the alliance. Additionally, because it is impossible to know all of a firm's capabilities before alliances are formed,

© Michael Reynolds/EPA/Landov

China's Sichuan Changhong Electric Company experienced a problematic alliance with Apex Digital in the United States, leading to substantial losses for the firm.

participants in alliances often discover that the partner's competencies are not as strong or complementary as assumed.

Firms also may be unwilling to share important resources as assumed when the alliance was formed.[30] For example, Pixar's market power grew considerably during the time of its alliance with Disney because of the substantial success of their jointly produced animated films, so Pixar likely became unwilling to share its creative talent with Disney, at least under the old arrangement. When the alliance ended, Disney may have needed Pixar more than Pixar needed Disney.

Effectively managing alliances can reduce some of their risks. But it isn't easy to manage the risks of alliances, as evidenced in the demise of successful alliances such as those between Disney and Pixar and between Amazon.com and Toys "R" Us. Some firms use detailed contracts to try to guard against opportunistic behavior by a partner. While a detailed contract can help, it isn't possible to identify and then specify in a contract all partner actions that are acceptable while they cooperate as alliance partners.[31]

In 2004, the leading Chinese manufacturer of television sets, Sichuan Changhong Electric Company, announced a huge loss estimated at approximately $500 million. The loss was attributed largely to declining sales in the United States because of the 25 percent tariffs imposed by the U.S. government and a financial scandal involving its major alliance partner in the United States. The partner, Apex Digital, which supposedly owed Changhong almost $468 million, accounted for much of Changhong's loss. Apex acted as a distributor of Changhong products to such customers as Wal-Mart. Thus, problems with overseas alliance partners can have a substantial negative effect on a firm's performance.[32]

Indeed, the best action that most firms can take is to attempt to develop a trusting relationship. Trust is the best preventive medicine against opportunistic behavior. In addition, trust promotes the sharing of resources and even the willingness to cooperate with and help alliance partners. We emphasize the importance of trust in our discussion of managing alliances.

Managing Strategic Alliances

Given the importance of strategic alliances and their potential effects on firm performance, businesses have started to emphasize the management of alliances as a way to develop a competitive advantage and create value for their shareholders.[33] As a result, firms are even creating units with the responsibility of managing their multiple strategic alliances.[34] The actions required to successfully manage alliances and their outcomes are shown in Figure 9.1.

Selecting partners is the first step in managing alliances to make them successful. If an incompatible partner is selected, the alliance is likely to fail. Furthermore, the firm should understand its partner well enough to ensure that it has the resources desired. An important part of the analysis and selection of a

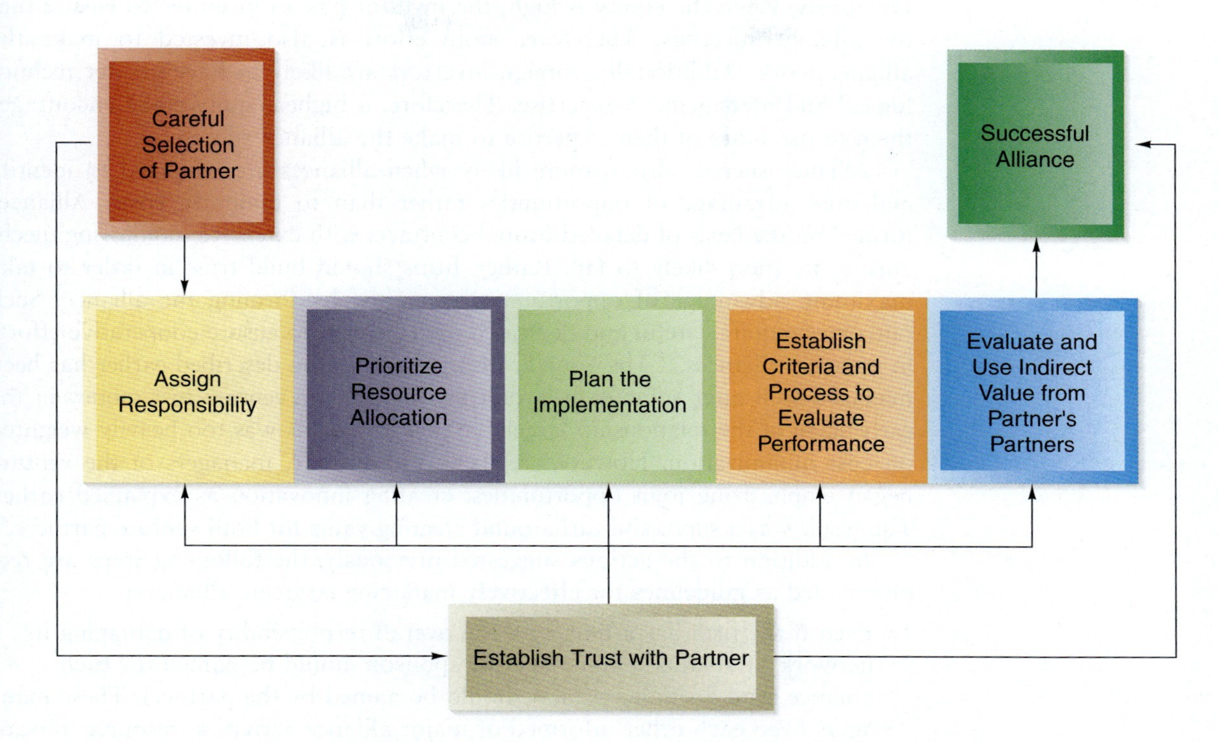

partner is to understand the context in which the partner operates, its competitive landscape, and the institutional forces (such as banks and government policies) with which it must deal (especially for international alliances).[35]

After selecting the partner and starting the alliance, each partner must access the resources desired from the other partner and learn the knowledge needed to successfully use the alliance. If either or both partners fail to achieve their goals, the alliance will fail. To increase the probability of alliance success, then, both partners must provide access to resources and even be willing to help the other partner learn as needed. The willingness to help partners may require extra effort until trust between them grows. Firms should attempt to build trust with the intent of establishing social capital in the alliance.[36] Trust is the base for social capital, which in turn leads to cooperation between partners. Social capital implies that firms will help their partners gain value from an alliance. Of course, the partner is expected to reciprocate. Because of the difficulty in building trust and social capital, firms often form alliances with former partners with whom social capital already exists.

One measure of an alliance's success, in addition to its longevity, is the extent to which knowledge is transferred between partners and integrated into the alliance operations. Integrating separate knowledge sets is important because doing so helps produce synergy and innovation.[37] Thus, alliance managers should invest time and effort to ensure that both partners learn (add knowledge) from the alliance and that their two complementary knowledge stocks are integrated to create value in the alliance.

According to some recent research, firms would do well to pay careful attention to equity investments in the alliances. The failure rate is high in alliances where the foreign investors have a low equity investment. However, the success rate is higher when the foreign investor makes a large equity investment.[38] Obviously, when the equity is high, the investor has an incentive to ensure that the alliance succeeds. Therefore, more effort is also invested to make the alliance work. Additionally, foreign investors are likely to have greater technological and management expertise. Therefore, a higher equity stake encourages them to use more of their expertise to make the alliance successful.

Alliance success also is more likely when alliances are managed to identify and take advantage of opportunities rather than to minimize costs. Alliances formed on the basis of detailed formal contracts with extensive monitoring mechanisms are more likely to fail. Rather, firms should build trust in order to take maximum advantage of opportunities generated by forming the alliance. Such outcomes require careful and dedicated management to ensure cooperative efforts in strategic alliances.[39] The Sony/Ericsson joint venture described earlier has been managed well after some early problems. In fact, the venture lost money in the early stage of the relationship largely because the focus was too heavily weighted on cost minimization. However, realizing the mistake, managers of the venture began emphasizing joint opportunities, creating innovation as explained earlier. The result was a successful turnaround creating value for both venture partners.[40]

In addition to the actions suggested previously, the following steps are recommended as guidelines for effectively managing strategic alliances:

1. Even if the firm has a unit with the overall responsibility of managing its network of alliances, a manager or sponsor should be named for each alliance (and a similar person should be named by the partner). These managers keep each other informed of major alliance activities, resource allocations, and outcomes.
2. The organization should analyze the alliance's priority within its resource allocations and ensure the commitment needed for each alliance to succeed.
3. A clear plan for implementing the alliance should be created and activated after the partners have agreed to the alliance.
4. The means for analyzing the performance of the alliance and distribution of performance outcomes to the partners should be clearly established. Important stakeholders' interests need to be considered when establishing the performance criteria.
5. When evaluating an alliance's value, the partners' partners in other alliances should be considered. The indirect network of partners from other alliances may be of value for future alliances or in providing indirect value through the benefits derived by the firm's partner.[41]

Summary

The primary purpose of this chapter is to explain how a firm can develop and manage strategic alliances to develop or maintain a competitive advantage. In doing so, we examined the following topics:

- A **strategic alliance** is a relationship between firms in which the partners agree to cooperate in ways that provide benefits to each of them. In an **equity alliance,** each partner owns a specified percentage of the equity in a separate venture. These ventures are often called **joint ventures.** In a **nonequity alliance,** a contractual relationship is established between two or more firms for them to share resources or capabilities.

- Firms form alliances for many reasons. Alliances can be helpful for entering new markets (product or geographic), especially those that are restricted (such as by governments). Alliances can be useful for sharing the risks of entering the markets or in developing new products. In some cases, alliances help firms expand their economies of scale and market power. Strategic alliances are often helpful in meeting competitive challenges, especially when they enable firms to gain access to **complementary resources** or learn new capabilities. Finally, strategic alliances have played a major role in the recent outsourcing trend.
- Strategic alliances can be established at the business level. They may be **vertical alliances** across separate primary activities in the value chain or **horizontal alliances** between competitors at the same stage of the value chain.
- Corporate-level strategic alliances include those for facilitating diversification and/or those designed to create synergy. Additionally, franchising is a type of corporate-level strategic alliance.
- International strategic alliances have become highly common for entering new foreign markets. Often, these alliances are used as a means to outsource primary or secondary activities to firms operating in countries with lower labor costs. Although they facilitate learning about new markets, the cultural differences between participating firms make international strategic alliances quite risky.
- While strategic alliances can provide several benefits to the partners, they also carry some potentially important risks. A major risk is the potential for opportunism by one of the partners. There is a high alliance failure rate, often because of differences in corporate or national cultures and due to information asymmetries. Differences in culture may produce conflicts, and information asymmetries can lead to inaccurate assumptions about resources and capabilities held by partners.
- To increase the probability of success, strategic alliances need to be managed. First, firms should take great care in selecting compatible partners that have the resources needed. It is also important to examine the amount of equity used in forming an alliance. After the alliance is formed, the partners should establish trust to ensure the transfer of resources and learning. They should also assign responsibilities within the firm, develop priorities for allocating resources, plan for an alliance's implementation, and develop means for evaluating its performance and distribution of performance outcomes to partners.

Key Terms

complementary resources 188
cooperative strategy 186
equity alliance 186
horizontal strategic alliance 190
joint venture 187
nonequity alliance 187
strategic alliance 186
vertical strategic alliance 190

Discussion Questions

1. What is a strategic alliance and what are the differences between equity and nonequity alliances?
2. Why do firms form alliances? Explain.
3. What are vertical and horizontal business-level alliances?
4. What are corporate-level strategic alliances?
5. Why do firm commonly use strategic alliances to enter international markets?
6. What are the major risks involved in forming strategic alliances?
7. What can firms do to manage strategic alliances in ways that will increase their probability of success?

Endnotes

1. R. D. Ireland, M. A. Hitt, & D. Vaidyanath, 2002, Alliance management as a source of competitive advantage, *Journal of Management,* 28: 413–446.
2. S. S. Lui & H.-Y. Ngo, 2004, Trust and contractual safeguards on cooperation in non-equity alliances, *Journal of Management,* 30: 471–485; T. B. Folta & K. D. Miller,

2002, Real options in equity partnerships, *Strategic Management Journal,* 23: 77–88.
3. M. Schifrin, 2001, Partner or perish, *Forbes,* May 21: 28; M. Gonzales, 2001, Strategic alliances, *Ivey Business Journal,* 66(1): 47–51.
4. M. J. Leiblein & J. J. Reuer, 2004, Building a foreign sales base: The roles of capabilities and alliances for entrepreneurial firms, *Journal of Business Venturing,* 19: 285–307.
5. R. Narula & G. Duysters, 2004, Globalisation and trends in international R&D alliances, *Journal of International Management,* 10: 199–218.
6. R. J. Arend, 2004, Volatility-based effects on shareholder value: Alliance activity in the computing industry, *Journal of Management,* 30: 487–508.
7. Nokia to increase R&D in China in effort to revive market share, *Wall Street Journal Online,* http://www.wsj.com, May 21.
8. M. A. Hitt, M. T. Dacin, E. Levitas, J.-L. Arregle, & A. Borza, 2000, Partner selection in emerging and developed market contexts: Resource-based and organizational learning perspectives, *Academy of Management Journal,* 43: 449–467.
9. P. Dussauge, B. Garrette, & W. Mitchell, 2004, Asymmetric performance: The market share impact of scale and link alliances in the global auto industry, *Strategic Management Journal,* 25: 701–711.
10. F. T. Rothaermel & D. L. Deeds, 2004, Exploration and exploitation alliances in biotechnology: A system of new product development, *Strategic Management Journal,* 25: 210–221.
11. M. J. Mol, P. Pauwels, P. Mattyssens, & L. Quintens, 2004, A technological contingency perspective on the depth and scope of international outsourcing, *Journal of International Management,* 10: 287–305.
12. Andrea Pininfarina: Chief executive, Pininfarina Group, Italy, 2004, *Business Week Online,* http://www.businessweek.com, June 7; G. Edmondson, 2003, A talk with Pininfarina's driver, *Business Week Online,* http://www.businessweek.com, March 3.
13. P. Saparito, C. C. Chen, & H. J. Sapienza, 2004, The role of trust in bank–small firm relationships, *Academy of Management Journal,* 47: 400–410.
14. M. Kotabe, X. Martin, & H. Domoto, 2003, Gaining from vertical partnerships: Knowledge transfer, relationship duration, and supplier performance improvement in the U.S. and Japanese automotive industries, *Strategic Management Journal,* 24: 293–316.
15. B. Orwall, 2004, Can Disney still rule animation after Pixar? *Wall Street Journal Online,* http://www.wsj.com, February 2.
16. G. Edmondson & M. Ihlwan, 2004, Hyundai and DaimlerChrysler: Driving in different directions, *Business Week Online,* http://www.businessweek.com, May 3; G. Edmondson, B. Bremner, K. Kerwin, & C. Palmeri, 2004, Daimler: Now for the next repair job, *Business Week,* April 26: 58.
17. J. B. Barney, 2002, *Gaining and Sustaining a Competitive Advantage,* Upper Saddle River, N.J.: Prentice Hall.
18. G. K. Price & J. M. Connor, 2003, Modeling coupon values for ready-to-eat breakfast cereals, *Agribusiness,* 19(2): 223–244.
19. Barney, *Gaining and Sustaining a Competitive Advantage,* 351.
20. J. S. Harrison, M. A. Hitt, R. E. Hoskisson, & R. D. Ireland, 2001, Resource complementarity in business combinations: Extending the logic to organizational alliances, *Journal of Management,* 27: 679–699.
21. D. Lei, M. A. Hitt, & R. A. Bettis, Dynamic core competences through meta-learning and strategic context, *Journal of Management,* 22: 547–567.
22. P. J. Brews & C. L. Tucci, 2004, Exploring the structural effects of internetworking, *Strategic Management Journal,* 25: 429–451.
23. J. Yang, 2003, One step forward for Japan's chipmakers, *Business Week Online,* http://www.businessweek.com, July 7.
24. L. J. Flynn, 2003, EchoStar deal lets SBC offer satellite TV in phone bill, *New York Times Online,* http://www.nytimes.com, July 22.
25. J. Wilgoren, 2003, In the urban 7-Eleven, the Slurpee looks sleeker, *New York Times Online,* http://www.nytimes.com, July 13.
26. S. C. Michael, 2003, First mover advantage through franchising, *Journal of Business Venturing,* 18: 61–80; S. C. Michael, 2002, Can a franchise chain coordinate? *Journal of Business Venturing,* 17: 325–342.
27. J. Lu & P. W. Beamish, 2004, International diversification and firm performance: The s-curve hypothesis, *Academy of Management Journal,* 47: 598–609; M. A. Hitt, R. E. Hoskisson, & H. Kim, 1997, International diversification: Effects on innovation and firm performance in product diversified firms, *Academy of Management Journal,* 40: 767–798.
28. C. Hymowitz, 2003, European executives give some advice on crossing borders, *Wall Street Journal Online,* http://www.wsj.com, December 2.
29. D. C. Hambrick, J. Li, K. Xin, & A. S. Tsui, 2001, Compositional gaps and downward spirals in international joint venture management groups, *Strategic Management Journal,* 22: 1033–1053.
30. Hitt, Dacin, Levitas, Arregle, & Borza, op. cit.
31. M. A. Hitt, M. T. Dacin, B. B. Tyler, & D. Park, 1997, Understanding the differences in Korean and U.S. executives' strategic orientations, *Strategic Management Journal,* 18: 159–167.
32. C. Buckley, 2004. Leading Chinese TV exporter has huge loss, *New York Times Online,* http://www.nytimes.com, December 28.
33. Ireland, Hitt, & Vaidyanath, op. cit.
34. J. H. Dyer, P. Kale, & H. Singh, 2001, How to make strategic alliances work, *MIT Sloan Management Review,* 42(4): 37–43.
35. M. A. Hitt, D. Ahlstrom, M. T. Dacin, E. Levitas, & L. Svobodina, 2004, The institutional effects on strategic alliance partner selection in transition economies: China versus Russia, *Organization Science,* 15: 173–185.
36. K. Starkey & S. Tempest, 2004, Bowling along: Strategic management and social capital, *European Management Review,* 1: 78–83.
37. S. Rodan & C. Galunic, 2004, More than network structure: How knowledge heterogeneity influences managerial performance innovativeness, *Strategic Management Journal,* 25: 541–562.
38. C. Dhanaraj & P. W. Beamish, 2004, Effect of equity ownership on the survival of international joint ventures, *Strategic Management Journal,* 25: 295–305.
39. J. H. Dyer & C. Wujin, 2003, The role of trustworthiness in reducing transaction costs and improving performance: Empirical evidence from the United States, Japan and Korea, *Organization Science,* 9: 285–305.
40. J. L. Schenker, 2003, Sony Ericsson posts loss despite sales gain, *New York Times Online,* http://www.nytimes.com, July 16.
41. K. E. Klein, 2004, Fine-tune that alliance, *Business Week Online,* http://www.businessweek.com, February 10.

GLOSSARY

A

acquisition a transaction in which a firm buys a controlling interest in another firm with the intention of either making it a subsidiary business or combining it with its current business or businesses

acquisition strategy an action plan that the firm develops to successfully acquire other companies

administrative innovation a new way of organizing and/or handling the organizational tasks firms use to complete their work

B

balanced scorecard provides a framework for evaluating the simultaneous use of financial controls and strategic controls

benchmarking the process of identifying the best practices of competitors and other high-performing firms, analyzing them, and comparing them with the organization's own practices

business-level strategy an action plan the firm develops to describe how it will compete in its chosen industry or market segment

C

capabilities result when the firm integrates several different resources to complete a task or a series of related tasks

competitive advantage when the firm's core competencies allow it to create value for customers by performing a key activity *better* than competitors or when a distinctive competence allows it to perform an activity that creates value for customers that competitors can't perform

competitive M-form an organizational structure in which there is complete independence between the firm's divisions

competitive rivalry the set of actions and reactions between competitors as they compete for an advantageous market position

complementary resources resources that each partner brings to the partnership that, when combined, allow for new resources or capabilities that neither firm could readily create alone

complementors the network of companies that sell goods or services that are complementary to another firm's good or service

cooperative M-form an organizational structure in which horizontal integration is used so that resources and activities can be shared between product divisions

cooperative strategy an action plan the firm develops to form cooperative relationships with other firms

core competencies capabilities the firm emphasizes and performs especially well while pursuing its vision

corporate entrepreneurship an organization-wide reliance on entrepreneurship and innovation as the link to solid financial performance

corporate relatedness achieved when core competencies are successfully transferred between some of the firm's businesses

cost leadership strategy an action plan the firm develops to produce goods or services at the lowest cost

country specific or location advantages advantages that concern the desirability of producing in the home country versus locating production and distribution assets in the host country

D

demographic trends changes in population size, age structure, geographic distribution, ethnic mix, and income distribution

differentiation strategy an action plan the firm develops to produce goods or services that customers perceive as being unique in ways that are important to them

distinctive competencies core competencies that differ from those held by competitors

divestiture a transaction in which businesses are sold to other firms or spun off as independent enterprises

due diligence the rational process by which acquiring firms evaluate target firms

E

economic trends the direction of the economy in which a firm competes or may choose to compete

economies of scale the improvements in efficiency a firm experiences as it incrementally increases its size

economies of scope cost savings that the firm accrues when it successfully shares some of its resources and activities or some of its core competencies between its businesses

entrepreneurial culture encourages employees to identify and exploit new opportunities

entrepreneurial opportunities circumstances suggesting that new goods or services can be sold at a price exceeding the costs incurred to create, make, sell, and support them

entrepreneurs people who recognize entrepreneurial opportunities and then take risks to develop an innovation to pursue them

entrepreneurship a process of "creative destruction" through which existing products, methods of production, or ways of administering or managing the firm are destroyed and replaced with new ones

equity alliance an alliance in which each partner owns a percentage of the equity in a venture that the firms have jointly formed

exporting the process of sending goods and services from one country to another for distribution, sale, and service

external environment a set of conditions outside the firm that affect the firm's performance

F

financial controls focus on shorter-term financial outcomes

financial economies cost savings or higher returns generated when the firm effectively allocates its financial resources based on investments either inside or outside the firm

focus strategy an action plan the firm develops to produce goods or services to serve the needs of a specific market segment

focused cost leadership strategy an action plan the firm develops to produce goods or services for a narrow market segment at the lowest cost

focused differentiation strategy an action plan the firm develops to produce goods or services that a narrow group of customers perceive as being unique in ways that are important to them

foreign direct investment a process through which a firm directly invests (beyond exporting and licensing) in a market outside its home country

franchising the licensing of a good or service and business model to partners for specified fees (usually a signing fee and a percentage of the franchisee's revenues or profits)

functional structure an organizational structure consisting of a CEO and a small corporate staff

G

general environment the trends in the broader society that influence an industry and the firms in it

geographic-area divisional structure a decentralized organizational structure that enables each division to focus on a geographic area, region, or country

global matrix structure an organizational structure in which both functional and product expertise are integrated into teams so the teams will be able to quickly respond to requirements in the global marketplace

global strategy an action plan that the firm develops to produce and sell standardized products in different markets

global trends changes in relevant emerging and developed country global markets, important international political events, and critical changes in cultural and institutional characteristics of global markets

greenfield venture a venture in which a firm buys or leases land, constructs a new facility and hires or transfers managers and employees, and then independently launches a new operation (usually a wholly owned subsidiary) without involvement of a partner

H

horizontal acquisition the purchase of a competitor competing in the same market or markets as the acquiring firm

horizontal strategic alliance an alliance that involves cooperative partnerships in which firms at the same stage of the value chain share resources and capabilities

human capital includes the knowledge and skills of those working for the firm

I

industry a group of firms producing similar products

innovation the development of something new—a new good, a new type of service, or a new way of presenting a good or service

intangible resources assets that contribute to creating value for customers but are not physically identifiable

integrated cost leadership/differentiation strategy an action plan the firm develops to produce goods or services with a strong emphasis on both differentiation and low cost

internal environment the set of conditions (such as strengths, resources and capabilities, and so forth) inside the firm affecting the choice and use of strategies

internal-coordination or administrative advantages advantages that make it desirable for a firm to produce the good or service rather than contracting with another firm to produce or distribute it

J

joint venture a separate business that is created by an equity alliance

L

leveraged buyout (LBO) a restructuring strategy in which a party buys all or part of a firm's assets in order to take the firm or a part of the firm private

liability of foreignness the costs and risks of doing business outside a firm's domestic market

licensing the process of entering an international market by leasing the right to use the firm's intellectual property—technology, work methods, patents, copyrights, brand names, or trademarks—to a firm doing business in the desired international market

M

market power power that exists when the firm sells its products above competitive prices or when its costs are below those of its primary competitors

merger a transaction in which firms agree to combine their operations on a relatively equal basis

mission defines the firm's core intent and the business or businesses in which it intends to operate

multidivisional (M-form) structure an organizational structure in which the firm is organized to generate either economies of scope or financial economies

multidomestic strategy an action plan that the firm develops to produce and sell unique products in different markets

multiproduct strategy an action plan that the firm develops to compete in different product markets

N

nonequity alliance a contractual relationship between two or more firms in which each partner agrees to share some of its resources or capabilities

O

operational relatedness achieved when the firm's businesses successfully share resources and activities to produce and sell their products

opportunities conditions in the firm's external environment that may help the firm reach its vision

organizational culture the set of values and beliefs that are shared throughout the firm

organizational structure specifies the firm's formal reporting relationships, procedures, controls, and authority and decision-making processes

outsourcing acquiring a capability from an external supplier that contributes to creating value for the customer

P

political/legal trends the changes in organizations and interest groups that compete for a voice in developing and overseeing the body of laws and regulations that guide interactions among firms and nations

primary activities inbound logistics (such as sources of parts), operations (such as manufacturing, if dealing with a physical product), sales and distribution of products, and after-sales service

process innovations new means of producing, selling, and supporting goods and services

R

related-party transactions paying a person who has a relationship with the firm extra money for reasons other than his or her normal activities on the firm's behalf

resources the tangible and intangible assets held by the firm

S

simple structure an organizational structure in which the owner/manager makes all of the major decisions and oversees all of the staff's activities

social capital includes all internal and external relationships that help the firm provide value to customers and ultimately to its other stakeholders

sociocultural trends changes in a society's attitudes and cultural values

stakeholders individuals and groups who have an interest in a firm's performance and an ability to influence its actions

strategic alliance a relationsp between firms in which the partners agree to cooperate in ways that provide benefits to each firm

strategic business unit (SBU) a semiautonomous unit of a diversified firm with a collection of related businesses

strategic business unit (SBU) M-form an organizational structure in which the divisions within each SBU concentrate on transferring core competencies rather than on sharing resources and activities

strategic controls focus on the content of strategic actions rather than on their outcomes

strategic entrepreneurship the process of taking entrepreneurial actions using a strategic perspective by combining entrepreneurial and strategic management processes to enhance the firm's ability to innovate, enter new markets, and improve its performance

strategic intent the firm's motivation to leverage its resources and capabilities to reach its vision

strategic leaders the individuals practicing strategic leadership

strategic leadership developing a vision for the firm, designing strategic actions to achieve this vision, and empowering others to carry out those strategic actions

strategic management the ongoing process companies use to form a *vision, analyze* their external environment and their internal environment, and select one or more *strategies* to use to create value for customers and other stakeholders, especially shareholders

strategy an action plan designed to move an organization toward achievement of its vision

strategy implementation the set of actions firms take to use a strategy after it has been selected

strengths resources and capabilities that allow the firm to complete important tasks

substitute products goods or services that perform similar functions to an existing product

support activities provide support to the primary activities so that they can be completed effectively

switching costs the one-time costs customers incur when they decide to buy a product from a different supplier

T

takeover a specialized type of acquisition in which the target firm does not solicit the acquiring firm's offer

tangible resources valuable assets that can be seen or quantified, such as manufacturing equipment and financial capital

technological trends changes in the activities involved with creating new knowledge and translating that knowledge into new products, processes, and materials

threats conditions in the firm's external environment that may prevent the firm from reaching its vision

top management team the group of managers charged with the responsibility to develop and implement the firm's strategies

transnational strategy an action plan that the firm develops to produce and sell somewhat unique, yet somewhat standardized products in different markets

V

value chain consists of the structure of activities that firms use to implement their business-level strategy

value the satisfaction a firm's product creates for customers; can be measured by the price customers are willing to pay for the firm's product

vertical acquisition the purchase of a supplier or distributor of one or more of a firm's goods or services

vertical strategic alliance an alliance that involves cooperative partnerships across the value chain

vision contains at least two components—a mission that describes the firm's DNA and the "picture" of the firm as it hopes to exist in a future time period

W

weaknesses the firm's resource and capability deficiencies that make it difficult for the firm to complete important tasks

worldwide divisional structure a centralized organizational structure in which each product group is housed in a globally focused worldwide division or worldwide profit center

NAME INDEX

H

I

J

K

L

M

N

O

P

Q

R

S

T

V

W

X

Y

Z

COMPANY INDEX

Q

R

S

T

U

V

W

X

Y

SUBJECT INDEX

A

B

C

D

E

F

G

H

I

J

N

O

P

Q

R

S

T

U

V

W

W